Casebook for
Clinical
Supervision

Casebook for
Clinical Supervision

A COMPETENCY-BASED APPROACH

Edited by

Carol A. Falender and Edward P. Shafranske

American Psychological Association
Washington, DC

Third Printing, April 2014

Published by
American Psychological Association
750 First Street, NE
Washington, DC 20002
www.apa.org

To order
APA Order Department
P.O. Box 92984
Washington, DC 20090-2984
Tel: (800) 374-2721; Direct: (202) 336-5510
Fax: (202) 336-5502; TDD/TTY: (202) 336-6123
Online: www.apa.org/books/
E-mail: order@apa.org

In the U.K., Europe, Africa, and the Middle East, copies may be ordered from
American Psychological Association
3 Henrietta Street
Covent Garden, London
WC2E 8LU England

Typeset in Goudy by Circle Graphics, Inc., Columbia, MD

Printer: Maple-Vail Book Manufacturing Group, Binghamton, NY
Cover Designer: Naylor Design, Washington, DC
Technical/Production Editor: Tiffany L. Klaff

The opinions and statements published are the responsibility of the authors, and such opinions and statements do not necessarily represent the policies of the American Psychological Association.

Library of Congress Cataloging-in-Publication Data

Casebook for clinical supervision : a competency-based approach / edited by Carol A. Falender and Edward P. Shafranske. — 1st ed.
       p. ; cm.
   Companion v. to: Clinical supervision / Carol A. Falender and Edward P. Shafranske. c2004.
   Includes bibliographical references.
   ISBN-13: 978-1-4338-0342-0 (alk. paper)
   ISBN-10: 1-4338-0342-9 (alk. paper)
   1. Clinical psychologists—Supervision of. 2. Clinical competence. I. Falender, Carol A. II. Shafranske, Edward P. III. Falender, Carol A. Clinical supervision. IV. American Psychological Association.
   [DNLM: 1. Psychology, Clinical—organization & administration. 2. Clinical Competence. 3. Personnel Management.   WM 105 C337 2008]
   RC467.7.C39 2008
   362.2'04250683—dc22

                                                             2007048173

British Library Cataloguing-in-Publication Data

A CIP record is available from the British Library.

Printed in the United States of America
First Edition

CONTENTS

CONTRIBUTORS

Veronica Barenstein, PhD, Director, Family and Couples Therapy program, Semel Institute for Neuroscience and Human Behavior, David Geffen Medical School, University of California, Los Angeles

Judith S. Beck, PhD, Director, Beck Institute for Cognitive Therapy and Research, Bala Cynwyd, PA; Clinical Associate Professor of Psychology in Psychiatry, University of Pennsylvania, Philadelphia

Stephen H. Behnke, JD, PhD, Director, Ethics Office, American Psychological Association, Washington, DC

Cynthia Belar, PhD, ABPP, Executive Director for Education, American Psychological Association, Washington, DC; Professor Emeritus, University of Florida, Gainesville

Kanika D. Bell, PhD, Assistant Professor, Department of Psychology, Clark Atlanta University, Atlanta, GA

Phillippe B. Cunningham, PhD, Professor, Family Services Research Center, Department of Psychiatry and Behavioral Sciences, Medical University of South Carolina, Charleston

Carol A. Falender, PhD, independent practice; Clinical Professor, Department of Psychology, University of California, Los Angeles; Adjunct Professor, Pepperdine University, Los Angeles, CA

Nadine J. Kaslow, PhD, ABPP, Professor, School of Medicine, Department of Psychiatry and Behavioral Sciences, Emory University, Atlanta, GA

Gerald P. Koocher, PhD, ABPP, Dean and Professor, School for Health Studies, Simmons College, Boston, MA

Derek Milne, PhD, Director, Doctorate in Clinical Psychology, University of Newcastle, Newcastle Upon Tyne, England; Northumberland, Tyne, and Wear National Health Service Trust, England

J. Christopher Muran, PhD, Chief Psychologist, Beth Israel Medical Center; Associate Professor, Albert Einstein College of Medicine, New York, NY

Natalie Porter, PhD, Professor, California School of Professional Psychology, Alliant International University, San Francisco, CA

Jeff Randall, PhD, Assistant Professor, Family Services Research Center, Department of Psychiatry and Behavioral Sciences, Medical University of South Carolina, Charleston

Michael Rothman, PhD, Beth Israel Medical Center; Assistant Professor, Department of Psychiatry and Behavioral Sciences, Albert Einstein College of Medicine, New York, NY

Jeremy D. Safran, PhD, Professor and Director of Clinical Training, Department of Psychology, New School for Social Research, New York, NY; faculty, New York University postdoctoral program in psychotherapy and psychoanalysis

Joan E. Sarnat, PhD, ABPP, private practice, Berkeley, CA; personal and supervising analyst and faculty member, Psychoanalytic Institute of Northern California, San Francisco

Edward P. Shafranske, PhD, ABPP, Professor and Director of the PsyD program in clinical psychology, Pepperdine University, Los Angeles, CA

Christopher Stevens, PhD, Beth Israel Medical Center, New York, NY

Cal D. Stoltenberg, PhD, David Ross Boyd Professor, Department of Educational Psychology, University of Oklahoma, Norman

Luis A. Vargas, PhD, Associate Professor, Department of Psychiatry, University of New Mexico School of Medicine, Albuquerque

FOREWORD

STEPHEN H. BEHNKE

It is my pleasure to introduce the *Casebook for Clinical Supervision: A Competency-Based Approach.* The editors, Carol A. Falender and Edward P. Shafranske, have been addressing issues related to the supervisory relationship for many years. Their influence has been particularly strong in shaping the psychology laws and regulations in their home state of California, but the effects of their work have been felt across the country. In this volume Falender and Shafranske have gathered the thoughts of individuals with national reputations for their writings in this and other areas of psychological practice to address the supervisory role from a practitioner's perspective.

It would be fair to pose the question, "Why an introduction from a psychologist whose primary work is in ethics?" Reviewing the table of contents reveals why this introduction makes perfect sense to the editors. Their approach views supervision as a multifaceted relationship that encompasses clinical, legal, and ethical aspects, each of which merits careful consideration and all of which are to be incorporated into the supervisory encounter. Clinical supervision is the primary means by which psychologists and their supervisees ensure that their legal and ethical responsibilities to clients, the profession, and the public are fulfilled. Building on theory and research, this volume provides clinical perspectives on how these ethical responsibilities are put into practice in a clinically appropriate and sensitive manner that will minimize exposure to legal and ethical liability.

The title contains two essential concepts: supervision in a clinical context and developing competence. Each of the chapters elaborates on some aspect of one or both of these concepts. The first three chapters address an aspect of supervision as a *process*—the process of becoming competent, the process of developing as a supervisor, and the process of conducting psychotherapy. These chapters reveal an orientation toward supervision that resists a static understanding by focusing on growth and development that occur over time.

The next three chapters (chaps. 4–6) explore aspects of the supervision relationship: personal factors and countertransference, issues of diversity, and ruptures in the alliance. These chapters examine the role of supervisor and supervisee characteristics and address a powerful yet understudied phenomenon: the supervisory relationship that has become broken. These chapters presume that supervision is at its heart a relationship and that an understanding of supervision must take into account what each partner brings to the endeavor and how the contribution of each is central to what occurs in the supervision.

Chapter 8 addresses legal and ethical aspects of supervision. These aspects, related yet distinct, are essential components of a supervisor's understanding of this work. Supervisors have ethical obligations both to their supervisees and to the patients treated by the supervisees, and failure to grasp this reality can expose both supervisor and supervisee to legal and ethical liability. Chapters 9 and 10 examine supervision in the context of the systems in which supervision inevitably occurs. These chapters highlight that understanding supervision cannot be confined to an examination of the individuals sitting in an office together and that systems and settings inevitably affect—either inhibiting or enhancing—the supervisory process. Chapter 11 includes what must be an essential component of any serious exploration of this subject: evaluation and enhancement. Discussions of supervision will prove fruitless if one has no way of evaluating whether supervision is having its intended effects and if one cannot adjust one's thinking accordingly, in terms of what that evaluation yields.

Supervision has been one of the more neglected areas of psychological practice. This volume is an important contribution to the field's understanding of what makes a good supervisor and what makes for good supervision. As such, it stands as a tribute to the deep and nuanced understanding Falender and Shafranske bring regarding the essential elements of a successful supervisory relationship.

Casebook for
Clinical
Supervision

1

BEST PRACTICES OF SUPERVISION

CAROL A. FALENDER AND EDWARD P. SHAFRANSKE

Since the publication of our book *Clinical Supervision: A Competency-Based Approach* (Falender & Shafranske, 2004), there has been a sea change toward competency-based approaches to supervision, not only in psychology but also in numerous other disciplines. The heart of this sea change is the development of comprehensive systems for identification of specific core competencies, corresponding best practices for both practice and supervision (Rubin et al., 2007), and their assessment (Kaslow et al., 2007). *Best practices* are an evolving distillation of the components associated with the highest quality supervision practice (Falender et al., 2004; Kilminster, Cottrell, Grant, & Jolly, 2007; National Council of Schools and Programs of Professional Psychology, 2007; Rice et al., 2007). They are practices which are increasingly agreed upon by supervisors as essential components of a successful supervision process. Competencies include establishment of the supervisory alliance, supervision contracting, dealing with strains and ruptures to the alliance, technical competence, diversity competence, evaluation and feedback, and legal and ethical competence.

Competency-based practices provide design, monitoring, and evaluation of supervisee development and supervision outcomes as well as a prototype for assessing competency throughout a psychologist's career.

Movement toward competency-based practice results from the confluence of a greater emphasis on consumer protection and quality assurance, and an increased focus on evidence-based practice (American Psychological Association [APA] Presidential Task Force on Evidence-Based Practice, 2006). The absence of specific supervision training in the graduate curriculum is highly problematic as licensure often marks the transition from supervisee to supervisor (Rodolfa et al., 1998; Scott, Ingram, Vitanza, & Smith, 2000). As a result, beginning supervisors are unprepared to assume their required supervisory responsibilities. Supervision is increasingly viewed as the key to implementation, fidelity, and transportability of evidence-based treatments (Baer et al., 2006).

In this chapter, we provide a brief summary of *Clinical Supervision* (Falender & Shafranske, 2004) and an overview of the chapters in the *Casebook for Clinical Supervision: A Competency-Based Approach*, with attention to best practices exemplified in each chapter.

BACKGROUND AND SUMMARY OF OUR MODEL[1]

In *Clinical Supervision* (Falender & Shafranske, 2004) we presented our framework for the practice of supervision. The present volume, the *Casebook*, is designed to facilitate translation of current theory, research, and tools on competencies into practice. Our intent is to explicate principles and competencies in *Clinical Supervision* and make them more immediately relevant to practice by presenting examples of best practices in each of the major competencies. Each subheading refers to a specific competency. Authors were selected strategically to correspond to the targeted competency areas, with the intent of demonstrating theory and research in actual practice. Despite abundant research in the past decade on clinical supervision, there has been no demonstration of high-quality supervision organized around competencies. The intent of the *Casebook* is to fill that gap and to provide case-based exemplars[2] of competency-based supervision for all levels of supervisors—from those in training through seasoned professionals. Through the use of the *Casebook* in conjunction with *Clinical Supervision* supervisors can significantly enhance their competency in research, theory, and practice of clinical supervision. The volumes can be used individually or as a set, because they are complementary, each reinforcing the other. Each chapter of *Clinical Supervision* corresponds to one in the *Casebook* so that the reader can view how the theory and research of competency is demonstrated in practice.

---

[1]The following section is adapted from *Clinical Supervision: A Competency-Based Approach* (Falender & Shafranske, 2004).
[2]All authors have complied with the ethical standard of confidentiality in all case materials.

CLINICAL SUPERVISION: DEFINITION, PILLARS, AND SUPERORDINATE VALUES

In *Clinical Supervision* (Falender & Shafranske, 2004), we defined *supervision* as

> a distinct professional activity in which education and training aimed at developing science-informed practice are facilitated through a collaborative interpersonal process. It involves observation, evaluation, feedback, and facilitation of supervisee self-assessment, and the acquisition of knowledge and skills by instruction, modeling, and mutual problem solving. In addition, by building on the recognition of the strengths and talents of the supervisee, supervision encourages self-efficacy . . . [and] is conducted in a competent manner in which ethical standards, legal prescriptions, and professional practices are used to promote and protect the welfare of the client, the profession, and society at large. (p. 3)

Supervision is built on three interrelated pillars: the supervisory relationship, inquiry, and educational praxis. These pillars exist in synergistic confluence, either enhancing or compromising the process of supervision. The *supervisory relationship* provides the foundation for the development of an alliance in which individual and shared responsibilities in the supervision of clinical practice will be achieved. *Inquiry* refers to processes facilitating critical understanding of the therapeutic process, and it fosters in the supervisee enhanced awareness of professional and personal contributions. *Educational praxis* provides the multiplicity of learning strategies tailored to enhance supervisees' knowledge and skills.

Four superordinate values inform supervision: integrity-in-relationship, ethical values-based practice, appreciation of diversity in all its forms, and science-informed practice. These values are integral to clinical competence and influence every aspect of the supervisory process. *Integrity-in relationship* relates to a state of completeness and moral incorruptibility. Corruptions, whether from ethical violations (i.e., boundary violations), supervisory incompetence, or inattention to supervisory responsibilities, compromise the integrity of the relationship and, subsequently, the therapy the supervisee is conducting. *Ethical values-based practice* refers to the profound role of supervisors as role models for their supervisees. Supervisors assist supervisees in targeted exploration of values as the impact human decision making, but without moving into psychotherapy or counseling roles. Ethics and competence are yoked together, two sides of the same coin. The third value, *appreciation of diversity in all its forms*, is an expression of the profession's respect for people's rights and dignity (APA "Ethical Principles of Psychologists and Code of Conduct" [hereafter referred to as the APA Ethics Code], 2002, Principle E; see also the APA Web site version at http://www.apa.org/ethics/). We believe that diversity competence includes self-awareness of multiple factors by both supervisor and supervisee in the context of the client's presentation. It is an interactive conceptual process. Components include belief systems, biases, assumptions, values, expectations, and worldviews. Diversity competent supervision requires the practice of appropriate, relevant, and sensitive assessment and intervention strategies and skills, while taking into account the larger milieu of organization, society, and sociopolitical variables.

Science-informed practice refers to the core value of psychology, the integration of science and practice. Increasingly, integrating science and practice means following evidence-based practices and integrating knowledge, skills, and values associated with these practices into conceptualization and treatment. An example would be if the supervisor, supervisee, and client were of differing or even same ethnicity, religion, socioeconomic status, and so forth, the role of the clinical supervisor is to integrate perspectives and biases each introduces to ensure understanding and accommodation to the needs of the client. Or, a supervisor might be highly protective of a supervisee, so much so that he does not allow the supervisee to develop autonomy or a sense of confidence in his or her clinical interventions. Unless the supervisor gains insight into his protection of this particular supervisee—that it is based in the supervisor's own personal factors, for example, viewing the supervisee as a son or daughter—his behavior could hinder the development of the supervisee.

Taking a stance of inquiry, learning to frame questions, engaging in critical thinking, testing hypotheses, and formulating conclusions emerge from the process of following a science-informed practice, and supervisees will learn these skills if their supervisors instill in them the importance of the competency science-informed practice.

Our premise is that, together, the definition, pillars, and superordinate values are essential components of best practices of supervision and are foundational principles to both volumes, *Clinical Supervision* (Falender & Shafranske, 2004) and the *Casebook*. These components represent a movement from a purely hierarchical supervision process, or intervention, to one that is strength-based and that builds on the process of collaborative and interpersonal growth and development of both the supervisee and supervisor, established from the onset of supervision. Introduction of self-assessment transforms responsibility for evaluation from the supervisor to a shared task between supervisor and supervisee. The supervisor holds power through evaluation and gatekeeping, determining whether the supervisee will progress to the next level of professional development and ensuring the safety of the client.

COMPETENCY-BASED SUPERVISION

In Falender and Shafranske (2007), we defined *competency-based supervision* as

> an approach that explicitly identifies the knowledge, skills, and values that
> are assembled to form a clinical competency and develops learning strate-

gies and evaluation procedures to meet criterion-referenced competence standards in keeping with evidence-based practices and requirements of the local clinical setting. (p. 233)

This definition transforms competence into a working process and a structure for establishing and monitoring ongoing supervision practice.

Narratives in this *Casebook* are designed to provide supervisors at all levels insight into the complexity and creativity of applying a competency-based model to the supervision process. Supervisors will gain insight on how theoretical and metatheoretical aspects serve as an implicit foundation and permeate supervision.

Best practice areas define the practice of supervision. Construction of the supervision contract is the foundation, as we discuss in more detail in the section "Supervisory Contract and Alliance" (chap. 1, this volume). The supervisory alliance is then established through the process of contract development and is strengthened with added transparency through feedback, evaluation, and attention to client outcomes. Supervisors are responsible for establishing the alliance and identifying and repairing strains and ruptures. Best practices for supervision include cognizance of the role of personal factors and diversity in all aspects of therapy and supervision, management of countertransference, and identification and use of parallel process. *Parallel process* refers to the dynamics of the therapeutic relationship stimulating and being reflected within the supervisory relationship, or conversely, the dynamics of the supervisory relationship being reenacted in the therapeutic relationship with the client. The supervisor practices with knowledge, skills, and value of legal and ethical standards.

Competency-based approaches in psychology have a long history (APA, 2006; Peterson, 1992), but specific competencies were not articulated until the 2002 Competencies Conference: Future Direction in Education and Credentialing in Professional Psychology, sponsored by the Association of Psychology Postdoctoral and Internship Centers (Kaslow et al., 2004), a product of which was a description of supervisor competencies (Falender et al., 2004; see also Exhibit 1.1, this volume) and the subsequent Benchmarks Conference, which elaborated the cube model with foundational and functional competencies (Rodolfa et al., 2005). In *Clinical Supervision* (Falender & Shafranske, 2004), we added to these efforts by laying out a framework for translation of much supervision research to competencies and a transformational approach to supervision.

Our competency-based approach provides an explicit framework and method to initiate, develop, implement, and evaluate the processes and outcomes of supervision. Emphasis is on the ability to apply knowledge and skills in the real world and use performance outcomes as criteria for evaluating supervisees and programs. The explicit approach instills a deliberate quality in development of learning goals and objectives, with specific processes by which

EXHIBIT 1.1
Supervision Competencies Framework

Knowledge
1. Knowledge of area being supervised (psychotherapy, research, assessment, etc.).
2. Knowledge of models, theories, modalities, and research on supervision.
3. Knowledge of professional/supervisee development (how therapists develop, etc.).
4. Knowledge of ethics and legal issues specific to supervision.
5. Knowledge of evaluation, process outcome.
6. Awareness and knowledge of diversity in all of its forms.

Skills
1. Supervision modalities.
2. Relationship skills—ability to build supervisory relationship/alliance.
3. Sensitivity to multiple roles with supervisee and ability to perform and balance multiple roles.
4. Ability to provide effective formative and summative feedback.
5. Ability to promote growth and self-assessment in the trainee.
6. Ability to conduct own self-assessment process.
7. Ability to assess the learning needs and developmental level of the supervisee.
8. Ability to encourage and use evaluative feedback from the trainee.
9. Teaching and didactic skills.
10. Ability to set appropriate boundaries and seek consultation when supervisory issues are outside the domain of supervisory competence.
11. Flexibility.
12. Scientific thinking and the translation of scientific findings to practice throughout professional development.

Values
1. Responsibility for client and supervisee rests with the supervisor.
2. Respectful.
3. Responsible for sensitivity to diversity in all its forms.
4. Balance between support and challenging.
5. Empowering.
6. Commitment to lifelong learning and professional growth.
7. Balance between clinical and training needs.
8. Value ethical principles.
9. Commitment to knowing and using available psychological science related to supervision.
10. Commitment to knowing one's own limitations.

Social Context Overarching Issues
1. Diversity.
2. Ethical and legal issues.
3. Developmental process.
4. Knowledge of the immediate system and expectations within which the supervision is conducted.
5. Awareness of the sociopolitical context within which the supervision is conducted.
6. Creation of climate in which honest feedback is the norm (both supportive and challenging).

Training of Supervision Competencies
1. Coursework in supervision including knowledge and skill areas listed.
2. Has received supervision of supervision including some form of observation (videotape or audiotape) with critical feedback.

EXHIBIT 1.1
Supervision Competencies Framework (*Continued*)

Assessment of Supervision Competencies
1. Successful completion of course on supervision.
2. Verification of previous supervision of supervision documenting readiness to supervise independently.
3. Evidence of direct observation (e.g., audiotape or videotape).
4. Documentation of supervisory experience reflecting diversity.
5. Documented supervisee feedback.
6. Self-assessment and awareness of need for consultation when necessary.
7. Assessment of supervision outcomes—both individual and group.

Note. From "Defining Competencies in Psychology Supervision: A Consensus Statement," by C. A. Falender et al., 2004, *Journal of Clinical Psychology, 60,* p. 778. Copyright 2004 by the American Psychological Association.

learning is accomplished. The first step is identification of setting-specific competencies related to local clinical requirements and knowledge of the clinical literature regarding competencies relevant to contemporary clinical practice. Once selected, the requisite knowledge, skills, and values are assembled, forming competencies identified and the initial focus of supervision. For example, a first session with a client requires a variety of listening skills, knowledge of diagnoses and decision trees, risk assessment, diversity competence, and interpersonal skills. Once competencies are defined, identification of strengths and areas requiring additional work by supervisees can be mutually developed through self-assessment, observation, and feedback. In addition to setting specific objectives, we advocate specific individual assessment and collaborative goal setting. The process of developing site-specific and individual competencies is collaborative and enhances alliances and communication.

SUPERVISORY CONTRACT AND ALLIANCE

Components of best practices of supervision are woven through all of the chapters in the *Casebook*. At the heart of the supervision process, structurally and ethically, is the supervision contract developed through collaboration of supervisee and supervisor. In forming the contract together, they determine goals, tasks required to accomplish these (Bordin, 1983), and roles of the supervisor and supervisee in the process. The supervisory alliance, a best practice across theoretical orientations, is achieved through the contract development and the creation of an emotional bond marked by mutual respect, empathy, acceptance, and encouragement to experiment. Self-assessment, feedback, and evaluation structure the contract, direct the development of the supervisee, and maintain the focus on client outcome.

Ruptures, Repair, Personal Factors, and Parallel Process

In the course of supervision, there will be times when strains and even ruptures to the relationship develop. The supervisor is responsible for identifying and repairing strains and ruptures in the supervisory alliance as well as for identifying and managing transference and countertransference of the supervisee—and supervisor—in the triad of client(s), supervisee–therapist, and supervisor. Attention to parallel processes (or isomorphism for cognitive therapists) is a supervisory responsibility. A caustic interaction between client and therapist–supervisee may be reenacted between supervisee–therapist and supervisor, or a conflict that was unresolved between supervisor and supervisee–therapist may be reenacted in the client's therapy.

Diversity Competence in Supervision

A supervisory competence and best practice is diversity competence. Excellent supervision practice is infused with knowledge, skills, values, and attitudes regarding diversity of the supervisor him/herself, of the supervisee, and of the client(s) and how these interact. Supervisors are required to self-assess multiple identities and attitudes, biases, and assumptions and to address how multiple diversity factors interact with power and privilege inherent in the supervisory role.

Ethical and Legal Competence

In ethical supervision, there is a premise of competence and metacompetence (Falender & Shafranske, 2007). Supervisors engage in informed consent for supervision (Thomas, 2007), model ethical problem solving (Gottlieb, Robinson, & Younggren, 2007), infuse diversity competence (Allen, 2007), and engage in ethical practice (Barnett, 2007). Elaboration of supervisory competencies and provision of formative evaluation and feedback results in increased transparency of the supervision process and attention to the ethical standard of autonomy (APA Ethics Code; APA, 2002). All of these aspects are formalized in the contract, clarifying for the supervisee multiple aspects of expectations, requirements, evaluation, and confidentiality. The highest ethical duty of the supervisor is protecting and ensuring the well-being of the client. As a result, ideally, the supervisor obtains direct information from the client for the purposes of supervision. This may come in the form of client report forms (Worthen & Lambert, 2007), live observation, or video or audio review of client sessions.

The results of a study of physicians reported for disciplinary action (Papadakis et al., 2005) support the critical importance of the supervisor's tracking, monitoring, and providing constructive feedback to the supervisee. Retrospective analysis of practicing physicians referred to disciplinary boards revealed that those same students engaged in significantly more unprofessional behavior as medical students and were less responsive to feedback. Use of a competency-based model and best practices of supervision would have resulted in early identification of performance discrepancies, corrective feedback, and if no change occurred, disciplinary action, probation, and even expulsion from medical school.

THE CASEBOOK

The chapters that follow provide models for supervisors to implement the best practices outlined in the preceding sections. Chapter 2, "A Competency-Based Approach to Supervision," by Nadine J. Kaslow and Kanika D. Bell, describes cross-racial supervision in a university-affiliated, large, urban public hospital serving a predominantly African American teen population. The chapter highlights the application of general principles of competency-based supervision. It provides insight into the multiple levels of integration in construction of a collaborative supervisory alliance, drawing on vicissitudes of previous supervision and supervisee struggles. Kaslow and Bell demonstrate the intricate interplay of the supervisory alliance, developmental considerations, and individual and cultural diversity factors. Their interaction is punctuated with abundant reflection, self-assessment, and constructive feedback, which translate to a supervision prototype for the supervisee to internalize and emulate. The supervisor's initiation of discussion of personal and cultural factors illuminates the complexity of the supervisee's struggles vis-à-vis clients who share some aspects of her multiple identities. That the supervisor and supervisee coauthored the chapter is a metaphor for the process of their development together.

In chapter 3, "Developmental Approaches to Supervision," Cal D. Stoltenberg describes how his supervisory interventions can be guided by a metatheoretical integrated developmental model. The supervisor engages in ongoing developmental assessment paired with supervisee self-assessment, and both of these processes inform supervisory interventions and structure the supervisory alliance. Combining supervisee report with joint review of videotaped session, Stoltenberg tracks domains attending to subjective experience of the supervisee and discrepancy from supervisor observations. Effective use of metaphor assists the supervisor as he tracks and evaluates case conceptualization, supervisee perception of supervision, and interventions.

In chapter 4, "Psychotherapy-Based Approaches to Supervision," the three authors, Judith S. Beck, Joan E. Sarnat, and Veronica Barenstein, present theoretically distinct supervisory interactions that share significant common factors but which highlight their unique differences. Beck demonstrates how the cognitive supervisor identifies and frames particular data to establish the supervisory alliance and direct the change process. She outlines parallel processes in conceptualization; planning for client interventions and for therapist–supervisee difficulties; and competencies relevant to the client and supervisee cognitions, problems, and coping. Sarnat proceeds from a psychodynamic approach, with significant attention to the supervisory alliance addressing supervisee behavior when the supervisor suspects personal factors or parallel process may be interfering with clinical work. Through description of supervisor process and its translation into supervision behavior, client behavior is addressed. Barenstein's approach encapsulates group supervision and parallel process, or isomorphism in family systems work, laying out the elaborate process of supervision when one supervisee is at an impasse in her work with a client.

Edward P. Shafranske and Carol A. Falender, in chapter 5, "Supervision Addressing Personal Factors and Countertransference," provide a nuanced approach to the identification and management of countertransference in supervision. In the context of respecting boundaries, the supervisor explores the enactment of the countertransference and provides the supervisee structure to elaborate, understand the dynamic, and respond in the clinical session to the stimuli that provoked the disproportionate reaction in the therapist–supervisee.

In chapter 6, "Supervision, Culture, and Context," Luis A. Vargas, Natalie Porter, and Carol A. Falender illustrate how contextual and systemic diversity factors enlarge the supervisory lens, informing the process. Supervisee and supervisor personal diversity multiple identities, and corresponding self-knowledge, frame approaches to conceptualization and therapy. The supervisory alliance is developed through consideration of the supervisee–supervisor–client triad and how the worldviews and preconceptions of each direct the therapy. Several supervisor approaches to contextual factors, biases, and belief structures toward the client, and personal diversity statuses, are described.

For Jeremy D. Safran, J. Christopher Muran, Christopher Stevens, and Michael Rothman, in chapter 7, "A Relational Approach to Supervision: Addressing Ruptures in the Alliance," attention to strains and ruptures goes beyond merely focusing on repair and the subsequent strengthened alliance; for them, even more important is the enhanced understanding of construction of events and self-awareness regarding working with one's own feelings and reactions, and the impact on relating.

In chapter 8, "Addressing Ethical and Legal Issues in Clinical Supervision," Gerald P. Koocher, Edward P. Shafranske, and Carol A. Falender describe circumstances in which legal and ethical dilemmas occur in supervision. The authors lay out the importance of the supervisory contract, which involves reaching contextual agreement on the limits of supervision and the ethical and legal framework. Supervisee vulnerabilities, multiple relationships, and boundary crossings are all placed in the perspective of supervisor competencies, with attention to best-practice problem-solving strategies for resolution.

Two specific applications in local clinical settings are provided by Philippe B. Cunningham and Jeff Randall in chapter 9, "Multisystemic Approaches to Supervision: Tales of Woe (Cultural Nonconnect) in Supervision and Understanding the Fit," and Cynthia Belar in chapter 10, "Supervisory Issues in Clinical Health Psychology." Cunningham and Randall show the convergence of evidence-based treatment and model-driven evidence-based supervision. They illustrate this with multisystemic therapy, an evidence-based intervention for youth diagnosed with conduct disorder and their families. They discuss best practices of supervisory alliance, attention to parallel process, strains and ruptures to the supervisory alliance, and dealing with cultural therapeutic impasses. Belar translates competency-based supervision to health psychology and behavioral medicine settings, with their unique challenges. She outlines the elaborate modeling and developmental assessment of progress that occurs in the context of supervisee self-assessment and the complexity of the range of competencies required for practice. Immediate demands and specific intrinsic circumstances of the local setting are integrated with multiple best practices, including a highly articulated definition of the supervision process, use of personal factors, and a strong supervisory alliance.

Finally, in chapter 11, "Evaluating and Enhancing Supervision: An Experiential Model," Derek Milne describes a developmental schema for monitoring, evaluation, and quality improvement in supervision. By tracking the behaviors that occur in the therapy session and in supervision, Milne defines the role of the supervisor in assisting the supervisee to engage in clinical exploration to enhance clinical skills. He describes cycles of experiencing, reflecting, and conceptualizing that occur before planning and experimenting, higher level functions, are implemented. Specific skills, knowledge, and values with respect to clinical work are identified in the process and are gradually assembled to form competencies. This model is also useful in providing a tool for self-evaluation of the supervisor's competencies by identifying which interventions are used, which are successful, and which modifications of behavior are most effective with particular supervisees and, ultimately, clients.

Together, these *Casebook* chapters provide supervisors and supervisees with a firsthand look at the process of supervision and how to implement it. Best practices are described in each chapter, with alliance, strains, feedback, evaluation, and self-assessment as common themes.

REFERENCES

Allen, J. (2007). A multicultural assessment supervision model to guide research and practice. *Professional Psychology: Research and Practice, 38,* 248–258.

American Psychological Association. (2002). Ethical principles of psychologists and code of conduct. *American Psychologist, 57,* 1060–1073.

American Psychological Association. (2006). *APA Task Force on the Assessment of Competence in Professional Psychology. Final report.* Washington, DC: Author.

APA Presidential Task Force on Evidence-Based Practice. (2006). Evidence-based practice in psychology. *American Psychologist, 61,* 271–285.

Baer, J. S., Ball, S. A., Campbell, B. K., Miele, G. M., Schoener, E. P., & Tracy, K. (2006). Training and fidelity monitoring of behavioral interventions in multisite addictions research. *Drug and Alcohol Dependence, 87,* 107–118.

Barnett, J. E. (2007). In search of the effective supervisor. *Professional Psychology: Research and Practice, 38,* 268–272

Bordin, E. S. (1983). Supervision in counseling: II. Contemporary models of supervision: A working alliance based model of supervision. *The Counseling Psychologist, 11,* 35–42.

Falender, C. A., Cornish, J. A., Goodyear, R., Hatcher, R., Kaslow, N. J., Leventhal, G., et al. (2004). Defining competencies in psychology supervision: A consensus statement. *Journal of Clinical Psychology, 60,* 771–787.

Falender, C. A., & Shafranske, E. P. (2004). *Clinical supervision: A competency-based approach.* Washington, DC: American Psychological Association.

Falender, C. A., & Shafranske, E. P. (2007). Competence in competency-based supervision practice: Construct and application. *Professional Psychology: Research and Practice, 38,* 232–240.

Gottlieb, M. C., Robinson, K., & Younggren, J. N. (2007). Multiple relations in supervision: Guidance for administrators, supervisors, and students. *Professional Psychology: Research and Practice, 38,* 241–247.

Kaslow, N. J., Borden, K. A., Collins, F. L., Forrest, L., Illfelder-Kaye, J., Nelson, P. D., et al. (2004). Competencies Conference: Future directions in education and credentialing in professional psychology. *Journal of Clinical Psychology, 60,* 699–712.

Kaslow, N. J., Rubin, N. J., Bebeau, M. J., Leigh, I. W., Lichtenberg, J. W., Nelson, P. D., et al. (2007). Guiding principles and recommendations for the assessment of competence. *Professional Psychology: Research and Practice, 38,* 441–451.

Kilminster, S., Cottrell, D., Grant, J., & Jolly, B. (2007). AMEE Guide No. 27: Effective educational and clinical supervision. *Medical Teacher, 29,* 2–19.

National Council of Schools and Programs of Professional Psychology. (2007). *Competency developmental achievement levels (DALs) of the National Council of Schools and Programs in Professional Psychology (NCSPP).* Retrieved January 15, 2008, from http://www.ncspp.info/DALof%20NCSPP%209-21-07.pdf

Papadakis, M. A., Teherani, A., Banach, M. A., Knettler, T. R., Rattner, S. L., Stern, D. T., et al. (2005). Disciplinary action by medical boards and prior behavior in medical schools. *The New England Journal of Medicine, 353,* 2673–2682.

Peterson, R. L. (1992). The social, relational, and intellectual context of the core curriculum and the San Antonio conference. In R. L. Peterson, J. D. McHolland, R. J. Bent, E. Davis-Russell, G. E. Edwall, K. Polite, et al. (Eds.), *The core curricu-*

lum in professional psychology (pp. 3–12). Washington, DC: American Psychological Association.

Rice, F., Cullen, R., McKenna, H., Kelly, B., Keeney, S., & Richey, R. (2007). Clinical supervision for mental health nurses in Northern Ireland: Formulating best practice guidelines. *Journal of Psychiatric and Mental Health Nursing, 14,* 516–521.

Rodolfa, E. R., Bent, R., Eisman, E., Nelson, P., Rehm, L., & Ritchie, P. (2005). A cube model for competency development: Implications for psychology educators and regulators. *Professional Psychology: Research and Practice, 36,* 347–354.

Rodolfa, E. R., Haynes, S., Kaplan, D., Chamberlain, M., Goh, M., Marquis, P., et al. (1998). Supervisory practices of psychologists—Does time since licensure matter? *The Clinical Supervisor, 17,* 177–183.

Rubin, N. J., Bebeau, M., Leigh, I. W., Lichtenberg, J. W., Nelson, P. D., Portnoy, S., et al. (2007). The competency movement within psychology: An historical perspective. *Professional Psychology: Research and Practice, 38,* 452–462.

Scott, K. J., Ingram, K. M., Vitanza, S. A., & Smith, N. G. (2000). Training in supervision: A survey of current practices. *The Counseling Psychologist, 28,* 403–422.

Thomas, J. T. (2007). Informed consent through contracting for supervision: Minimizing risks; enhancing benefits. *Professional Psychology: Research and Practice, 38,* 221–231.

Worthen, V. E., & Lambert, M. J. (2007). Outcome-oriented supervision: Advantages of adding systematic client tracking to supportive consultation. *Counseling and Psychotherapy Research, 7,* 48–53.

2

A COMPETENCY-BASED APPROACH TO SUPERVISION

NADINE J. KASLOW AND KANIKA D. BELL

This chapter is coauthored by the supervisor (Nadine J. Kaslow) and the supervisee (Kanika D. Bell), which reflects the partnership that characterizes effective supervisory endeavors. We offer a collaborative, integrative, and competence-based perspective on supervision. The dominant perspective guiding our approach to supervision is a competency-based model (Falender & Shafranske, 2004) that incorporates multiple approaches, most notably developmental (Stoltenberg, McNeill, & Delworth, 1998; Worthington, 1987), process-oriented (Bernard, 1997; Holloway, 1995), attachment theory (Neswald-McCalip, 2001; Pistole & Watkins, 1995), and psychotherapy based. Given that many psychologists (29%–35%; Norcross & Goldfried, 2005) and postdoctoral fellows (79%; Logsdon-Conradsen et al., 2001) self-identify as integrationists, under our approach both the supervisor and the supervisee integrate multiple theoretical orientations: attachment theory, object relations, interpersonal, family systems, existential or humanistic, psychoeducational, and cognitive behavior. We advocate for an integrative model, as we believe it offers a more comprehensive and flexible approach that can be tailored to the unique needs of each individual client. This integrative approach requires that each member of the dyad engage in developing competence and share with the other member of the team competence in multiple perspectives in case conceptualization and integration. The collaborative-, integrative-, and competency-based approach to supervision keeps at the forefront issues of development, gender, and culture as related to the supervisor, the supervisee, and the clients being served. In addition, transference and counter-transference dynamics and interpersonal process issues are focal.

In this chapter, we present our thoughts on a competency-based approach to supervision. We address various supervisory processes areas, including those related to the creation of an effective supervisory alliance and optimal learning environment, the inclusion of developmental considerations, and the ways in which diversity issues impact the process. The strengths and limitations of this perspective from the supervisee's point of view are enumerated, with particular attention paid to the potential for mentoring, the emphasis on empowerment, the safety of the supervisory relationship, and the opportunity to develop competence as a supervisor. Illustrative supervisor–supervisee narratives are presented with regard to the context of supervision, supervision goals and processes, and evaluation and outcomes. We close the chapter recommendations for competency-based approaches to supervision that underscore the collaborative aspect of the supervisory relationship.

DESCRIPTION OF THE SUPERVISION APPROACH

This section provides a description of the supervision approach. We focus on content areas, key supervisory processes, and strengths and limitations of the model.

Content Areas

Given the integrative nature of the competency-based model, interactions between supervisor and supervisee focus on the sociodemographics, history, biological status, behavior, cognition, affect, current interpersonal interactions, transference dynamics, and environmental context of the family, group, or client; how the therapist's personal history and life affect his or her encounters with the client; and the interactional patterns between the therapist and the client, the therapist and supervisor, and the therapist and other professionals working with the client. The supervisor enables the supervisee to gain greater familiarity with an integrative conceptual approach. Various forms of psychotherapy integration may be explored (e.g., common factors, technical eclecticism, theoretical integration, assimilative integration), depending on the particulars of the client (Stricker & Gold, 2003).

Processes

This section focuses on three processes that are key to the competency-based approach to supervision: creating an effective supervisory alliance and an optimal learning environment, considering developmental factors, and attending to individual and cultural diversity. A fourth process, related to evaluation and outcomes, is described in a later section. These processes reflect the major goals of this approach to supervision.

Creating an Effective Supervisory Alliance and an Optimal Learning Environment

Consistent with Winnicott's (1965) work on holding environments (i.e., the caregiver provides a supportive and empathic interpersonal environment that helps the child reduce anxiety, assume age-appropriate autonomy, and develop a meaningful sense of self) that facilitate healthy development and with attachment theory's emphasis on secure attachments for healthy personal and interpersonal functioning (Bowlby, 1988; West & Sheldon-Keller, 1994), this approach to supervision expects the supervisor to possess a range of personal and professional qualities to set the tone for an effective supervisory alliance and create an optimal learning environment. With regard to personal qualities, competency-based supervisors exhibit the capacity to be accepting, collaborative and nonauthoritarian, attentive, empathic and understanding, supportive and warm, encouraging, interpersonally sensitive, socially skilled, dependable, motivated, calm and able to self-regulate, adaptable and flexible, genuine, open-minded, imaginative and creative, self-aware, effective at conflict management, respectful of boundaries, trustworthy, and highly ethical. They demonstrate enumerable working alliance qualities, including the ability to establish an emotional bond that is characterized by support, trust, respect, care, and role clarity; foster collaboration and teamwork; develop an agreement on goals and tasks; acknowledge mistakes and share errors; work through and resolve conflicts; use appropriate self-disclosure; appreciate the dynamics of the supervisory relationship; and convey an understanding of the interpersonal characteristics (including attachment styles) that both parties bring to the relationship. Furthermore, competency-based supervisors are interested in the "person of the therapist," which includes the supervisee's reactions to the client, how one's own personal biases influence one's perceptions and responses, the ways in which one's personal dynamics influence the therapeutic and supervisory relationships, and parallel process phenomenon.

Taking Developmental Factors Into Consideration

The level of development of each party impacts her or his expectations, behavior, and learning. For example, postdoctoral fellows typically benefit most from supervision that acknowledges that they are transitioning to professional young adulthood and as a result are in the process of creating a more coherent and integrated sense of self separate from authority figures (Kaslow & Deering, 1994; Kaslow, McCarthy, Rogers, & Summerville, 1992). They most appreciate supervisors who engage with them collaboratively, and they value the collaborative relationships they form with their clients and with other care providers (Friedman & Kaslow, 1986).

Attending to Diversity

Supervision conducted in accord with a competency-based model addresses how the diversity characteristics of supervisor and supervisee influence events in supervision, examines the interaction among different forms of diversity, and challenges biases and behaviors indicative of the key "isms" (racism, sexism, heterosexism, ageism). Because both supervision and therapy itself occur within social, historical, political, and economic contexts, both supervisor and supervisee use this knowledge to guide the assessments, interventions, and consultations being performed in the context of supervision. Current guidelines on multiculturalism, sexual orientation, age, and so on (American Psychological Association, 2003, 2004; American Psychological Association, Division 44/Committee on Lesbian, Gay, & Bisexual Concerns Task Force, 2000) inform the supervision and the clinical work being supervised. Supervisees and supervisors also are evaluated (i.e., they evaluate one another) with regard to their knowledge, skills, and attitudes in working with diverse individuals (Daniel, Roysircar, Abeles, & Boyd, 2004; Pope-Davis & Coleman, 1997).

Strengths and Limitations of the Approach

This section offers both the supervisor's and the supervisee's perspective on strengths and limitations of a collaborative, integrative, and competency-based approach to supervision. The balance of the advantages and challenges of this model need to be considered in its implementation.

Perspective of the Supervisor

This supervisory approach has many positive attributes. A competency-based model provides clarity about the knowledge, skills, and attitudes that need to be acquired through the supervisory process at each developmental stage and in each functional competency (i.e., intervention) domain (Kaslow, 2004; Kaslow et al., 2004; Rodolfa et al., 2005). Attention also is paid to core foundational competencies, such as professionalism, ethics, and individual and cultural diversity. The focus in supervision is not just on building technical competence but also on addressing personal and interpersonal factors (Falender & Shafranske, 2004). The emphasis on an integrative model is intellectually stimulating and allows for flexibility in conceptualization and intervention on the basis of the needs of the particular client and the personal predilections of both the supervisor and the supervisee. The model places a high value on self-assessment, as well as on both formative and summative feedback, all of which are essential to the growth process (Falender & Shafranske, 2004). The collaborative nature of the approach makes it more rewarding and personally meaningful for both parties. One potential limitation of this approach is that it requires resources in terms of time, commitment, and investment on both the supervisor and the supervisee and the institution in which the supervision occurs. A second potential challenge is that the focus on an integrative model may not be focused enough and there may be tensions in the dyad if one party espouses an integrative orientation and the other has a focused theoretical framework.

Perspective of the Supervisee

From the perspective of the supervisee, a primary strength of the collaborative competency-based approach is its potential for mentoring (Johnson & Huwe, 2003). Supervisees appreciate the empowering balance of autonomy giving, support, and education. Competency-based supervision favorably compares with other models in that there is less overt management and more individualized training. Through attention to personal factors, it provides a safe context to process professional struggles, as well as a secure environment to disclose personal challenges that may impact one's professional life and functioning. Such a supervisory relationship also encourages and supports self-assessment. This might entail reflecting on biases and their impact on clinical encounters; processing countertransference reactions; and attending to interpersonal style and how it influences interactions with peers, colleagues, and clients.

Another key element is the value placed on the potential for developing supervisory skills (Falender et al., 2004). Supervisees find it empowering to be entrusted with the supervision of a more junior colleague and invaluable to have a supervisory relationship that emphasizes their becoming a competent supervisor. One of the hopes of this approach is that the supervisor serves as a role model for effective supervisory processes.

One potential limitation of the approach is that it may be time consuming. In addition, it may not be well-suited to certain theoretical orientations because of the process orientation. Furthermore, it requires a good supervisory relationship because it places demands on the interpersonal relationship.

AN EXAMPLE OF THE APPROACH

Below is an example of the supervision that involved the two authors: the supervisor and the supervisee, who is a postdoctoral fellow. The narrative covers a broad array of topics, including an integrative perspective that is developmentally informed, attention to diversity, contracting, alliance and learning environment, role of mentoring, person of the therapist, self-assessment, assessment of competence, feedback processes, and supervisory competence. These topics are key to the approach to supervision espoused in this chapter. When each topic is addressed in the narrative described below, it is noted in capital letters in parentheses.

Context of the Supervision

The authors work in a university-affiliated, large, urban public hospital that serves a predominantly African American population. The group therapy work supervised was associated with a clinical–research project funded by the Centers for Disease Control and Prevention, National Center for Injury Prevention and Control, on the assessment and treatment of African American women who were abused, suicidal, and low-income (Grady Nia Project). The supervisor, a Caucasian female, has worked in the setting for 15 years. The supervisee is an African American woman new to the hospital. The interaction highlighted here occurred during the year of her postdoctoral fellowship in psychology.

Supervision Goals and Processes

Goals

There were a variety of goals to this supervisory process. We aimed to engage in a collaborative relationship and use a developmentally informed integrative and competency-based approach to guide our efforts. We were committed to creating a meaningful working alliance that would support a facilitative learning environment. Doing so involved crafting a supervisory contract; bolstering the competence of the supervisee in the domains of intervention and supervision; focusing on the person of the therapist, including emphasizing the value of self-assessment; addressing diversity considerations; assessing the supervisee's competence incorporating both formative and summative feedback; and engaging in mentoring activities to support the supervisee's professional development.

Competency-Based Contracting, Feedback, and Evaluations

At the outset of the supervision, a contract was mutually developed that included the pertinent core domains of competence; activities associated with each competency domain; and expected knowledge, skills, and attitudes to be exhibited at the end of each 6-month period. This contract served as the basis for the supervisee's summative self-assessment at the

6-month and 1-year evaluation points, as well as the supervisor's summative assessment of the trainee at those same times. The supervisee had the opportunity to evaluate the supervisor on these same competency domains, allowing for parallel assessments. Informal, formative feedback in accord with the competency-based contract was offered in an ongoing fashion and often occurred simultaneously with the sharing of self-assessment feedback from each party.

Supervisor: [First meeting.] K, here is a format for a competency-based contract for our supervision. It includes the domains of competence relevant to our work on the Grady Nia Project: service [psychological assessment, intervention, consultation], scholarship and research, supervision that you provide, professional development, and other competencies. I want you to consider over the next week what activities you want to undertake related to each of the domains and what you would like to accomplish over the next 6 months. Next week, we can review your thoughts, complete the contract together, and agree on your roles, responsibilities, and performance expectations. (CONTRACTING)

Supervisee: [Second meeting.] It makes most sense to plan my activities and track my progress taking into account my future career goals. I am interested in both an academic and a clinical career, so I am glad that professional development is something that we can focus on, as I need help figuring out what I want to do next. Given what I am seriously considering, I hope that we can spend time focused on my supervision of others and publishing some research, as well as becoming more skilled in group therapy. I have never had the opportunity before to do ongoing supportive therapy groups or outpatient groups with highly traumatized people with few resources. (CONTRACTING)

Supervisor: It sounds then like our clinical focus should be on group work. Tell me more about what group therapy experiences you have already had, and what was helpful to you in the prior supervision you received on your group work and in your other clinical endeavors. (ALLIANCE AND LEARNING ENVIRONMENT)

Supervisee: My past group therapy work was with children and adolescents. I never did one in a hospital setting or with an audience that wasn't captive. Unfortunately, the supervision for my prior group work wasn't very helpful. Half of it was done by people who did not have much more experience than me clinically or who had different professional backgrounds, and thus we had dissimilar agendas for the groups. One supervisor micromanaged the group and was punitive in her recommended approach. It would have been more useful if my past supervisors and I had discussed the goals for the group work and the outcomes. Although my group therapy work wasn't well supervised, other supervisors' feedback has been invaluable. This has been from people who shared their own experiences with me and told me about their mistakes, balanced affirming and critiquing my efforts, made me feel appropriately confident, and acknowledged diversity issues. Oh, and I remember, I did have one really excellent group therapy supervisor. His passion was group therapy with adolescents and he was very interested in me personally, and in my developing an identity as a therapist and how I could bring myself into the therapy. (ALLIANCE AND LEARNING ENVIRONMENT)

Supervisor: Thanks for sharing that. I have a better sense of where you are starting in terms of your group therapy work with this population. If at any time the group therapy supervision isn't at the right level for you or isn't helpful enough, let me know. We can always alter our approach. I trust we will need to do so, as the groups are often complex, given the women we serve. (ALLIANCE AND LEARNING ENVIRONMENT)

Given that you are a postdoctoral fellow, I don't feel the need to micromanage your work. However, since this work is unfamiliar to you, I will share my insights with you regarding dealing with abused women, suicidal women, and women who frequently are in crisis and need to be managed primarily in an outpatient setting despite their often serious Axis I and Axis II problems. We can develop some general goals for the group work that can guide your efforts, but usually it is most effective if these goals are developed collaboratively with the groups' members themselves. (DEVELOPMENTAL)

I hope we can freely discuss issues of gender, race, and class on an ongoing fashion. I highly value culturally relevant assessments and interventions. I recall from when you interviewed here that we share this commitment. (DIVERSITY)

As far as the professional development focus of our work, I will do my best to help you sort out what you would like to do after completing your fellowship. We can discuss those issues as often as you would like. I agree that as you become clearer about your career trajectory, we can shift the emphasis of our work together and modify our expectations accordingly. (MENTORING)

I was sorry to hear that a number of your supervision experiences related to group work were unfavorable. Please let me know if our interactions do not feel positive or helpful. If this occurs, it is useful to me to hear your suggestions for improving our communication and work together. (ALLIANCE AND LEARNING ENVIRONMENT) I want you to know that if I have concerns about your work, I will share those with you in an ongoing fashion, so there won't be any surprises when the formal feedback comes. I will do my best to give you positive feedback along the way. (ONGOING ASSESSMENT OF COMPETENCE)

Don't hesitate to ask me for the good feedback, and I will provide you concrete examples of how you are progressing within each competency domain. (ONGOING ASSESS-MENT OF COMPETENCE)

Supervisee: [2 months into the supervision.] I feel like I know how to deal with the psychological and emotional needs of the women fairly well. We are establishing strong bonds, where they trust me and enjoy coming to group, and I like doing group. But I struggle with helping them with their basic deprivations; they are homeless, jobless, fighting to get their children back, and have serious health problems. I don't know how to assist them in accessing the resources they need. I am frustrated about this. (SELF-ASSESSMENT)

Supervisor: We can talk about how to help the women gain more resources than those available to them through the Resource Room and our social worker. But my sense is you know how to do that. I wonder if what might be more useful for you would be to reflect on the feelings their deprivation stirs up in you. (PERSON OF THE THERAPIST)

When I first came here, I felt overwhelmed by what felt like endless needs that could not be met and had rich White person's guilt. (PERSON OF THE THERAPIST, DIVERSITY)

Supervisee: I feel middle-class Black person's guilt. Even though we are of the same race, our lives are different. I don't know anything personally about searching for food on the streets, a real issue for many of these women. (PERSON OF THE THERAPIST, DIVERSITY)

Supervisor: How do you think the women respond to the class difference? How do you think this issue can be addressed best with them? (DIVERSITY)

Supervisee: Interestingly, they are proud of my accomplishments but don't seem to identify with them. They assume White women will be able to achieve what I have achieved. Someone in the group even asked me how my mama reacted to me finishing the PhD. I try to find ways we are similar and do appropriate self-disclosure. But I am careful about that. There are some ways in which I am similar to the women in the group that I haven't shared. What the women respond to best is my genuine empathy, regardless of whether it comes from experience. (DIVERSITY, PERSON OF THE THERAPIST)

Supervisor: Would it be helpful for us to discuss the things you have considered disclosing but have chosen not to do so? (PERSON OF THE THERAPIST)

Supervisor: [3 months into the supervision.] I have been giving you informal feedback along the way, and you have done the same with me. We both know that the formal evaluation of your performance doesn't occur until the 6-month point. But, as I mentioned when we first started meeting, it is helpful to have more formalized feedback at the midpoint. So, would you like us to do that today, or to have a chance to think about it and focus on the feedback in more depth next week? (FEEDBACK—FORMATIVE)

Supervisee: Let's do it now, but I appreciate your giving me the option.

Supervisor: It would be best if we review each competency domain we had intended to focus upon and consider your strengths, as well as areas for improvement. . . . Now that we've talked about the assessment and consultation aspects of the service contract, let's focus on the intervention part concerning the two groups and the individual therapy you have been doing. What are your intervention strengths? (SELF-ASSESSMENT)

Supervisee: My strongest strengths would be my ability to empathize and just listen. I try to avoid giving too much advice and lecturing the women. They've had enough of that in their lives. I want to communicate that this therapeutic environment is safe, one in which they feel comfortable being honest and expressing themselves. (SELF-ASSESSMENT)

Supervisor: You are gifted at creating a holding environment for the women that is both healing and empowering. I also believe you employ active intervention techniques that are important to the therapeutic work. I am curious about your reflections on additional strategies you use that help the women. (INTEGRATIVE APPROACH)

Supervisee: I do try various interventions, but not in a textbook fashion. I am not sure if my openness to an assortment of techniques and the way I blend interventions associated with different orientations is a strength or a weakness. (INTEGRATIVE APPROACH)

Supervisor: You raise a good point. Would it feel more like a positive attribute if we worked on your developing a better articulated integrated theoretical model? Having such a framework would increase the chance that your interventions felt less piecemeal and more synthesized. This is an optimal stage of your development for you to frame your own model, and I'm willing to guide you in that effort. (INTEGRATIVE APPROACH)

Supervisee: That would be helpful. I have been trying to find a way to piece together intervention techniques that I feel are useful from different schools of thought and, thus, define for myself an integrative orientation. (INTEGRATIVE APPROACH)

Supervisor: Sounds like we agree that this should be a priority area for us over the next several months. At the 6-month point, we can assess your sense of your capacity to formulate such a model and thoughtfully use the model to inform your interventions. You have the theoretical base, clinical acumen, and technical skills to create and utilize such a guiding framework. (ONGOING ASSESSMENT OF COMPETENCE)

Supervisee: [After reviewing all competency domains.] I like getting this comprehensive feedback at the midpoint. It is more beneficial to my development than waiting until the 6-month period. It gives me a better gauge of where I am, and what I still need to accomplish during the postdoc year. (ONGOING ASSESSMENT OF COMPETENCE)

Supervisee: [4 months into the supervision.] I've noticed something fascinating about the groups. The women speak differently when the other postdoc isn't there. They express more hostility towards Whites and make more comments about racism. They really like her and probably think it would be rude to say those things in front of her. They don't realize that she has worked with this population for a long time and is aware of the devastating effects of prejudice even though she has not experienced it personally. Most African Americans assume that other African Americans have experienced racism; it binds us across class I suppose. Maybe they think that she will misinterpret their anger and take offense. I don't want to talk with her, because the reality is that Black people act differently sometimes when White people aren't around. There is nothing she can do to change that. (DIVERSITY)

Supervisor: [After an examination of the supervisee's reluctance to discuss this with her cotherapist.] I appreciate your reluctance.

However, I think this is a relatively common phenomenon here and definitely worth exploring more with your cotherapist. I encourage you two to dialogue about this. It is important that she know what is going on in the group when she is not there, including things that relate to race, racism, and racially informed transferences. It is essential that you two explore what her interpersonal contributions may be to their perception. Even if you two conclude that there is nothing about her interactions that reflect a problem in cultural competence, I know as a White person working here, that there are always ways in which people can give me feedback that helps me more effectively converse with people very different from me in terms of race and class. Also, I am willing to talk with you two about this together. (DIVERSITY)

Supervisee: I don't think it would be necessary for you to meet with us, because I don't want her to feel she has done something wrong or insensitive. (DIVERSITY)

Supervisor: I realize and recognize that. However, just as you need to be biculturally or triculturally competent working here, so do I and so does she. So if she doesn't hear about this and reflect on how she can increase her cultural sensitivity, we deny her an important learning experience. (DIVERSITY)

Supervisee: I am still uncomfortable, partly about bringing this to a peer. But, I see the relevance, including just telling her we discussed this in group and in supervision. (SELF-ASSESSMENT, DIVERSITY)

Supervisor: I think too that as a postdoc, it is an important developmental issue to have these difficult conversations. How can I help you do so? (DEVELOPMENTAL)

Supervisee: [Next session.] I talked with her this week. She was eager to hear what I had to say; it was something she had thought about. She recognizes the differences between herself and the clientele at the hospital. She thanked me and we decided that when these issues emerge in the future, we will try to talk about them more directly. (DIVERSITY)

Supervisor: This sounds excellent; an important step for both of you. My bet is that not only will each of you grow from this conversation, but your cotherapy relationship will deepen, and your capacity to help the women in the group deal with racial differences and similarities will be enhanced. (DIVERSITY, DEVELOPMENTAL)

Supervisee: [5 months into the supervision.] I'm glad we are meeting today to address group on Friday. I realize that many of the women we serve have Axis II pathology, and I am comfortable dealing with that. But when a group member is floridly psychotic or in a full manic episode, it can become difficult to manage her and the rest of the group's reactions. Last Friday, X was in some sort of psychotic episode. We were surprised by her presentation because she had never behaved that way in all of the time she has been seen here. Based on her past records, she carries a diagnosis of paranoid schizophrenia, but here she was in a manic episode with psychotic features. She wore several layers of clothing, had makeup smeared on her face, and had no impulse control. She was remarkably paranoid and cursed out other group members. My main concern, other than her safety, was that the rest of the group would misinterpret her erratic behavior as aggression toward them. I got her admitted because she was in no position to go home from group. The group witnessed a fellow member being escorted by security down the hall to the inpatient unit. I debriefed the group after the incident and gave the women a chance to process their feelings. Fortunately, the women understood that this was not X's intentional behavior. They realized she was not trying to hurt their feelings, which was great because X was shouting hurtful things to them. Since Friday, I have gone to the unit to check on X and let her know that we are thinking about her. (INTERVENTION COMPETENCE)

Supervisor: I'm impressed with how you handled the situation. I wonder what impact it had on you. Whenever there is a crisis, it is important to reflect upon what you learned. (DEVELOPMENTAL, SELF-ASSESSMENT, PERSON OF THE THERAPIST)

Supervisee: That's an interesting question, because much of the debriefing I had to do that evening was for a group helper! She cried after group because she was offended and scared by X's behavior. It wasn't X's actions that affected me as much as the group helper's! I had to remember that I am in a supervisory role to the group helpers. She had never seen a psychotic episode like that, so she took X's aggressive language personally. I assured her that although one needs to have somewhat of a thick skin when working with the severely mentally ill, it is common to have feelings about crises. Her reaction made me realize that everyone in the group is emotionally invested, not just the participants. (SUPERVISORY COMPETENCE)

Supervisee: [6-month evaluation.] I need help job hunting. I have realized that psychologists are not sought on Monster.com, nor are positions posted in obvious places most of the time. My mentors have stressed networking, but I don't really know anyone professionally in Atlanta, as I did not go to school or internship here. (MENTORING)

Supervisor: Let's talk about your expertise and potential positions of interest to you. Now that you have passed the licensing exam, are halfway through the postdoc, and have done a great job, this aspect of your development should be central. (MENTORING)

Supervisee: I like the population here at the hospital. I have always been interested in working with underserved groups. My favorite things are assessments and group therapy with an inpatient or forensic populations. (SELF-ASSESSMENT, MENTORING)

Supervisor: I concur that those are areas of strength for you. It is evident that you like working with the clients here. Let's talk about possibilities and people to connect with in some of these areas. I am willing to contact people on your behalf. Bring your vita to supervision next week and we can revise it for the job market. As we discussed in the postdoc seminar, most people's CV's need to be modified as they transition to the real world. (MENTORING, ONGOING ASSESSMENT OF COMPETENCE)

Supervisee: Our discussion in the seminar was helpful. I learned some basics about what to put in and take off, but I would benefit from individual help. (MENTORING)

Supervisor: Over the week, I will think about people for you to contact. You can get your vita ready. (MENTORING)

Supervisee: [2 weeks later.] I changed my vita and it looks pretty good. I had some difficulty contacting the professionals you directed me to. I'm a bit scared of cold-calling people. I would like to know specifics about how certain people got their jobs and what their duties entail, but I don't know if they would feel comfortable sharing that information. I would appreciate people sharing the nuts-and-bolts stuff. (MENTORING)

Evaluation and Outcomes

In both an ongoing fashion and at discrete and predetermined time points (e.g., every 3 months), the supervisor and supervisee directly assess the positive and problematic aspects of the supervisory relationship and process, supervisory learning environment, and outcomes of the clinical work being supervised. Discussions focus on both parties' comfort with the relationship, agreement on supervisory objectives and effectiveness in achieving the stated goals, perceptions about each person's openness to feedback and willingness to use this input to make changes, trainee's views about the evaluative process and the supervisor's interpersonal style and professional competence, supervisor and supervisee's views on the extent to which the supervision enhanced the supervisee's professional competence, and a joint assessment of the supervisory impact (Falender & Shafranske, 2004; Lehrman-Waterman & Ladany, 2001). The trainee provides a written evaluation of the supervisor according to the same core competency domains on which he or she is evaluated as a supervisee. On the basis of the joint assessment of the supervisory relationship and process, the parties mutually determine modifications needed to improve the alliance and learning environment. A plan of action is put into place to ensure alterations are made to the satisfaction of both concerned.

Using the contract as a guide, the supervisor, supervisee, and supervisee's supervisee provide feedback on the trainee's functioning in each core competency domain. Feedback includes attention to factual knowledge, clinical skills, judgment, interpersonal attributes (e.g., openness, flexibility, positivity, cooperativeness, willingness to accept and use feedback, awareness of impact on others, ability to deal with conflict, acceptance of personal responsibility, ability to express feelings effectively and appropriately, and awareness of personal strengths and limitations and the need for continuing professional education), capacity to extend clinical skills to new situations and contexts, ethical sensitivity, cultural competence, and development of a primary professional identity as a psychologist (Frame & Stevens-Smith, 1995; Friedman & Kaslow, 1986; Overholser & Fine, 1990; Stigall et al., 1990). Many supervisors who practice from a competency-based framework incorporate standard assessment tools of such constructs as the working alliance and multicultural competence (Bernard & Goodyear, 1998; Falender & Shafranske, 2004). Supervisors recognize the importance of using objective criteria when providing feedback, communicating input clearly and directly, attending to the power dynamics inherent in the supervisory relationship, and ensuring that all feedback is offered in a humane fashion (Cormier & Bernard, 1982; Porter & Vasquez, 1997).

Given that the focus of this approach is on the supervisee's competence, one key element of the evaluation is the assessment of the clinical outcomes of the work being conducted (Ellis & Ladany, 1997; Stein & Lambert, 1995). Such an evaluation must occur in a fashion that is both formative and summative. Attention is paid to the link between the supervisee's clinical knowledge, skills, and attitudes and the progress made by the client with regard to alleviating symptom distress and improving interpersonal relations and social role performance. Audiotapes, videotapes, review of detailed process notes, cotherapy, or live supervision are supervisory methods that facilitate the assessment of client outcomes and their link to the supervisee's performance. The next section of narrative illustrates various aspects of the assessment of competence in our supervisory work.

> *Supervisor:* [Month 7 (time of the writing of this chapter).] As we have talked about previously, today we will review your self-assessment, my feedback on your performance, and your supervisee's feedback about you. We can review this by competency domain and then use the integrated input to inform our discussion of your goals and activities for the next 6 months. For each domain, let's examine the activities you have completed to date, how you met your goals in this domain, and your areas of strength and ways in which you can improve. We need to talk about how I can help facilitate these improvements. (ONGOING ASSESSMENT OF COMPETENCE)

The following are excerpts from the review for two domains: direct service and supervision provided by the supervisee; there is not space in this chapter to review all other domains—scholarship and research, professional development, other competencies, and involvement in training activities.

> *Supervisee:* [After describing direct service activities completed to date.] I am doing well on the psychodiagnostic assessments, but clearly I need more exposure to projective tests. I would like to get more experience witnessing or participating in forensic evaluations. I am enjoying and doing well with the inpatient groups. Nia groups are going well, but I may have initially underestimated the basic level needs of the women. I can relate to some of their struggles as Black women or depressed persons, but I have often felt powerless when I did not have answers about key things, like how to obtain food, shelter, employment. In terms of consultation, I had the pleasure, thanks to you, of involvement with a local nonprofit organization having problems due to personal disputes between two of its managerial staff members. Unfortunately, one disputant is no longer employed with the organization, but I enjoyed problem solving with the facility's director. I hope to consult more in the future. I didn't realize that problem solving and mediation were strengths of mine. I hope to develop these skills further. (SELF-ASSESSMENT)

> *Supervisor:* You have accomplished a great deal in the direct service domain. I am extremely pleased with your performance. I concur with your assessment of your strengths. As you can see from my evaluation, I would add the following. You are gifted

at forming a strong therapeutic alliance with your clients. Some of our most challenging clients have formed secure attachments to you, are more engaged in treatment than they have ever been, and are improving the quality of their lives. You handle crises in a calm and responsible fashion, do a good job of establishing and monitoring therapeutic goals and applying therapeutic strategies effectively, and have managed terminations professionally. I appreciated your willingness to volunteer to do that consultation. Next time I need assistance with such work, I will invite you. I concur that you have very strong skills in negotiation. These have served you well on the interdisciplinary clinical and research teams on which you work. I really appreciate your sensitivity to diversity considerations in all aspects of the assessment, intervention, and consultation process. You have done an excellent job of raising diversity issues in supervisions, seminars, and team meetings. You have an impeccable sense of professional ethics; that matters a great deal to me. (ONGOING ASSESSMENT OF COMPETENCE, DIVERSITY)

Supervisee: It is good to hear that the evaluation of my strengths is expanding. It is nice to know that at this level of training, I am continuing to improve. I am saying this based on supervisor evaluations over time. It is good to know that I have gained more competence in more areas. (ONGOING ASSESSMENT OF COMPETENCE)

Supervisor: Yes, a longitudinal perspective on one's professional development can be a very gratifying experience. You are right where you should be professionally, and I am confident that you will continue to grow and develop because of your sincere commitment to the learning process and to your own professional growth. (MENTORING)

Supervisee: What do you think about what I named as weaknesses and what would you add? (ONGOING ASSESSMENT OF COMPETENCE)

Supervisor: I think your self-assessment is quite accurate with regards to both your strengths and areas for improvement. Another area that we could potentially focus on more in supervision would be in terms of using empirical data to guide your interventions. Because of our need to focus on addressing the women's day-to-day needs and concerns, as well as your reactions to their plights, we have not taken enough time to consider what the evidence base might add to your conceptualization and intervention armamentarium. (ONGOING ASSESSMENT OF COMPETENCE)

Supervisee: That's true. I think what would be helpful to me would be more conversations about my evolving integrative theoretical perspective and how to ensure that the interventions I conduct reflect this unified approach to psychotherapy and the associated research.(SELF-ASSESSMENT, INTEGRATION)

I really value being a supervisor. I like being in the position to supervise more junior colleagues. It is a great opportunity for me, given that being a supervisor is part of what I want to do professionally. I think it is helpful to the students to have someone supervise them who is close to their level of development. As a supervisor, I am very accessible, which is important given the severity of the pathology and crises of our clients. I tend to my supervisee's personal–professional needs, as well as deal with the client issues. I do a good job helping them to process their feelings regarding their work. (SELF-ASSESSMENT, PERSON OF THERAPIST)

Supervisor: I have been impressed in our weekly conversations about your supervision by your dedication to the process, warm and engaging style as a supervisor, comfort sharing your knowledge with your supervisee, and desire to hone your supervisory skills. As we review the feedback you received from your supervisee, it is obvious that she was impressed by the quality of the supervisory relationship; your knowledge about and sensitivity to both ethical and legal considerations and individual and cultural diversity; and your capacity to effectively impart your knowledge, skills, and attitudes to her regarding interventions and consultations. (ONGOING ASSESSMENT OF COMPETENCE, PERSON OF THE THERAPIST, DIVERSITY)

Supervisee: We got along great; her written and oral feedback to me is consistent with my perception of the relationship. It was challenging to me early on asserting myself as the expert in the room. She asked a lot of questions right off about what she was supposed to do, because she had never worked with individuals with such severe psychiatric disorders before. I want to improve my ability to assess a supervisee's developmental level early on, so I know what they are and are not ready for. (SELF-ASSESSMENT)

Supervisor: That is a good area for us to focus on over the next few months. I don't have any other things I think you need to work on, as you seem developmentally on track for where you should be. You just need more experience, and as you supervise a broader range of individuals, more supervisory challenges will emerge. You have been fortunate that your first experience has been with such a good trainee. It appears that each of you have grown a lot. (DEVELOPMENTAL)

CONCLUSION AND RECOMMENDATIONS

Our coauthoring of this chapter reflects the approach to supervision we recommend, namely a collaborative endeavor with the supervisor guiding the supervision and the supervisee playing a major role in the coconstruction of the relationship and the work. Although we believe that all competency-based approaches to clinical supervision must be collaborative, we recognize that the form this collaboration will take will depend on a multitude of factors, including the developmental stage of both participants, the context in which the supervision is conducted and in which the work being supervised occurs, the nature of the work itself, and the degree to which the supervisee's level of competence matches the expected level of competence. As the narrative shows, effective supervision requires the infusion of diversity considerations into all aspects of the work (Tummala-Narra, 2004).

The competency-based approach to supervision that is the focus of this chapter provides a framework for working with trainees who manifest competence problems. If developmentally informed expectations for knowledge, skills, and attitudes in each competency domain are clearly articulated but not met by a supervisee, a competency-based remediation plan must be put into effect. In addition to remediation activities that are educational in nature, such a plan may require personal psychotherapy (Elman & Forrest, 2004). Developing and implementing an appropriate remediation plan requires a level of supervisory competence; strong institutional and/or collegial support; and an appreciation of the complexities of the supervisory role as educator, mentor, and gatekeeper (Forrest, Elman, Gizara, & Vacha-Haase, 1999; Gizara & Forrest, 2004).

With the shift in the profession of psychology toward viewing supervision as a core competency (Falender et al., 2004), more attention needs to be paid to devising and implementing education and training programs in a competency-based approach to supervision at the graduate school, internship, postdoctoral, and continuing professional education levels. For these training efforts to be most beneficial, the knowledge base about supervision processes must be expanded and enhanced. For example, common and distinguishing factors among supervisory approaches need to be articulated. Our field also would benefit from a richer perspective on supervision methods that reflect integrative theoretical approaches and the meaningful synthesis of science and practice (Falender & Shafranske, 2004). Greater delineation of optimal processes for formative and summative evaluation would be useful (Falender & Shafranske, 2004). It would be advisable for the profession to identify the degree and nature of competence expected for supervisees in each core competency domain at each stage of development. Similarly, developmental levels of supervision competence of the supervisor need to be better understood. Furthermore, a consensus needs to be secured regarding when a supervisee's performance is incompetent, that is, when it falls below the acceptable threshold in any of the core competencies. Qualitative and quantitative research methodologies should be used to advance the profession's knowledge about these issues. Unfortunately, there has been a dearth of empirical work conducted on supervision in general and on a competency-based approach to supervision more specifically.

In closing, we hope that our chapter mirrors to some extent the supervisory process—that is, that it combines didactic information with personal sharing. The emphasis on theory integration and competencies is more didactic in nature, whereas the focus on interpersonal processes, transference and countertransference dynamics, the supervisory relationship, and the career development of the supervisee is more personal in nature. We recognize, however, the challenge of presenting narrative, as the reader is not privy to what comes before and after the narrative presented or the affective tone of the interactions. Our conversations are intended as guides to be adapted for each supervisory relationship.

REFERENCES

American Psychological Association. (2003). Guidelines on multicultural education, training, research, practice, and organizational change for psychologists. *American Psychologist, 58,* 377–402.

American Psychological Association. (2004). Guidelines for psychological practice with older adults. *American Psychologist, 59,* 236–260.

American Psychological Association, Division 44/Committee on Lesbian, Gay, & Bisexual Concerns Task Force. (2000). Guidelines for psychotherapy with lesbian, gay, and bisexual clients. *American Psychologist, 55,* 1440–1451.

Bernard, J. M. (1997). The discrimination model. In J. C. E. Watkins (Ed.), *Handbook of psychotherapy supervision* (pp. 310–327). New York: Wiley.

Bernard, J. M., & Goodyear, R. K. (1998). *Fundamentals of clinical supervision* (2nd ed.). Needham Heights, MA: Allyn & Bacon.

Bowlby, J. (1988). *A secure base: Parent–child attachment and healthy human development.* New York: Basic Books.

Cormier, L. S., & Bernard, J. M. (1982). Ethical and legal responsibilities of clinical supervisors. *The Personnel and Guidance Journal, 60,* 486–491.

Daniel, J. H., Roysircar, G., Abeles, N., & Boyd, C. (2004). Individual and cultural diversity competency: Focus on the therapist. *Journal of Clinical Psychology, 80,* 755–770.

Ellis, M. V., & Ladany, N. (1997). Inferences concerning supervisees and clients in clinical supervision: An integrative review. In J. C. E. Watkins (Ed.), *Handbook of psychotherapy supervision* (pp. 447–507). New York: Wiley.

Elman, N., & Forrest, L. (2004). Psychotherapy in the remediation of psychology trainees: Exploratory interviews with training directors. *Professional Psychology: Research and Practice, 35,* 123–130.

Falender, C. A., Cornish, J. A. E., Goodyear, R., Hatcher, R., Kaslow, N. J., Leventhal, G., et al. (2004). Defining competencies in psychology supervision: A consensus statement. *Journal of Clinical Psychology, 80,* 771–786.

Falender, C. A., & Shafranske, E. P. (2004). *Clinical supervision: A competency-based approach.* Washington, DC: American Psychological Association.

Forrest, L., Elman, N., Gizara, S., & Vacha-Haase, T. (1999). Trainee impairment: Identifying, remediating, and terminating impaired trainees in psychology. *The Counseling Psychologist, 27,* 627–686.

Frame, M. W., & Stevens-Smith, P. (1995). Out of harm's way: Enhancing monitoring and dismissal processes in counselor education programs. *Counselor Education and Supervision, 35,* 118–129.

Friedman, D., & Kaslow, N. J. (1986). The development of professional identity in psychotherapists: Six stages in the supervision process. In F. W. Kaslow (Ed.), *Supervision and training: Models, dilemmas, and challenges* (pp. 29–49). New York: Haworth Press.

Gizara, S. S., & Forrest, L. (2004). Supervisors' experiences of trainee impairment and incompetence at APA-accredited internship sites. *Professional Psychology: Research and Practice, 35,* 131–140.

Holloway, E. L. (1995). *Clinical supervision: A systems approach.* Thousand Oaks, CA: Sage.

Johnson, W. B., & Huwe, J. M. (2003). *Getting mentored in graduate school.* Washington, DC: American Psychological Association.

Kaslow, N. J. (2004). Competencies in professional psychology. *American Psychologist, 59,* 774–781.

Kaslow, N. J., Borden, K. A., Collins, F. L., Forrest, L., Illfelder-Kaye, J., Nelson, P. D., et al. (2004). Competencies conference: Future directions in education and credentialing in professional psychology. *Journal of Clinical Psychology, 80,* 699–712.

Kaslow, N. J., & Deering, C. G. (1994). A developmental approach to psychotherapy supervision of interns and postdoctoral fellows. *Psychotherapy Bulletin, 29,* 20–23.

Kaslow, N. J., McCarthy, S. M., Rogers, J. H., & Summerville, M. B. (1992). Psychology postdoctoral training: A developmental perspective. *Professional Psychology: Research and Practice, 23,* 369–375.

Lehrman-Waterman, D., & Ladany, N. (2001). Development and validation of the evaluation process within supervision inventory. *Journal of Counseling Psychology, 48,* 168–177.

Logsdon-Conradsen, S., Sirl, K. S., Battle, J., Stapel, J., Anderson, P. L., Ventura-Cook, E., et al. (2001). Formalized postdoctoral fellowships: A national survey of postdoctoral fellows. *Professional Psychology: Research and Practice, 32,* 312–318.

Neswald-McCalip, R. (2001). Development of the secure counselor: Case examples supporting Pistole and Watkins's (1995) discussion of attachment theory in counseling supervision. *Counselor Education and Supervision, 41,* 18–27.

Norcross, J. C., & Goldfried, M. R. (Eds.). (2005). *Handbook of psychotherapy integration* (2nd ed.). New York: Oxford University Press.

Overholser, J. C., & Fine, M. A. (1990). Defining the boundaries of professional competence: Managing subtle cases of clinical incompetence. *Professional Psychology: Research and Practice, 21,* 462–469.

Pistole, M. C., & Watkins, C. E. (1995). Attachment theory, counseling process, and supervision. *The Counseling Psychologist, 23,* 457–478.

Pope-Davis, D. B., & Coleman, H. L. K. (1997). *Multicultural counseling competencies: Assessment, education and training, and supervision.* Thousand Oaks, CA: Sage.

Porter, N., & Vasquez, M. (1997). Covision: Feminist supervision, process, and collaboration. In J. Worell & N. G. Johnson (Eds.), *Shaping the future of feminist psychology: Education, research, and practice* (pp. 155–171). Washington, DC: American Psychological Association.

Rodolfa, E. R., Bent, R. J., Eisman, E., Nelson, P. D., Rehm, L., & Ritchie, P. (2005). A cube model for competency development: Implications for psychology educators and regulators. *Professional Psychology: Research and Practice, 36,* 347–354.

Stein, D. M., & Lambert, M. J. (1995). Graduate training in psychotherapy: Are therapy outcomes enhanced? *Journal of Consulting and Clinical Psychology, 63,* 182–196.

Stigall, T. T., Bourg, E. F., Bricklin, P. M., Kovacs, A. L., Larsen, K. G., Lorion, R. P., et al. (1990). *Report of the Joint Council on Professional Education in Psychology.* Washington, DC: The Joint Council on Professional Education in Psychology.

Stoltenberg, C., McNeill, B., & Delworth, U. (1998). *IDM supervision: An integrated developmental model for supervising counselors and therapists.* San Francisco: Jossey-Bass.

Stricker, G., & Gold, J. (2003). Integrative approaches to psychotherapy. In A. S. Gurman & S. B. Messer (Eds.), *Essential psychotherapies: Theory and practice* (2nd ed., pp. 317–349). New York: Guilford Press.

Tummala-Narra, P. (2004). Dynamics of race and culture in the supervisory encounter. *Psychoanalytic Psychology, 21,* 300–311.

West, M. C., & Sheldon-Keller, A. E. (1994). *Patterns of relating.* New York: Guilford Press.

Winnicott, D. W. (1965). *The maturational process and the facilitating environment.* New York: International Universities Press.

Worthington, E. L. (1987). Changes in supervision as counselors and supervisors gain experience: A review. *Professional Psychology: Research and Practice, 19,* 189–208.

3

DEVELOPMENTAL APPROACHES TO SUPERVISION

CAL D. STOLTENBERG

Over the years, a considerable amount of research and theorizing about the supervision process, including how trainees change over time, has examined the supervision process as being different from the processes both specifically involved in therapy and those conceived from the perspective of psychotherapy theory (e.g., Loganbill, Hardy, & Delworth, 1982). Generally, in these supervisory theories, an implicit stage theory of therapist development is assumed and supervisory behaviors that are thought to be consistent with the hypothesized level of development of the therapist are specified (Stoltenberg, McNeill, & Crethar, 1994; Worthington, 1987). Focus on therapist change over time from both a quantitative and qualitative perspective serves as the critical difference between developmental and other approaches to supervision (Falender & Shafranske, 2004). Central to a competency-based approach to supervision is the ability to accurately assess the trainee's competence within the context of his or her developmental status and trajectory. The integrated developmental model (IDM) provides a conceptual and empirical approach to development. This chapter briefly overviews the IDM and presents an example that shows how the approach can be implemented. The importance of assessing and intervening at different levels of supervisee development across domains (explained later) is highlighted.

Stoltenberg and Delworth (1987) and, later, Stoltenberg, McNeill, and Delworth (1998) have presented the most comprehensive and detailed model of therapist development and supervision to date, the IDM. The primary basis for this model includes the work of Hogan (1964), Loganbill et al. (1982), and Stoltenberg (1981); theories of human development; and several empirical studies of therapist development (see also Stoltenberg, 1993, 1997, 1998, and Stoltenberg, McNeill, & Crethar, 1995, for expansions of aspects of the IDM). The IDM uses three overriding structures to monitor trainee development through three levels (plus a final integrated level) across various domains of clinical training and practice, thus integrating quantitative and qualitative processes and providing markers to assess development across domains.

The three structures are self and other awareness (with both cognitive and affective components), motivation, and autonomy. These three structures are the developmental markers for change in the therapist-in-training over time across eight domains of professional activity. The *self and other awareness* structure indicates where the trainee is in terms of self-preoccupation, awareness of the client's world, and enlightened self-awareness. The cognitive component includes the content and quality of the thought processes, whereas the affective component accounts for the emotional experience of the trainee moving from anxiety-based uncertainty and lack of confidence (Level 1); through emotional reactions to the client, including empathy (Level 2); and culminating in an awareness of one's personal emotional experience (including an insightful emotional reaction to the client and awareness of countertransference), empathy with the client, and an ability to reflect on the experience (Levels 3 and 3i; see Table 3.1). *Motivation* reflects the trainee's interest, investment, and effort expended in clinical training and practice. The *Autonomy* structure addresses the degree of dependence or independence demonstrated by trainees over time. A particularly important aspect of this approach is the recognition that a trainee is likely to be functioning at different developmental levels for various domains of professional activity.

CONTENT AREAS AND PROCESSES

The domains of professional activity can be conceptualized in varying degrees of specificity. Stoltenberg et al. (1998) offer the following categories: intervention skills competence, assessment techniques, interpersonal assessment, client conceptualization, individual differences, theoretical orientation, treatment goals and plans, and professional ethics (American Psychological Association [APA] Ethics Code; APA, 2002; see also the APA Web site version at http://www.apa.org/ethics/). Although each could be further reduced to more specific domains, the general categories serve to high-

TABLE 3.1
Developmental Levels and Structures

Level	Motivation	Autonomy	Self and other awareness
1	Motivated	Dependent; need for structure	Cognitive: limited self-awareness; Affective: performance anxiety
2	Fluctuating between high and low; confident and lacking confidence	Dependency–autonomy conflict; assertive vs. compliant	Cognitive: focus on client; understand perspective; Affective: empathy possible, also over-identification
3	Stable; doubts not immobilizing; professional identity is primary focus	Conditional dependency; mostly autonomous	Cognitive: accepting and aware of strengths and weakness of self and client; Affective: aware of own reactions and empathy
3i	Stable across domains; professional identity established	Autonomous across domains	Personalized understanding crosses domains; adjusted with experience and age

Note. From *IDM Supervision: An Integrated Developmental Model for Supervising Counselors and Therapists* (pp. 28–29), by C. D. Stoltenberg, B. W. McNeill, and U. Delworth, 1998, San Francisco: Jossey-Bass. Copyright 1998 by Cal D. Stoltenberg. Reprinted with permission of the author.

light the fact that one must carefully attend to the focal activity in which the trainee is engaging to adequately assess the developmental level at which the trainee is functioning at any given time. *Intervention skills competence* address the trainee's confidence in and competence in carrying out therapeutic interventions. *Assessment techniques* address the trainee's confidence in, and ability to conduct, psychological assessments. *Interpersonal assessment* extends beyond a formal assessment and includes the use of self in conceptualizing a client's interpersonal dynamics. *Client conceptualization* incorporates, but is not limited to, diagnosis. This domain goes beyond an axis diagnosis and involves the therapist's understanding of how the client's characteristics, history, and life circumstances blend to impact adjustment. *Individual differences* includes an understanding of ethnic, racial, gender, and cultural influences on individuals, as well as the idiosyncrasies that form the person's personality. *Theoretical orientation* involves formal theories of psychology and psychotherapy as well as eclectic approaches and personal integration. *Treatment goals and plans* addresses how the therapist conceptualizes and organizes his or her efforts in working with clients in the psychotherapeutic context. Finally, *professional ethics* addresses how professional ethics and standards of practice are intertwined with personal ethics in the development of the therapist (see Exhibit 3.1).

According to the IDM, the twin processes of assimilation and accommodation induce a trainee's upward movement. Piaget (1970) described *assimilation* as the process of fitting reality into one's current cognitive organization. *Accommodation*, however, was defined as significant adjustments in cognitive organization that result from the demands of reality. Piaget considered assimilation and accommodation to be closely interrelated in every cognitive activity (Miller, 1989). Attempts to assimilate involve minor changes in the individual's cognitive structures as he or she adjusts to new ideas, whereas accommodation involves the formation of new constructs through the loosening of old ones.

Additional models of development provide other ways of viewing the process of therapist development. For example, Anderson's (1985, 1996) model of cognitive development describes changes from novice to expert status that includes more abstract representations in memory of relevant processes and pattern match. In addition, the ability to reason forward from known information, rather than reason backward from a problem statement, constitutes change from novice to expert. Expanding this to the clinical realm, one can see expert therapists engaging in forward thinking, leading to diagnosis and treatment from recognition of patterns displayed by clients with regard to personality characteristics, environmental circumstances, and therapist reactions to the client. Novice therapists are more likely to focus in on specific presenting problems or therapeutic processes and reason backward,

EXHIBIT 3.1
Integrated Development Model Structures and Domains

Overriding structures
- Self and other awareness
- Cognitive
- Affective
- Motivation
- Autonomy

Specific domains
- Intervention skills competence
- Assessment techniques
- Interpersonal assessment
- Client conceptualization
- Individual differences
- Theoretical orientation
- Treatment goals and plans
- Professional ethics

Note. From *Supervising Counselors and Therapists: A Developmental Approach* (p. 36), by C. D. Stoltenberg and U. Delworth, 1987, San Francisco: Jossey-Bass. Copyright 1987 by Cal D. Stoltenberg. Reprinted with permission of the author.

without recognizing broad patterns. Similarly, the concept of "schema development" (Gagné, Yekovich, & Yekovich, 1993) captures processes similar to what is delineated in the IDM regarding therapist development.

Essentially, the IDM suggests assimilation occurs within levels (Level 1, *novice,* through Level 3i, *expert*) and accommodation occurs between levels. In terms of cognitive development, initial formulation of simplistic schemata reflecting one's understanding of clients and the therapeutic process are refined into more encompassing concepts with more broadly associated links to other schemata. For the present case study, I used a practicum rating form for trainees (a rough estimate of developmental level) prior to and after the supervision experience. A rather extensive case conceptualization format provides the supervisor with useful information about the supervisee's clients and, more importantly, forces trainees to collect a broad spectrum of information about their clients, on which to build a conceptualization. Another measure was used, the evaluation of supervision form to evaluate the supervisee's perception of supervision.

Supervisory interventions, as one might expect, should vary according to the developmental level of the trainee (for any given domain). The IDM uses five categories of supervisory interventions to classify supervisor strategies. These are depicted in Table 3.2. Facilitative interventions are appropriate

TABLE 3.2
Supervision Interventions

Intervention strategy	Purposes
Facilitative: nurturing atmosphere; conducive to growth, warmth, liking, respect; conveys trust	Reduces anxiety; allows for reflection and introspection
Confrontive: highlights discrepancies; compares and contrasts emotions, beliefs, and behaviors	Examination and comparison; achieve congruence
Conceptual: theories, principles, substantive content; gives meaning to events, ties together isolated events	Integrate theory and research; analytical thinking
Prescriptive: specific plan of action; direct intervention; prescribes treatment or specific instructions; eliminates certain behaviors	Gives guidance; ensures client welfare; satisfies dependency
Catalytic: promotes change; gets things moving; highlights, defines, articulates, or enhances meaning; processes comments	Stirs things up, promotes reflection and integration

Note. Originally adapted from "Toward a General Theory of Consultation," by R. R. Blake and J. S. Mouton, 1978, *Personnel and Guidance Journal, 56,* p. 330. Copyright 1978 by the American Counseling Association. Adapted with permission. Adaptation for *Supervision Interventions* (handout included in workshop materials), by E. Hardy and C. Loganbill for, 1984, for *Psychological Supervision* (workshop), Iowa City: University Counseling Service, Iowa Memorial Union, University of Iowa. Copyright 1984 by E. Hardy and C. Loganbill. Adapted with permission of the authors.

across levels. For Level 1 trainees, in addition, prescriptive and conceptual interventions are useful. In late Level 1, catalytic interventions can be appropriate. For Level 2, in addition to facilitative interventions, confrontive, conceptual, and catalytic interventions are used regularly. For Level 3, facilitative interventions remain important; confrontive interventions are occasionally used; and conceptual and catalytic remain useful.

STRENGTHS AND LIMITATIONS OF THE APPROACH FROM THE POINT OF VIEW OF THE SUPERVISEE

Entry-level knowledge and skills are expected of the trainees, with higher degrees of each consistent with more advanced levels. Values of the trainee should reflect consistency with the APA Ethics Code (APA, 2002). Reactions to the approach have been consistently positive, with an appreciation for the explicit acknowledgement of variability in knowledge and skills across levels of trainees. Some anxiety on the part of the trainee is expected, and desired, as a motivating influence on the trainee's development (consistent with Piaget's [1970] concept of "disequilibrium"). This can (and should) result in some level of discomfort for the trainee on an ongoing basis so as to stimulate growth (overly comfortable people do not grow). Typically, the process of engaging in learning psychotherapy provides sufficient motivating anxiety that additional stress need not be applied by the supervisor. Common challenges reflect accurate assessment of developmental level for the various domains of professional practice in play during any given supervisory relationship (or any given session). In addition, being flexible in one's ability to respond to the appropriate developmental level for the different domains (often within one session) is challenging. Within the context that I conduct supervision, informal formative evaluation is ongoing, with summative evaluations given at midsemester (oral) and end of the semester (written).

DIVERSITY ISSUES IMPACTING THE SUPERVISORY PROCESS

The supervisor can function most effectively when he or she is aware of the personal and professional values that impact his or her practice. Awareness of one's own cultural background, that of the supervisee, and those of the clients are all important in enabling the creation of an effective supervision environment. Assessing the effects of culture in addition to, and apart from, therapist development is necessary. Gender differences are also important variables to monitor in the supervisory (and therapeutic) relationship.

EXPECTED FUTURE DEVELOPMENTS AND DIRECTIONS

I maintain that this approach is not bound to any one therapeutic orientation, but research has not yet been conducted across all current approaches. The content of supervision, however, will differ by therapeutic orientation, although the process should remain fairly consistent. I expect clinical and research advances to largely fit into the overall framework of this model.

AN EXAMPLE OF THE APPROACH

The following example describes the context in which the supervision occurred, the goals and processes, and the evaluation and outcomes.

Context of the Supervision

The supervision relationship occurred in our Counseling Psychology Clinic, which functions as a community mental health center in a city with a population close to 100,000. The clinic serves a breadth of clientele with diverse cultural backgrounds, ages, and socioeconomic statuses. Clients' presenting problems are typical of community mental health centers with a wide range of chronicity and diagnostic categories and tending to have clients near the lower end of the economic spectrum. Services provided include individual counseling and psychotherapy, family therapy, and marital therapy, in addition to a wide range of assessment services, all with sliding scale fees. Therapists are either master's students in community counseling or school counseling programs, or doctoral students in counseling psychology. Master's students spend their 1st year in the program engaged in practica at the clinic, whereas doctoral students spend a minimum of 2 full years in practica at the clinic (3 full years if they enter with a bachelor's degree but not a master's degree). All supervision of doctoral students is provided on site by faculty in the counseling psychology program. Supervision of master's students is provided by advanced doctoral students as part of a practicum in clinical supervision.

For the present case study, the student supervisee was a 28-year-old single Caucasian man in his 2nd year of the program. He was originally from the Midwest and grew up in a family of limited financial means. He entered with a master's degree in counseling (having had practica in his prior program) and experience working with an adolescent population. His primary theoretical orientation was client centered, although he had experience with cognitive behavioral, relational–cultural, and narrative approaches. During the course of this supervision relationship, lasting over 4 months (one semester), he worked primarily with individual clients, although he also had two married couples in his caseload. He worked with a cotherapist (female doctoral student, 1 year behind him in the program) when engaging in couples therapy.

I was the supervisor in the case study. I am a married Caucasian man (51 years old at the time of the supervision), and I also grew up in the Midwest in a rural setting, in a blue-collar farm family. I have a PhD in counseling psychology and have been active in clinical supervision for 23 years. I am a professor in the program, as well as the director of training. At the time of this supervision relationship, I was responsible for eight supervisees (seeing them weekly for individual supervision and group supervision or case conference). My therapy orientation is integrative, relying on client-centered, cognitive behavior, and psychodynamic theories to inform my work with clients. As noted earlier, my orientation to supervision is developmental, following the IDM.

Supervision Goals and Processes

The supervisee had completed his 1st full year in the doctoral program, which included two long semesters and the summer session in practicum. I have supervised 2nd-year students in our program for 18 years, occasionally picking up other supervisees with less experience, but usually focusing on this group. Our students go through the program as a cohort, so the trainee had been in practicum for the entire year with the same other seven students. Barring significant experience in counseling, psychotherapy, or assessment prior to entering the program (typically 5 years or fewer as a practicing master's-level therapist), I expect most supervisees in this practicum to be functioning at Level 2 in at least some domains and probably Level 1 in others. Although I had access to prior evaluations of the supervisee completed by other supervisors, I chose to meet with him first before looking over the evaluations so as to approach him with fresh eyes and not be overly influenced by the perceptions of others for our initial meeting.

As is typical for my supervisory sessions, our initial meeting was spent getting to know one another and discussing general training goals for the semester. One of the primary assumptions of the IDM is that therapists personalize their understanding of the therapy process and how they engage in it. As one's personal attributes and characteristics are important influences on one's behavior as a therapist, I find it important to focus considerable attention on getting to know the supervisee. During this session, the supervisee told me things about himself that he saw as important, discussed how he perceived himself as growing through the training process, and shared some expectations for our work together.

> *Supervisee:* I think I've grown a lot over the past year in my effectiveness as a therapist and for sure in my understanding about

5

SUPERVISION ADDRESSING PERSONAL FACTORS AND COUNTERTRANSFERENCE

EDWARD P. SHAFRANSKE AND CAROL A. FALENDER

We are never truly "neutral" observers and interpreters. In every word and comment we implicitly convey something of our own life experience, our standards and beliefs, something we feel about the patient as a human being. How could it be otherwise?

—Emanuel Peterfreund (1983, p. 108)

Psychotherapeutic work, no matter its theoretical perspective, involves human engagement and understanding. These complementary abilities—to relate to the other and to know the other—draw on a backdrop of countless interpersonal experiences for their performance. In addition to formal clinical training, such personal experiences shape the foundation of interpersonal competencies used in professional practice and influence in subtle and, at times, dramatic ways the therapist's ability to relate with empathy to the client and to fully participate in and effectively facilitate the therapeutic process. Clinical supervision provides one crucial entry point by which the supervisee will come to appreciate the intersection of personal and professional factors, internalize professional attitudes, and develop approaches to more effectively bring the 'person' of the therapist as an ally into the service of the treatment. We open this discussion emphasizing the normative and ever-present contributions of personal factors to clinical practice, and we reserve the term *countertransference* for more carefully delineated phenomena that require more pointed examination within supervision and management within the therapeutic relationship. We further discriminate *objective countertransference* (reactions of the psychotherapist induced by the client's maladaptive perceptions, affects, and behavior, which are consistent with the responses of significant others in the client's life) from *subjective countertransference* (uncharacteristic and, at times, maladaptive reactions of the psychotherapist emanating from personal factors). We then present an orienting approach to personal factors and describe a process model to explicitly address countertransference in supervision.

THEORETICAL OVERVIEW

Clinical supervision provides a setting for novice clinicians to explore the nature of their personal reactions and the impact such reactions have on the therapeutic process. Integral to this supervisory task is the use of a theoretical framework in which the influence of personal factors, subjective and objective countertransference reactions, and mutually constructed enactments can be understood.

Personal Factors

Each of us, as psychologists, well before we ever entered graduate school or met our first client, formed fundamental ways of relating to others. We assimilated family and culture-bound styles of interpersonal relating, formed attitudes and beliefs about human nature, and absorbed the worldviews and mores of the ethnic, social, political, cultural, intellectual, gendered, economic, and spiritual communities in which we inhabit. These inescapable frameworks of identity, forged out of interaction with our surroundings, establish fundamental assumptions about self and others, instill ethical values, and furnish a feeling or sense of being at home in the world. Not solely products of internalization, our personal identities reflect dynamic, emergent sources of meaning and motivation, which result in continuity of self-experience and self-agency over time. As we assimilate new experience into our inherited social reality, we may question (or even reject) aspects originating in our given multicultural identities; however, the imprint of these seminal influences remains. Personal perspectives, commitments, and loyalties emerge out of the dialectic between freely authoring our lives and our historical and cultural embeddedness. These personal factors influence professional work, as clinical understanding inevitably draws from the multicultural sources shaping our identities.

Our perspectives are not only shaped by forces of individual psychology but are influenced by the loyalties we hold to the particular social worlds that contributed to the formation of our identities. Fowers (2001) suggested "being loyal is inherently exclusionary and discriminatory" (p. 269) and leads to partiality:

> It [loyalty] emphasizes our embeddedness in family, culture, and nation and that we are unavoidably partial to these groups. Our attachment to

these groups and the way of life in which we have been socialized is deeper than abstract reason and more compelling than most calculations of consequences. (p. 279)

Such loyalties engender notions of difference and may delimit our ability to fully understand and to empathize with others' worlds of experience. For example, internalized homophobia (Gelso, Fassinger, Gomez, & Latts, 1995; Hayes & Gelso, 1993) may influence our ability to understand the other and may perpetuate expressions of prejudice.

Supervision provides a context to develop appreciation for the personal factors that inform clinical understanding and engagement with clients. Central to this task is demonstrating in practice that our understanding is always perspectival and bears the "inescapable influence of personal interests, commitments, and the cultures out of which personal meaning is constructed" (Falender & Shafranske, 2004, p. 83). In addition to affecting one's understanding of another's experience, influences of history and culture impact styles of interpersonal relating, particularly in respect to the expression of emotion and mores regarding interpersonal conduct. Through careful examination of points of *subjective conjunction* (when the supervisee believes to be in sync with the worldview of the client) and *subjective disjunction* (when the supervisee experiences confusion, disbelief, or disagreement about the client's perspective), the role of personal factors can be elucidated, because it is in self-perceived moments of heightened empathy or disconnection when the contributions of the therapist's implicit meaning system are most apparent. The intention of bringing into awareness the persistent influence of personal factors is consistent with the multicultural guidelines of the American Psychological Association (APA; 2003) which recognize that as cultural beings, psychologists (supervisees and their supervisors) may hold attitudes and beliefs that can detrimentally influence their perceptions of interactions with individuals who are different from themselves (p. 19). Differences in behavioral expectations based on cultural norms for interpersonal conduct, for example, accepting a gift or exchanging an embrace, contribute as well to the therapeutic relationship. In our view, personal factors derived from one's familial and multicultural identities continuously influence the therapeutic and supervisory processes.

Countertransference

Drawing on Kiesler (2001), we consider countertransference to be a class of clinical phenomena, unique among the personal factors experienced by psychotherapists, which refers to "distinctly different, unusual, or idiosyncratic acts or patterns of therapist experience and/or actions toward a client [that constitute] deviations from baselines [in the therapist's usual practice]" (pp. 1061–1062). Similar to all personal factors, countertransference influences the conduct of therapy; however, unique to these phenomena is their potential to heighten emotional reactivity in the therapist, prompting not only intense affective states but also resulting in nonreflective and, at times, unintended actions. Such actions, when in the extreme, may threaten the therapeutic alliance and imperil the treatment. Whereas the interplay of personal factors in the usual course of treatment allows for discussion, correction, and reinterpretation of misunderstandings and misattunements, the therapeutic dyad under the influence of countertransference (often related to transference) holds the possibility of rapid acceleration of forms of engagement or enactments, which further strains the alliance and foreclose meaningful therapeutic collaboration. This is particularly the case when working with clients who present histories of severely compromised interpersonal relationships and difficulties in maintaining self-regulation. Norcross (2001) observed that

> Most theoretical orientations place considerable emphasis on the inner work of the therapist—how to constructively harness the intense, conflictual, and often painful reactions of working with difficult people— even if they do not invoke the term (Safran & Muran, 2000). All theoretical traditions, moreover, recognize the therapist's contribution to the treatment process and the need for therapist self-care when experiencing the looming despair, sudden rage, or boundary confusion that is all part of countertransference. (p. 981)

Although agreement might be obtained among clinicians with respect to describing the behavioral manifestations and phenomenology of countertransference, controversy has swirled around its origins, nature, and value.

Countertransference has been broadly applied to refer to the personal reactions of the psychotherapist; however, originally it was more narrowly defined. Freud (1910/1957) conceived of countertransference as "a result of the patient's influence on [the physician's] unconscious feelings" (p. 144) and concluded, "no psychoanalyst goes further than his own complexes and internal resistances permit" (p. 145). From this perspective, countertransference was seen as a manifestation of the therapist's transference in response to the client and an obstacle to be overcome (p. 144). Freud later added to his conceptualization the notion that the doctor may use his or her unconscious mind to understand the patient's unconscious mind. Like a double helix, the notions of countertransference as a hindrance to treatment and as a vehicle for understanding have been intertwined throughout the development of the concept (Epstein & Feiner, 1979, p. 490). Although a comprehensive review of the use and meaning of the term is beyond the scope of this chapter, the following summary presents major theoretical perspectives appearing in the clinical literature, which offer hypothetical models to employ within supervision.

Freud's (1910/1957) original emphasis on the activation of the therapist's transference remains a salient perspective (Brenner, 2006). For example, Luborsky and Barrett (2006), following their review of the literature, proposed the therapist's responses to the patient were based on significant patterns of relating in the therapist's life. Similarly, Gelso and Hayes (2007) conceptualized these dynamics in terms of the *countertransference interaction hypothesis* in which "countertransference results from the interaction of particular patient actions or triggers (words, intimations, characteristics, behaviors) with particular therapist conflicts and vulnerabilities" (pp. 131–132). This perspective emphasizes the role of subjective countertransference (Spotnitz, 1969), in which the unresolved conflicts in the therapist are seen to contribute to inappropriate and defensive reactions on the part of the therapist manifested by avoidance.

An alternative perspective was presented in Heimann's (1950) pivotal article, which expanded countertransference to "cover all of the feelings" (p. 81) the therapist has toward the client and provided an important tool to understand the client's unconscious. In this totalistic perspective, countertransference originated in the client and reflected unconscious pressure exerted into the therapist by way of projection identification, thus stimulating heightened emotional reactions in the clinician. Although controversy remains as to the relative contributions of the client and the therapist in the production of such mental contents in the therapist (Gabbard, 1995; Jacobs, 1999), "most contemporary Kleinians now accept the notion that the therapist's countertransference may reflect the patient's attempt to evoke feelings in the therapist that the patient cannot tolerate" (Gabbard, 2001, p. 285; see also role-responsiveness theory [Sandler, 1976]). Relevant to this perspective is Winnicott's (1949) notion of *objective countertransference*, in which the therapist's reactions are seen to be responses to "the actual personality and behavior of the patient based on objective observation" (p. 45) and reflect reactions generally evoked in others by the client's maladaptive behavior (Hafkenscheid, 2003; Kiesler, 2001). Important to our discussion, the totalistic or comprehensive perspective encourages the exploration of countertransference and places emphasis on its beneficial aspects in gaining awareness of the client's intrapsychic life as well as the interpersonal impacts and pressures enacted within the therapeutic relationship.

An intersubjective perspective, which considers experience to be socially constructed, imports a postmodern sensitivity that emphasizes the contributions of both the client and the therapist to shape each other's responses. *Countertransference* (and *transference*) may be viewed as "an inexplicably intertwined mixture of the *clinical* participants' subjective reactions to one another" (Dunn, 1995, p. 723), and clear distinctions between the psychotherapist's countertransference and the client's transference become blurred. Rather than conceiving of reactions as the products of isolated minds, an intersubjective perspective recognizes an individual's reactions to be the products of the interaction, influenced by self-experience and contextual factors. Drawing on social constructivism from a psychoanalytic relational point of view (Hoffman, 1983, 1991) and the model of the "analytic third" from a contemporary neo-Kleinian–Bionian perspective (Ogden, 1994, 2005), countertransference is seen as a mutually constructed phenomenon emanating out of the intrapsychic and interpersonal interactions within the therapeutic encounter. An emphasis within supervision, drawing on this approach, would view the emotional reactions and behaviors of the supervisee to be important data reflecting not only the dynamic interactions between the client and therapist but also involving the contributions of the supervisor (Corpuz, Falender, & Shafranske, 2006).

Countertransference may be viewed globally to include all of the personal reactions of the therapist to the client, as products of their interpersonal interactions. Such reactions may also be understood to reflect the therapist's unconscious transference to the client, or alternatively, as the contents of the client's mental life that have been projected onto and contained by the therapist. No matter the specific interpretative stance taken, countertransference is an important area for exploration within clinical supervision and management within psychotherapy training.

THE SUPERVISORY PROCESS

The process of supervision bears the responsibility of ensuring the highest level of patient care, while simultaneously affording the supervisee with an opportunity to practice, leading to development of clinical competence. The task of learning psychotherapy is difficult on many levels because of its complexity and the unique interpersonal and psychological demands placed on the therapist. Psychotherapy is often stressful, despite what is usually conveyed in clinical texts, and this is particularly the case for the novice clinician. The experienced psychotherapist, on the one hand, develops over time skills at living with "the pressure of person on person, with its attendant anxieties, satisfactions, cautions, and effort" (L. Friedman, 1988, p. 6). The supervisee, on the other hand, faces every session with a degree of doubt in himself or herself and uncertainty as to what to expect in the clinical interaction. Supervision provides a vehicle to process the wide range of personal reactions that are stimulated in the consulting room, to foresee and correct any possible mishandling of the case, and to provide support to the supervisee in developing abilities to understand and to engage the client in a meaningful therapeutic process. Whereas deficits in knowledge and technical skill may be readily addressed through additional training, shortcomings in fundamental interpersonal skills; conflicts arising from unresolved psychological issues;

unproductive reactions when working with difficult patients; or biases, inflexibility, and prejudice pose particular challenges. In our view, a supervisory working alliance must be in place and a modicum of trust developed to address personal factors and countertransference with the supervisee. We also suggest that a preparatory phase can be initiated that will assist in establishing a strong foundation on which personal factors can be addressed. Included within this preparation are the following:

- *Alliance:* Through the mutual identification of training goals and objectives and consensus on the means to achieve the goals, a respectful, cordial, and collaborative relationship is initiated.
- *Supervisory contract:* The expectation that personal factors and countertransference will be addressed in supervision is discussed and incorporated into the supervisory contract. The development of self-awareness of personal factors affecting the therapeutic process, the ability to use consultation effectively, and the ability to manage countertransference reactions are explicitly identified as professional competencies to be developed in clinical raining and supervision.
- *Explicit orientation to personal factors:* The supervisor introduces the conceptual framework for understanding the role of personal factors in the conduct of psychotherapy as well as in supervision. Emphasis is placed on the normative nature of the confluence of personal and professional factors in psychological practice. Exposure to selected theoretical and empirical literature as well as personal supervisor discussion and personal disclosure encourage openness to this dimension of practice.
- *Modeling:* The supervisor models appropriate disclosure in briefly sharing how aspects of his or her own multicultural identities contribute to clinical practice.
- *Initial exploration of personal factors and strengths:* In training activities and in individual supervision, the supervisee and supervisor initiate exploration of personal factors and signature strengths that contribute positively to the supervisee's competence.

Following this opening phase, it is important that exploration of personal factors be consistently addressed within supervision, or the meta-message will be communicated that issues related to multicultural diversity and individual differences do not really matter. Of particular importance is the development of the understanding that everyone is located within multiple cultural locations and that attention to multicultural issues is not only a matter of clinical relevance, it is a professional responsibility (APA, 2003). Fowers (2001) wrote the following:

> This attachment to culture is an unavoidable part of being human and the ambiguities, tensions, and conflicts of being a participant in culture are just as present among mainstream Americans as among members of minority groups. Matters of culture are important whether we are working with a member of another cultural group or someone who shares much of our own cultural background. . . . Culture is not about people from other groups; it is a powerful part of all of our identities. (p. 277)

In our view, it is important to place emphasis on the multiple cultures in which we are embedded, for instance, gender, religion or spirituality, age, ableness, economic status, and so on, and to consider individual differences not as static entities but rather as dynamic dimensions, which have meaning between individuals. Such a process of exploration is not about categorization but is rather about thoughtful reflection about the dynamic contexts in which these cultures interact, particularly with the clinical setting.

Management of Countertransference

Exploration and management of countertransference are best accomplished on the foundation of a well-established supervisory alliance in which consideration of personal factors has been routinely encouraged. Such a foundation can be further enhanced by supervisor modeling in which supervisors disclose examples of the countertransference pressures they have faced when conducting psychotherapy. It is important for the supervisor at the beginning of the rotation to assess the supervisee's familiarity with the countertransference literature and to enhance understanding about the intersection of personal factors, multicultural identities, and countertransference; the ubiquitous nature of countertransference; the nature of enactments; the clinical contexts in which countertransference often is aroused; and the expectation to bring countertransference material into the supervision. Failure to address countertransference may lead to alliance ruptures in the therapeutic relationship and potentially in the supervisory relationship as well. The following points may be helpful reminders in establishing a context to process countertransference within supervision:

- Countertransference is a particular kind of personal factor that originates in a variety of clinical contexts; efforts to identify and to understand its nature and impact on the treatment is a clinical competency and is to be addressed in clinical supervision.
- Clinical competence includes the awareness of personal factors, which influence the therapeutic process, as well as skills in effec-

tively bringing countertransference reactions into the service of the treatment.

- Countertransference may elicit positive and/or negative responses in the therapist and take the forms of distinctly unusual, idiosyncratic, or uncharacteristic acts or patterns of therapist experience and/or actions toward a client, which may include enactments and parallel processes involving the supervisory relationship.

- Countertransference is an informer of the therapeutic process and can provide important insights into the client's relational world, the therapist's relational world, and the schemas or internal object relations affecting the clinical relationship. Both objective and subjective forms of countertransference may occur in the therapeutic process, which require differentiation and management.

- The supervisory alliance must be established before countertransference can be meaningfully addressed and managed.

- It is critical to maintain the boundary between supervision and psychotherapy when addressing countertransference reactions. Any exploration of supervisee personal factors must be specifically related to the conduct of the treatment provided by the supervisee.

- How supervisees address and manage countertransference reactions is more important than the fact that such reactions occur. Countertransference reactions may involve either avoidance or inappropriate overinvolvement, which serve self-protective and defensive functions.

Clinical supervision plays a crucial role in the management of countertransference by providing the supervisee a supportive and safe environment to identify and explore his or her personal reactions and to use clinical theories to organize understanding and to reinstate a productive therapeutic relationship. In many instances, supervisees will freely bring their countertransference reactions into supervision. Others are less likely to do so, because of inadequate understanding of countertransference, limited self-awareness, defensiveness, or lack of trust and safety in the alliance, among other reasons. Supervisors need to inquire into the supervisee's experience when departures from usual clinical conduct occur, when the supervisee reports or the supervisor observes distinctively unusual subjective states (boredom, confusion, irritation, excitement, fascination, arousal), or when treatment is not progressing. Gelso and Hayes (2002) identified five factors, personal and professional competencies, which are associated with the management of countertransference (see Table 5.1); each plays a crucial role in supporting the exploration and management of countertransference in supervision.

TABLE 5.1
Five Factors in Countertransference Management

Factor	Description
Self-insight	The extent to which the therapist is aware of his or her own feelings, including countertransference feelings, and understands their basis.
Self-integration	The therapist's possession of an intact, basically healthy character structure. In the therapy interaction, such self-integration manifests itself as a recognition of ego boundaries or an ability to differentiate self from other.
Anxiety	Refers to the therapist's ability to allow himself or herself to experience anxiety as well as management the internal skill to control and to understand anxiety so that it does not bleed over into their responses to patients.
Empathy	The ability to partially identify with and put one's self in the other's shoes; permits the therapist to focus on the patient's needs despite the difficulties the therapist may experience in the work. Also, empathic ability may be part of sensitivity to one's own feelings, including countertransference feelings, which in turn ought to prevent the acting out of countertransference.
Conceptualizing	The therapist's ability to draw on theory in the work and grasp ability theoretically the patient's dynamics in terms of the therapeutic relationship.

Note. Based on Gelso and Hayes (2002, pp. 420–421).

The exploration and management of countertransference may be accomplished through a collaborative process in supervision that involves identification of the indicators of countertransference, facilitation of self-reflective functions, elaboration of the possible origins and meanings of countertransference through the inclusion of theory, and development of metacommunication strategies to manage the countertransference.

A Process Model for Addressing Countertransference

Countertransference has been considered in the totalistic view to be an ongoing, pervasive influence within the therapeutic relationship. The spontaneous and disciplined responses of the psychotherapist originate from both personal and professional sources. Although theoretically these influences can be discriminated and their origins isolated, in practice these factors interpenetrate and are expressed globally as organizing principles. Even in instances in which discrete memories reveal specific dynamic starting points, mental contents immediately are associated within existing webs of meaning; as such, clear lines between personal and professional influence are difficult to identify. The psychologist will be in different states of mind in respect to countertransference at various points in the therapeutic process. That is not to imply that there are moments in which the clinician is either influenced or not by countertransference. In our view, it is more accurate to assume that personal factors are always in play, and from the totalistic perspective, countertransference is always present.

In our view, the more narrow definition of countertransference is more useful in clinical supervision, when monitoring supervisee behavior, particularly when considering Kiesler's (2001) criteria: "distinctly different, unusual, or idiosyncratic acts or patterns of therapist experience and/or actions toward a client [that constitute] deviations from baselines" [in the therapist's usual practice] (pp. 1061–1062). The impact on supervisee therapeutic behavior and on the therapeutic process may be of greater or lesser influence, depending on the extent to which the content evokes conflict in the psychologist. The development of a countertransference conceptual model to identify and to describe the states of mind or mental activities likely to occur under such influence contributes to the examination of the role of personal factors in psychological treatment. Bouchard, Normandin, and Séguin (1995) provide useful categories to classify such mental states or activities, based in part on an empirical research approach, the Countertransference Rating System developed by Normandin and Bouchard (1993). Although this approach is anchored in psychoanalytic terminology, we find that the phenomena that are described and the metacognitive process can be applied across theoretical perspectives. This model includes specific stages of processing and requires different interventions on the part of the supervisor.

The Objective–Rational State

In the objective–rational state, the clinician is participating in what is regarded (by the psychotherapist) as an objective observation of another's subjectivity. For example, Intern A is conducting an interview with a new client. As the client describes her long-standing depression and the chaos in her life, the trainee feels empathically moved and, in the moment, she feels that she has fully grasped her client's suffering. She reports to her supervisor with absolute certainty that she "gets this client" and believes that her perceptions are sound and that her understanding is objective. Bouchard et al. (1995), drawing on Buber (1970), characterized this as an "I–it mode" (p. 740), in which the clinician is mentally oriented toward observing from the outside rather than from the inside as a subject. Understanding the client is enhanced by the systematic observation of cognitions and behaviors, through the vicarious introspection of subjective experience, or through the analysis of one's identifications, in which the client may have projected disowned aspects of self onto the therapist through projective identification and other aspects of countertransference. Although the term *objective* is used in the title, we suggest that perception is never purely objective (the intern's perceptions are shaped by her subjective experience of empathy as well as by her developing skill in making clinical observations). The label of *objective* refers to the clinician's subjective experience of obtaining objective understanding. This is a state in which personal factors, although silently influencing the therapist, are not resulting in distinctive shifts in state of mind or in behavioral changes and remain almost invisibly in the background.

The Reactive State

The reactive state is one in which the psychologist is organizing experience primarily under the influence of countertransference. This state corresponds to the more narrow view of countertransference, which poses a hindrance to objectivity and results in distinctive, idiosyncratic states of mind and therapist behavior—states and behaviors that are out of the ordinary. In this state of mind, the capacity for objective–rational observation is suspended. It is a state primarily motivated by influences derived from personal, rather than professional, sources. Bouchard et al. (1995) suggested, from a psychoanalytic object relations perspective, that the manifestations of this state may result in impulsive, defensive–rational, or retrospective–defensive–rational reactions. These are states in which the clinician is under pressure to act or to defend against acting under the influence of the countertransference. In the dialogue from the case illustration, presented subsequently, the supervisee is in a heightened state of agitation, which limited her ability to bring into meaningful dialogue the client's behaviors; she was in a highly reactive state, feeling overwhelmed and angry.

The objective–rational state cannot be reentered under the state of countertransference without first recognizing the reactive state of mind and then processing within the reflective state, described in more detail below. The process of recognition commences when the clinician (or with the help of the supervisor in supervision) observes the discrepancy between his or her reactions in contrast to more usual forms of emotional, ideational, and behavioral responding. For example, if the therapist is in a unique state of agitation for which there is seemingly no external precipitant and only with a given client, this alerts the therapist that something unusual is going on. This awareness leads to a break in the immediacy of the enactment, and the clinician decenters from a reactive state and enters into a mode of reflection.

The Reflective State

This state is based on the ability of the clinician to make his or her own personal subjectivity the object of observation. In our view, this includes intentionality, curiosity, psychological-mindedness, nondefensiveness, and open-endedness, as well as other personal and professional capacities. The supervisee must have the capacity to maintain an awareness of the reactive state to examine the contents of the countertransference and to obtain a clinically useful understanding of the enactment. The supervisor assists by explicating and by encouraging the supervisee to nondefensively reengage in the state of mind that he or she was feeling during the session. The state comprises four distinct processes: *emergence, immersion, elaboration,* and *interpretation.*

Emergence. This subphase commences at the moment in which the psychotherapist gains a glimmer of awareness of countertransference responses. This awareness may reveal a shift in his or her emotions, thoughts, and behavior and sometimes is characterized by the recognition of being in an unusual state of mind, for instance, confusion, boredom, or fear. Essentially, emergence is a state in which the therapist is able to pause and think about his or her immediate experience. As the clinician is able to stay engaged with the experience (rather than avoiding or acting out of the state of mind), emergence of conscious self-awareness is supported. Supervision assists the novice clinician to pay attention to these glimmers of self-awareness, to contain emotional over-arousal, and to examine the meaning of the atypical states of mind or behavior they are experiencing in the therapeutic (or supervisory) relationship.

Immersion. This subphase concerns the intentional expansion of associations to the experience. By encouraging the supervisee to reflect on the salient moments in the session (as is facilitated in interpersonal process recall [Kagan, 1980]), associations such as memories, fantasies, and identifications, can be meaningfully brought into awareness.

Elaboration. Elaboration involves what Bouchard et al. (1995) referred to as "integrative elaboration" (p. 742). As the term implies, this subphase brings the supervisee's associations together within the context of clinical theory, which brings meaning to the experience of the countertransference and provides a means to understand the impacts on the therapeutic process.

Interpretation. This is the endpoint of the process of reflection and involves the development of a provisional understanding of the meaning and origins of the clinician's countertransference reactions. In supervision, the supervisor facilitates growth in the supervisee's self-reflective capacity and assists the novice psychotherapist to consider ways in which his or her reactions can be usefully brought into the service of the treatment.

Enhancing Self-Awareness and Clinical Use of Countertransference

Although initially developed for a psychoanalytic audience, the countertransference conceptual model provides a useful starting point for consideration of therapist competencies important to the management of countertransference, such as self-insight and self-integration (Hayes, Gelso, Van Wagoner, & Diemer, 1991; Van Wagoner, Gelso, Hayes, & Diemer, 1991). The components of the reflective state may be integrated into a heuristic, although not necessarily psychodynamic, process in supervision. The subphases of immersion and elaboration depict an approach to working with countertransference and personal factors that may be facilitated in supervision. Exploration of personal factors in supervision may be augmented by further study of the theoretical and research literature on countertransference (Friedman & Gelso, 2000; Hayes, 2004; Singer, Sincoff, & Kolligan, 1989) and clinical resources (Pope, Sonne, & Greene, 2006).

Following this process, supervision focuses on identifying strategies to address any difficulties arising from the countertransference. This may include judicious use of self-disclosure and engagement in metacommunication interventions, with the client focusing on repair of alliance strains or ruptures (see chap. 7, this volume, for a detailed discussion and chap. 5 of Falender & Shafranske [2004]).

AN EXAMPLE OF THE APPROACH

The following excerpt presents an important phase in a clinical case in which countertransference was significantly impacting the therapeutic process and illustrates the use of the countertransference conceptual model within supervision (which will be highlighted in the process commentary included in the brackets at the ends of narrative lines). As depicted in the transcript, the client, a Caucasian woman in her early 30s with depression with borderline features, related to the supervisee, a Caucasian female clinical psychology doctoral student in her mid-20s, in a highly dismissive tone, often criticizing or ignoring what seemed to be fairly empathic, supportive comments and symptom-focused interventions. In this phase of the treatment, the supervisee was aware that she was experiencing distinctive and idiosyncratic states of mind and was becoming aware that she was behaving in unusual ways during session, for instance, being curt in her tone, repeatedly glancing at the clock, and so on. The transcript begins with the supervisee in an agitated state of mind, immediately following a session with her client. In terms of the stages in the process model, the supervisee was in the emergent subphase (having already achieved a measure of self-awareness) and was beginning to process her reactions. The initial supervisor interventions were intended to facilitate immersion into the experience and entry into the subsequent elaboration subphase.

Supervisee: I am just so angry. I am fed up . . . I can't take this from her . . .

Supervisor: What are you experiencing right now, what's coming to mind, as you think of Shauna and your work with her? [This intervention aims to encourage immersion by facilitating self-reflection and directing attention to her associations.]

Supervisee: I hate it, what she does to me over and over . . .

Supervisor: Over and over?

Supervisee: Whatever I say, she rejects . . . when she was crying, I reflected, "You're feeling sad" and she says, "No, I'm not sad, I'm ah, somewhat sad, um unhappy"; then I confirm that, and she says, "No, I'm not really unhappy, I'm frustrated." Whatever I do, it's the same . . . I can't do anything . . . do anything right . . . earlier when we tried a CogB approach, she would just say, "Nothing helps" and not follow through; she was marginally compliant, and then she'd almost smile at me and say, "My problems are important . . . these baby steps don't help. I'm not like most people you see." Then I'd inquire and try to be empathic with her experience, and all I get back is, "I don't know," or "How is thinking about this going to help?" . . . [crying]

Supervisor: You feel you can't do anything right . . . [This focuses attention on her cognition and encourages exploration of her affective experience—both of which contribute to the generation of countertransference reactions.]

Supervisee: She makes me feel utterly powerless, empty, furious . . . what am I doing? . . . I should be feeling good, I passed preliminary orals, my boyfriend's moving out here, my other cases are going well, but it's too much, too much pressure, she makes me feel like . . . crying . . . I could be like her . . . I don't *want to be* in her state of powerlessness . . . empty, pathetic . . . my family was like hers, fractured, dysfunctional . . . it was like this with my brother, no matter what anyone did for him, he would reject it, he just f**d up over and over and no matter how much we loved him, he'd just . . .

Supervisor: Just . . . ? [This was a decision point for the supervisor: whether to encourage further immersion, which was leading to disclosure of personal material (associated to her countertransference reactions) or to shift the focus to how these emergent feelings were influencing her clinical functioning. This would shift the focus from personal exploration of the nature and origins of the countertransference to consideration of the clinical interaction. The decision was to encourage for the moment further immersion and elaboration; however, it was important to maintain attention on how personal factors were specifically influencing the therapeutic process.]

Supervisee: He'd just fail and fail and drink, none of us could succeed without feeling guilty about working hard . . . he'd reject whatever any of us tried to do to help . . . Jesus, where is all of this coming from, why am I thinking about this . . .

Supervisor: The transactions in the relationship with Shauna are triggering these reactions in you, including personal associations . . . you are really stirred up.

Supervisee: Right . . . it's like when I'm in the session, I freeze; I don't know what to do . . .

Supervisor: Perhaps we could look at what occurred in the last session more closely . . . you are finding yourself in a reactive mode . . . you're reacting. [The supervisor makes an attempt to redirect to the impact on clinical functioning and behavior in the session.]

Supervisee: She had been telling me about how her job was boring, beneath her, but she believed that all jobs, working for someone else would be that way . . . I had just reflected back what she had just said to me about feeling stuck, and I tried to empathize with her that she felt disappointed and stuck when she found that her job hadn't met her expectations . . . she goes on about all her talents [she is quite bright, multiple graduate degrees], but then she laments that nothing ever meets her expectations, nothing ever lives up to her ideas of how it should be . . . careers, husbands, men, friends . . . they all leave her . . . she had to go to [prestigious West coast university] and then back East to grad school and . . .

Supervisor: You're talking about her and moving away from your affects . . . I wonder if we could turn back to a specific moment in the last session . . .

Supervisee: Maybe, I don't want to think about it . . . to get back into that state . . .

Supervisor: Perhaps you and she are having a difficult time looking at the process that is transpiring between you and arousing reactions in you? [The supervisor alludes to a potential parallel in their modes of processing affect, including avoidance at looking at the material, which is characteristic of countertransference.]

Supervisee: I just am so frustrated.

Supervisor: I can sense your frustration. It's as if whatever you offer is rejected, spit out and you are . . .

Supervisee: Exactly, she just . . . it was the moment when she corrected me again, that she wasn't "sad" . . . she was "somewhat sad," I felt overwhelmed . . . I started asking questions, making suggestions; time was almost up, I just knew I was blowing it, and I suggested that she pay attention to her thoughts during the week and perhaps use her journal, and we could review the thoughts that were triggering her feelings and she says, "OK, but I don't think that'll help."

Supervisor: And . . .

Supervisee: I just wanted the session to end . . . I felt furious and powerless, and I just wanted to get out of there . . . like her friends, no wonder they bail on her, they can't stand her whining . . .

Supervisor: You're back in touch with your feelings, having reactions, which you don't usually have when you are conducting therapy, even with other challenging cases [I enumerate]; so there is a powerful dynamic or enactment that you may be caught up in, which can help us to understand the dynamics in the case. [The supervisor is attempting to facilitate further movement from immersion (and reactivity) to elaboration. In the elaboration phase, the raw material of the clinician's associations is brought into a meaningful theory—and, in our view, science-derived context.]

Supervisee: You're right; I know I'm so caught up in this.

Supervisor: Are you at a point where we can look at that together?

Supervisee: Yes, thanks, I feel better just being able to vent, to dump.

Supervisor: Like her?

Supervisee: Oh, like I just did to you, what she does to me . . . that's right, sometimes it's like she isn't even thinking in the session just dumping . . . she doesn't want to think . . . but I want her to think about what's going on [Parallel process emerges.]

Supervisor: Well, let's go back to a particular moment in the session, when you felt yourself becoming caught up in her process . . .

Supervisee: It's when she rejects my interest or any of my attempts to engage her in self-reflection . . . I get frustrated by her unwillingness to look at her behavior . . . her passivity, and I start feeling like I have to do something, like I have to fix her . . . but whatever I do, she spits out.

Supervisor: You are describing a repetitive pattern, a CCRT [Core Conflictual Relationship Theme (Luborsky, 1984)]; let's look at . . .

Supervisee: Then I get confused, and that's when the material from my family begins to . . . gets in the way . . . I can feel these intense feelings emerging . . . when my brother would fight with my father and lie about what he was doing or not doing, the whole family was in a turmoil . . .

Supervisor:	Another memory gets activated . . . let's look at those experiences for a moment, how might they connect in actuality with your client and her way of relating to you and others? [Supervisee becomes reactive, and the supervisor redirects her associations to the case. This reflects the overlap between processes of immersion and elaboration, which are demarked in theory, but are less purely differentiated in practice.]
Supervisee:	I think I can understand why all of her friends get tired and abandon her: They get fed up with all of the complaints.
Supervisor:	You are getting fed up with . . . what is she feeding you?
Supervisee:	A lot of crap . . . but really, as I think about it, it's her frustration, her feeling that no matter what she does it doesn't work out . . . then I feel powerless.
Supervisor:	Perhaps, you are experiencing the intensity of her powerlessness, which she wants you to get, to understand, and contain. [Projective identification comes to mind.]
Supervisee:	That's right . . . and I got confused in that session between her powerlessness, mine as a therapist, and in those past moments . . .
Supervisor:	How do you feel right now about Shauna?
Supervisee:	I feel empathy for her feelings of powerlessness . . . I think that's how she really feels, but I feel frustrated . . . it's like I can't stay with the feelings of frustration . . . I want her to do something about it
Supervisor:	So, how might you describe what happens in those moments of intensity . . . ?
Supervisee:	I think the pattern is that she comes in feeling depressed and looking to me to do something to fix her situation; when I empathize with her feelings, she rejects it because it doesn't really change her situation; I feel frustrated and shift into inquiry leading to problem solving, and she minimizes my attempts or puts me down . . . and I feel like her, misunderstood and . . . oh, I hadn't thought of that before . . . misunderstood, but I do understand.
Supervisor:	Tell me more. [Elaboration phase, moving toward the interpretive phase, which is characterized by integration of theory leading to consideration of future behavior.]
Supervisee:	I think I don't stay with her frustration for long, I shift to problem solving . . . And then she becomes rejecting, and then I really feel frustrated, out of control, ineffective . . .

Is this like projective identification ... that in specific moments I experience what underlies her experience ... ?

Supervisor: The intensity may suggest, among possibilities, that you are feeling in the moment, constructed in the moment out of both of your experiences, the intensity of trying hard and feeling that nothing works ... that she isn't obtaining what she wants and she is overwhelmed with fear that her needs will never be met ... you could think of this in terms of projective identification or consider that in these moments there is an enactment drawing from each of your experiences and being intersubjectively constructed.

Supervisee: That feels right ... actually, as I think of that, she fears that no one will understand how desperate she feels, since she feels she'll never be able to get it right.

Supervisor: And with you ...

Supervisee: I don't let her become desperate ... I counter it with suggestions that she rejects ...

Supervisor: Perhaps, the intensity of her experience has not found a place in the therapy?

Supervisee: Only in her rejecting my suggestions ... I don't want to feel her desperation ...

Supervisor: So, she makes you feel desperate ... rather than ...

Supervisee: Yes, I move out of empathizing with her and become like others in her life ... demanding that she just change ... it's hard to be with her frustration ... she does try, but if she doesn't get immediate success, she falls back into her depressive passivity ... I haven't really seen it so clearly before ... I guess it triggers my own stuff ... [The supervisee is able to discuss her reactions specific to the clinical material as formal aspects of countertransference. In the beginning of the session, she was primarily in a reactive state of mind; now, she is able to reflect on the impact of her personal reactions on the therapeutic process.]

Supervisor: How do you feel now, when you hold these thoughts in your mind?

Supervisee: Clear, I think I understand better, I'm not so mad, actually I feel some empathy for her ... I think I've been contributing to this pattern.

Supervisor: How so?

Supervisee: Feelings get triggered in me, when I sense her desperateness, and I think I react out of countertransference and shift to problem solving, putting it all back on her and the cycle of relating gets started.

Supervisor: Using the psychoanalytic model for a moment, how might you understand this? [This intervention is aiming at explicit integration of the theoretical and empirical literature into the discussion.]

Supervisee: This is an enactment and countertransference.

Supervisor: How do you understand countertransference . . . ?

Supervisee: Well, the countertransference part relates to my own personal experiences . . .

Supervisor: Might you also consider some of your responses as being outside of countertransference?

Supervisee: Well, realistically, I think most student therapists would feel frustrated.

Supervisor: Maybe even seasoned clinicians. . . . It reminds me of Winnicott's [1949] paper "Hate in the Countertransference," in which the idea of objective countertransference is introduced; you might want to read that paper.

Supervisee: It's been unclear whether I'm frustrated 'cause of past issues, or whether it's because this is a hard case and I'm new to this.

Supervisor: Let's look at how you can use the perspective you are taking to help Shauna.

Supervisee: Well, for one thing I'm not so mad, I feel like I've got my bearings.

Supervisor: How might that be expressed when you meet her next week?

Supervisee: Well, I'm going to try to really stay with where she is, rather than shifting quickly to problem solving, which I guess is a demand on her to get out of the feelings . . . Even just being able to think about this may help, what do you think?

Supervisor: I think you are right; it does help to be able to think and keep your bearings in session. What I hear you saying is that you will try to stay with her experience. It might be helpful to try to reinstate a measure of curiosity as well as empathy about the experience of her rejecting what you say; if you can be curious about the dynamic meaning and function, perhaps, it'll lead to her becoming increasingly curious about how she relates to you.

Following this supervision session, the supervisee was able in the next session with the client to be increasingly empathic and curious and to engage rather than withdraw when the client criticized her. She sought out additional reading and began to be even more interested in understanding this client's experience. They were able to continue to work with increased therapeutic effectiveness. The process model was effective in systematically leading the supervisor and supervisee through a process of metacognition, integrating direct experience and theory and leading to greater therapeutic effectiveness. Central to this work was the foundation of the supervisory alliance, which supported the exploration of the supervisee's countertransference. The countertransference conceptual model provided a systematic approach to process the emergence of the countertransference.

CONCLUSION

Clinical supervision provides a process and a relationship to enhance competence in psychotherapy. The development of self-awareness of the role of personal factors and the management of countertransference is essential. Supervisors assist in this development by setting clear expectations, modeling reflection-in-action, and facilitating processes that incorporate knowledge (theoretical and empirical literature), skills (through practice in session, cotherapy, process model, metacognition, etc.), and values (self-awareness and integrity).

REFERENCES

American Psychological Association. (2003). Guidelines on multicultural education, training, research, practice, and organizational change for psychologists. *American Psychologist, 58*, 377–402.

Bouchard, M.-A, Normandin, L., & Séguin, M.-H. (1995). Countertransference as instrument and obstacle: A comprehensive and descriptive framework. *The Psychoanalytic Quarterly, 64*, 717–745.

Brenner, C. (2006). *Psychoanalysis or mind and meaning*. New York: Psychoanalytic Quarterly.

Buber, M. (1970). *I and thou* (W. Kaufmann, Trans.). New York: Scribner. (Original work published 1923)

Corpuz, R., Falender, C. A., & Shafranske, E. P. (2006, June). *Use of parallel process and enactments to strengthen the supervisory alliance*. Paper presented at the International Interdisciplinary Conference on Clinical Supervision, Buffalo, NY.

Dunn, J. (1995). Intersubjectivity in psychoanalysis: A critical review. *The International Journal of Psychoanalysis, 76*, 723–738.

Epstein, L., & Feiner, A. H. (1979). Countertransference: The therapist's contribution to treatment—An overview. *Contemporary Psychoanalysis, 15,* 489–513.

Falender, C. A., & Shafranske, E. P. (2004). *Clinical supervision. A competency-based approach.* Washington, DC: American Psychological Association.

Fowers, B. J. (2001). Culture, identity, and loyalty. In B. D. Slife, R. N. Williams, & S. H. Barlow (Eds.), *Critical issues in psychotherapy* (pp. 263–280). Thousand Oaks, CA: Sage.

Freud, S. (1957). The future prospects of psychoanalytic therapy. In J. Strachey (Ed. & Trans.), *The standard edition of the complete psychological works of Sigmund Freud* (Vol. 11, pp. 139–152). London: Hogarth Press. (Original work published 1910)

Friedman, L. (1988). *The anatomy of psychotherapy.* Hillsdale, NJ: Analytic Press.

Friedman, S. M., & Gelso, C. J. (2000). The development of the inventory of countertransference behavior. *Journal of Clinical Psychology, 56,* 1221–1235.

Gabbard, G. O. (1995). Countertransference: The emerging common ground. *The International Journal of Psychoanalysis, 76,* 475–485.

Gabbard, G. O. (2001). A contemporary psychoanalytic model of countertransference. *Journal of Clinical Psychology, 57,* 983–991.

Gelso, C. J., Fassinger, R. E., Gomez, M. J., & Latts, M. G. (1995). Countertransference reactions to lesbian clients: The role of homophobia, counselor gender, and countertransference management. *Journal of Counseling Psychology, 42,* 356–364.

Gelso, C. J., & Hayes, J. A. (2002). The management of countertransference. In J. C. Norcross (Ed.), *Psychotherapy relationships that work* (pp. 267–283). New York: Oxford University Press.

Gelso, C. J., & Hayes, J. A. (2007). *Countertransference and the therapist's inner experience: Perils and possibilities.* Mahwah, NJ: Erlbaum.

Gelso, C. J., Latts, M. G., Gomez, M. J., & Fassinger, R. E. (2002). Countertransference management and therapy: An initial evaluation. *Journal of Clinical Psychology, 58,* 861–867.

Hafkenscheid, A. (2003). Objective countertransference: Do patients' interpersonal impacts generalize across therapists? *Clinical Psychology and Psychotherapy, 10,* 31–40.

Hayes, J. A. (2002). Playing with fire: Countertransference and clinical epistemology. *Journal of Contemporary Psychotherapy, 32,* 93–100.

Hayes, J. A. (2004). The inner world of the psychotherapist: A program of research on countertransference. *Psychotherapy Research, 14,* 21–36.

Hayes, J. A., & Gelso, C. J. (1993). Male counselors' discomfort with gay and HIV-infected clients. *Journal of Counseling Psychology, 40,* 86–93.

Hayes, J. A., & Gelso, C. J. (2001). Clinical implications of research on countertransference: Science informing practice. *Journal of Clinical Psychology, 57,* 1041–1051.

Hayes, J. A., Gelso, C. J., Van Wagoner, S. L., & Diemer, R. A. (1991). Managing countertransference: What the experts think. *Psychological Reports, 69,* 139–148.

Heimann, P. (1950). On counter-transference. *The International Journal of Psychoanalysis, 31,* 81–84.

Hoffman, I. (1983). The patient as interpreter of the analyst's experience. *Contemporary Psychoanalysis, 19,* 389–422

Hoffman, I. (1991). Discussion: Toward a social–constructivist view of the psychoanalytic situation. *Psychoanalytic Dialogues, 1,* 74–105.

Jacobs, T. J. (1999). Countertransference past and present: A review of the concept. *The International Journal of Psychoanalysis, 80,* 575–591.

Kagan, N. (1980). Influencing human interaction—eighteen years with IPR. In A. K. Hess (Ed.), *Psychotherapy supervision: Theory, research, and practice* (pp. 262–283). New York: Wiley.

Kiesler, D. J. (2001). Therapist countertransference: In search of common themes and empirical referents. *Journal of Clinical Psychology, 57,* 1053–1063.

Luborsky, L. (1984). *Principles of psychoanalytic psychotherapy.* New York: Basic Books.

Luborsky, L., & Barrett, M. S. (2006). The history and empirical status of key psychoanalytic concepts. *Annual Review of Clinical Psychology, 2,* 1–19.

Norcross, J. C. (2001). Introduction: In search of the meaning and utility of countertransference. *Journal of Clinical Psychology, 57,* 981–982.

Normandin, L., & Bouchard, M.-A. (1993). The effects of theoretical orientation and experience on rational, reactive, and reflective countertransference. *Psychotherapy Research, 3,* 77–94.

Ogden, T. H. (1994). The analytic third: Working with intersubjective clinical facts. *The International Journal of Psychoanalysis, 75,* 3–19.

Ogden, T. H. (2005). *This art of psychoanalysis: Dreaming undreamt dreams and interrupted cries.* London: Routledge.

Peterfreund, E. (1983). *The process of psychoanalytic therapy: Models and strategies.* Hillsdale, NJ: Analytic Press.

Pope, K. S., Sonne, J. L., & Greene, B. (2006). *What therapists don't talk about and why: Understanding taboos that hurt us and our clients.* Washington, DC: American Psychological Association.

Renik, O. (1993). Analytic interaction: Conceptualizing technique in light of the analyst's irreducible subjectivity. *The Psychoanalytic Quarterly, 62,* 553–571.

Renik, O. (1996). The perils of neutrality. *The Psychoanalytic Quarterly, 65,* 495–517.

Safran, J. D., & Muran, J. C. (2000). *Negotiating the therapeutic alliance.* New York: Guilford Press.

Sandler, J. (1976). Countertransference and role responsiveness. *International Review of Psycho-analysis, 3,* 43–47.

Singer, J. L., Sincoff, J. B., & Kolligan, J., Jr. (1989). Countertransference and cognition: Studying the psychotherapist's distortions as consequences of normal information processing. *Psychotherapy, 26,* 344–355.

Spotnitz, H. (1969). *Modern psychoanalysis of the schizophrenic patient.* New York: Grune & Stratton.

Van Wagoner, S., Gelso, C. J., Hayes, J. A., & Diener, R. (1991). Countertransference and the reputedly excellent therapist. *Psychotherapy, 28,* 411–421.

Winnicott, D. (1949). Hate in the countertransference. *The International Journal of Psychoanalysis, 30,* 69–75.

6

SUPERVISION, CULTURE, AND CONTEXT

LUIS A. VARGAS, NATALIE PORTER, AND CAROL A. FALENDER

Even after adoption of the "Guidelines on Multicultural Education, Training, Research, Practice, and Organizational Change for Psychologists" (American Psychological Association [APA], 2003), a culmination of decades of efforts, supervisors still find difficulty in adopting an integrated and contextual approach to diversity (Burkard et al., 2006; Falender & Shafranske, 2004; Hansen et al., 2006). In this chapter, we address the role of supervision in training therapists to be culturally responsive to the problems and needs of their clients and to firmly establish diversity as a core clinical and supervisory value (Falender & Shafranske, 2004). Three vignettes and a case example present the supervisor's role of integration of client, supervisee, and supervisor through a template of culture-based factors to determine how biases, belief systems, values, and specific realities impact supervisors' conceptualizations and their interventions (Falender & Shafranske, 2004). Examples of factors influencing the client, supervisee, and supervisor include the following:

- family characteristics and dynamics such as family organization and family life cycle;
- historical elements and processes such as migration history and acculturation;

- epistemological standpoints such as worldviews, beliefs about the nature of reality, problems of living, and concepts of self;
- faith-based beliefs such as religion and spirituality; and
- attitudes and values such as competition vs. cooperation, emotional restraint vs. expressiveness, independence vs. interdependence, control and dominance vs. harmony and egalitarianism.

The supervisory task involves a process of discovering sources of diversity to help the supervisee understand and appreciate the breadth of cultural contexts in which persons (including the client, supervisee, and supervisor) are situated. This process is quite a challenge because it requires that supervisors step outside of themselves to evaluate themselves according to the template of culture-based factors described earlier in this chapter, and then they assist their supervisees to do the same. These factors define and give order to our world and neither supervisor nor supervisee is likely to find this process an easy task. The idea that their culture-based beliefs, views, attitudes, and values are being examined, evaluated, or challenged either overtly or covertly by supervisors and clients can be a threatening experience for supervisees. As a result, it is important that the supervisor approach this task with tact, empathy, and support. For the purpose of this chapter, we define *culture* as the dynamic and active process of constructing shared meaning, as represented by shared ideas, beliefs, attitudes, values, norms, practices, language, spirituality, and symbols, with acknowledgement and consideration of positions of power, privilege, and oppression.

Global community psychology (Marsella, 1998) is a metapsychology that provides a systemic and contextual framework for understanding, assessing, and addressing the individual and collective psychological consequences of global events and forces by incorporating multicultural, multidisciplinary, and multinational knowledge, methods, and interventions. This approach is consonant with more naturalistic, qualitative, and contextual frameworks (Koss-Chioino & Vargas, 1999; Porter, 2005; Vargas, 2004) and raises the bar for supervisory self-awareness and contextual knowledge.

To illustrate, the first author's behavior is affected by a number of culturally based definitions of gender and gender roles (e.g., how gender is defined in the academic environment; in Mexican and American traditions; in Catholicism; in the Albuquerque, New Mexico, communities; by his biological family, his children, and his non-Latino wife and in-laws, and by social justice advocates). Similar multicultural influences could be described for the definitions and roles of "therapist," "professor," "husband," and "father." Individual descriptors of a client, therapist, or supervisor, such as African American, White, married, lesbian, disabled, poor, middle class, educated, uneducated, and so on, form multiplicative factors and are placed in a framework for systematically rethinking the impact of multicultural influences on the client (individual or family), therapist, and supervisor and their interaction. These premises underlie the culturally responsive supervisory process in the cases that follow.

- Culture and ethnicity are active, ongoing, ever-changing processes essential to be addressed in supervision.
- Clients, therapists, and supervisors are all influenced by multiple cultures–local, regional, national, and global.
- Supervisors must understand, appreciate, and respond to local and wide-ranging cultures that provide the context for, and influence the expression of, a client's (whether an individual's or a family's) behavior and mental and emotional processes.
- All therapies and their supervision are predicated on *epistemologies* (ways of understanding our world)—epistemologies are culturally based, and this must be addressed and integrated into supervision.

Providing culturally responsive supervision requires that the supervisor attend to the context in which services and therapy are provided and to the complex interactions between clients and therapists, among therapists' clients, between the therapist and the colleagues, and between therapists and their supervisors. The following describes three scenarios illustrating the contextual aspects to which a culturally responsive supervisor must attend including provision of a feminist, antiracist position.[1]

SUPERVISION FROM A CONTEXTUAL PERSPECTIVE

The first case attends to broader based, non-client-related interpersonal issues that are often overlooked in the supervisory process. Yet, these issues are critical to successfully engaging key staff members in the delivery systems in which a therapist works. These staff members can be indispensable to the therapist's goal of providing culturally responsive services because they know the local people and communities. The second case illustrates some of the difficulties arising from training models that emphasize cultural competence in such a way that students emerge with a sense of being experts in matters pertaining to cultural diversity or of having attained cultural competence. In both cases, the approach used was oriented toward the supervisee engaging in self-reflection and self evaluation—skills even more necessary when supervisees are eventually licensed as independent practitioners.

---

[1]Luis A. Vargas contributed the first two narrative case examples. Natalie Porter contributed the section on feminist, antiracist supervision. Carol A. Falender contributed the section on introducing diversity into supervision.

Recognized Versus Unrecognized Cultural Disparities

The first case involves a situation in which the supervisee is placed in a community that is culturally very different from the communities in which the supervisee previously worked. In this case, the supervisee struggled with whom to align: either the familiar non-American Indian contracted supervisor or psychology interns from another internship program or the American Indian clinic staff members. The appeal of aligning with the familiar staff and culture is evident in the supervisee's struggle. The second case involves a supervisee who enters a family therapy session with the sense that there is little cultural disparity because both the therapist and the clients are Latinos. The supervisory journey includes the supervisee's realization that there are multiple cultural differences (some not involving ethnicity) between the therapist and clients and even among the clients themselves, despite being a family. Also, the supervisee is, in part, responding to influences from her own disparate cultural upbringing (including what she was taught by her family and community and what she was taught in the U.S. educational system).

Case 1

An intern, Tim Jones, a European American from the Midwest, did an elective rotation at a mental health clinic in an American Indian reservation. Tim was interested in gaining clinical experience with culturally diverse populations and had sought out a number of clinical opportunities during his education to work with people from diverse cultures. He was particularly interested in working with Native Americans. The first author was his internship-assigned mentor. During his orientation visit to the clinic, his on-site supervisor, a non-American Indian contracted by the tribe, asked him whether he would like to join two other interns, also European Americans, from another internship program for group supervision during the lunch hour, as they had been doing for the previous 6 months. Tim observed that, during the lunch hour, they met behind closed doors in the supervisor's office, which faced an open area in the clinic. During the lunch hour, the American Indian staff members closed the clinic and ate together around a large table in the open area. During lunch, there was much teasing and bantering that reflected the strong camaraderie among the American Indian staff. I asked, from what he had observed, what he thought about the staff meeting in the open area and what meaning this seemed to have. Tim responded that he felt uncomfortable with the non-American Indian staff members separating themselves from the American Indian staff members. He believed that it was important to eat with the American Indian staff members. I suggested that he follow his best judgment and eat with them.

The following week, he said that he had informed the on-site supervisor that he preferred to join the American Indian staff members for lunch and scheduled his supervision with her for another time. He told me that he had become the brunt of some of the American Indians' teasing. He commented that he felt that they were not demonstrating the respect he thought he deserved as an intern who was just about to become a doctoral-level psychologist and wondered whether, perhaps, it was a better idea to join the others for group supervision. By doing so, he believed that he would be setting more appropriate professional boundaries. I inquired about what he thought was the American Indian staff members' intent in teasing him; he was not sure. I asked him to give this some thought and explore for himself what the intent might be.

At our next supervision session, he noted that the teasing seemed good-natured, not mean-spirited—a way of checking him out to see how genuine he was in his stated commitment to be a helper to their tribe and to genuinely engage in a helping relationship with the local Indian community. He felt that they were also testing him for what they saw as his air of elitism as a result of his formal education—in a sense, giving him the message that no one, even a doctor or professional therapist, should take himself or herself too seriously. He acknowledged that this was, in fact, an issue with which he had long struggled, pointing out that he was proud of attending prestigious universities throughout his education. I asked him what he felt he should do: continue to join the American Indian staff or attend the lunch-hour with the contract psychologist. He opted for the former, noting that he felt now that that was, in fact, the best course of action for him. With time, he came to feel accepted by these staff members, who seemed to be both surprised and pleased that he, unlike the other non-American Indian interns, had chosen to join them. Subsequently, these staff members took him under their wing. When he first began to eat with them, they had talked with him about their custom of putting some food aside for the spirits of their ancestors. Gradually, they taught him some of their other beliefs and customs. They invited him to their feast days and went with him on client home and school visits, while the other interns completed their rotations without having much of a sense about what happened outside the confines of the clinic and its therapy rooms. Tim felt that his work with his clients on the reservation was greatly enhanced by his relationship with the American Indian staff.

Case 2

Gabriela Sanchez came to her internship with an impressive set of credentials and a strong sense of being culturally competent, as a result of having taken several seminars and various workshops on cultural competence and publishing a couple articles with a well-known psychologist on cultural competence in clinical services. She was assigned an outpatient case of a young Latina adolescent who had grown up in a rural town in northern New Mexico. Gabriela was U.S. born; one of her parents was from Central America and the other was from South America. In her first session with the adolescent and her parents, Gabriela made a couple of generalizations about Latinos in an attempt to convey her sense of understanding of Latino culture so as to engage with the adolescent and her family. When Gabriela made a reference to their being "Latino," the father clarified rather indignantly that they were "Hispanic," which led the daughter to contradict her father: "You're Hispanics, I'm Chicana!" The father bristled at his daughter's disrespect and, Gabriela thought, glanced at her (Gabriela) as if he were blaming her for his daughter's disrespectful comment.

On making another generalization about "Latino" culture, the mother brusquely asked her, "Where are you from?" Gabriela remarked to me that the tone in the mother's voice conveyed a sense that her generalizations had not sat well with her. As we explored Gabriela's sense of herself at the moment that she tried to engage this family, Gabriela commented that she had been trying to convey to the family that she was culturally competent to treat them, because she had felt that the parents treated her as if she were their daughter and as if she were too young to understand their (the parents') point of view. Gabriela felt that the parents were not giving her a chance to demonstrate her competence as a psychologist and that if they did, she could show them that she was more than adequately trained to deal with the presenting problem.

I asked Gabriela whether there was a difference between wanting to prove one's expertise and competence and wanting to impose one's expert status, and I explained that I was asking because I was not sure whether she was trying to do the former or the latter. A bit annoyed at me, she curtly responded that she had wanted to prove her expertise. After a brief hesitation, she remarked that perhaps she felt a little resentful that they did not afford her the respect that she expected, especially because they were all Latinos and they should understand the value of *respeto* in Latino cultures. I suggested that perhaps we needed to look at the two ways that culture can express itself: in content (as in saying: "Latinos value *respeto*") and in context (as reflected in the mother's comment "Where are you from?"). I explored with Gabriela whether she believed that her behavior with the family had been culturally influenced by her training in U.S. universities and asked her whether she thought that she would have behaved differently were she in either her mother's or father's countries of origin dealing with a similar family in those countries. She said that she had never given this any thought and that, on reflection, she would have behaved differently— more deferentially to the parents. When I asked her why, she commented that parents in these countries would have viewed her behavior with the New Mexican family as somewhat of an affront to their positions as parents. She wondered aloud why she had never previously thought about how her behavior as a Latina psychologist was influenced by the U.S. context. This discourse opened the way to our engaging, in a collaborative manner, in an exploration of the cultures of the parents, the daughter, the therapist, the supervisor, and the varied contexts they and we occupied. Equally important were the emphases in our supervision session of minimizing hierarchy (e.g., supervisor vs. trainee) so as to encourage a transition to what would soon be collegial relationships with her fellow therapists and to minimize the potential for judgmental aspects in our behaviors as therapist and supervisor.

Feminist, Antiracist Supervision

Feminist supervision, illustrated in the example below, fosters therapy practices that promote the equal valuing and equality of all people and advocates for their full participation in society (American Psychological Association, Division 44/Committee on Lesbian, Gay, & Bisexual Concerns Task Force, 2000; Cammaert & Larsen, 1988; Larsen & Rave, 1995; Lerman & Porter, 1990; Porter & Vasquez, 1997). Like feminist therapy, it attends to the social context of women's lives and to structural barriers (e.g., sexism, racism, homophobia) and sociopsychological barriers (e.g., roles and stereotypes) that prevent social, economic, and political equality (Cammaert & Larsen, 1988).

The following principles of feminist supervision are based on those developed by the feminist supervision workgroup at the Shaping the Future of Feminist Psychology Conference (Porter & Vasquez, 1997). Feminist therapy and supervision

- are defined as mutually respectful, collaborative relationships in which client and supervisee autonomy are encouraged and diverse perspectives valued;
- attend to and validate the diversity of women's lives and context;
- attend to the social construction of gender and the role of language in maintaining a gendered society;
- facilitate the understanding of diversity, oppression, societal expectations and roles;
- encourage development of personal cultural identities;
- identify power differentials, within the therapy, within supervision, and within society, with the goal of client empowerment, including taking responsibility for one's actions;
- assist the supervisee in seeing his or her own privilege (e.g., White, heterosexual) and in using his or her greater power inappropriately; and
- assist supervisee self-reflection and examination by supervisor modeling of openness, authenticity, reflexivity, and self-monitoring.

Case 3

In this narrative, the supervision context and process are described, followed by a description of the supervisory interventions.

Client Background

Jackie, a 19-year-old college sophomore, attends a large state university 150 miles from her hometown, a small farming community. She is the youngest of three girls and the first to move so far away from her family to attend college. Her two older sisters are married and live near her parents. Jackie's father is a minister in an evangelical Protestant church, and her family is well-known not only in her small town but also in the wider farming community. Her sisters were both cheerleaders and prom queens at the local high school and community colleges. They each married after 2 years of college and are raising families in nearby communities. They and their families attend their father's church.

Jackie broke with family tradition by playing a sport rather than cheering for one. She received a scholarship to the university because of her academic achievement and soccer abilities. Jackie plans to major in sociology, with an eye to an advanced degree in social work. Her father has encouraged her education, remarking that his church could use an outreach ministry that helps the local church members.

She attends a church near the university that she likes very much, although it is a different denomination from the church in which she was raised. Jackie values her religious upbringing, although she is ambivalent about the strictness of her church. She is attracted to the more relaxed atmosphere of her current church but worries about which doctrine is "right."

Jackie spent time with several young men in high school and during her freshman year, mostly in small social groups, but did not feel any attraction beyond friendship toward any of them. She believed that sex should only occur after marriage, so she was not concerned about her lack of sexual feelings toward them. During the spring of her freshman year, she began to spend more time with a young woman, Beth, from her dormitory, who attended the same church. This friendship took a sexual turn one evening following a party where both had been drinking. At first, Jackie blamed her "weakness" on alcohol, but after several more sexual encounters, she realized that she felt stronger sexual and romantic feelings than she had ever felt before. She also felt ashamed and called off the relationship when she returned home for the summer.

Jackie came to the clinic about 6 weeks into the fall of her sophomore year. She had almost immediately reengaged with Beth in spite of her deep shame about violating her religious tenets and concerns about her parents finding out about her relationship. She vacillated between joy and pleasure, and shame and despondency. She had considered suicide as a way out but chose to seek therapy after speaking to a faculty member who had given a "gay-friendly" talk in her class.

Therapist Background

Karen, a 24-year-old heterosexual European American woman and 3rd-year graduate student, was assigned Jackie as a client in a university psychology training clinic. Karen had grown up in a suburb bordering an industrial and progressive city located in the center of a primarily agricultural state. Karen had been raised in a nonevangelical Protestant denomination that accepted openly gay and lesbian individuals as full members of the church, although their role in the ministry remained more controversial.

Supervision Session

This supervision session has occurred after the third therapy session. During the latest session, Jackie had described an argument with Beth that had precipitated their ending their relationship. Beth had requested that Jackie attend a campus event for gay, lesbian, bisexual, and transgendered (GLBT) students with her, and Jackie had refused, stating that she also resented Beth attending, because people might infer that they were both gay. Beth replied that they were both gay, which Jackie denied.

In supervision, Karen said that she did not know how to help Jackie address her denial or come to terms with her sexual orientation. Karen considered Jackie's denial a result of her fear of alienating her family and had provided this interpretation to Jackie in the session. Jackie had replied that it was God's disapproval that concerned her. Karen reported that Jackie had become distant and withdrawn for the remainder of the session, and that she (Karen) had struggled with her own feelings of ineffectiveness as she unsuccessfully attempted to reengage Jackie for the duration of the session.

As with all sessions, I began this supervision session by asking Karen for her specific goals. At the initial supervision session, Karen and I had established Karen's goals for supervision generally. Karen and I then began each session with Karen articulating what she hoped to accomplish in the specific supervisory session and its relationship to the broader set of goals. As supervisor, I may identify additional goals, which I offer with an explanation of their role within therapy or supervision. At the beginning of the supervision I outlined the process of feminist, multicultural therapy and supervision. Karen and I also spent some time describing ourselves to place us within a sociocultural framework, which allows us to subsequently examine (a) the biases Karen and I may inadvertently carry into therapy and supervision; (b) the impact of structural issues on the therapy and supervision (e.g., White or middle-class privilege), or ways in which power differences between the therapist and client, or supervisor and supervisee, affect the process; and (c) the impact of the client or supervisee's perceptions of these structural issues on the process.

Karen identified her goals for this session as figuring out how to help Jackie establish her own identity and differentiate herself from her family by acknowledging her relationship with Beth, her difficulties in individuating from her family, and ultimately her sexual orientation to herself and others. I asked Karen to evaluate to what extent her goals were congruent with those articulated by the client. Karen stated that she considered them congruent in that the client had initiated the exploration of her sexual feelings for Beth.

I asked Karen to consider whether her focus on Jackie's need to address her denial of her sexuality and "come out" emanated from Jackie or from her own beliefs as the therapist. I also wondered whether Karen was adequately recognizing the importance Jackie placed on her religious beliefs. Karen and I discussed the need to honor Jackie's values and priorities in spite of the conflicts and pain they brought about. Although from the therapist's perspective these beliefs might not seem to validate the "real" Jackie, respecting Jackie's culture required honoring her ability to establish her own value priorities. Together, Karen and I identified the need to provide Jackie with a safe place to find her own course without therapist pressure or bias.

Karen countered that Jackie had sought therapy following a class lecture that had described GLBT issues openly and positively, perhaps because she had hoped to encounter similar attitudes from a therapist. Karen proposed that Jackie's conflicted beliefs, values, and behaviors needed to be specifically addressed, albeit in a more open and less directive way than she originally considered. Karen agreed that she needed to monitor her own biases and reactions and needed to envision and accept more than one outcome to this discussion.

Karen and I developed a plan to more fully explore these issues in therapy that Karen would then propose to Jackie. The plan involved seeking out community resources and outside perspectives as well as continuing to delve into Jackie's feelings, fears, relationships, values, and cognitions in the context of her intersecting cultures that included family, religion, class, rural background, ethnicity, peer relationships, and gender. Jackie would meet with religious leaders whom she identified as having credibility for her; visit churches with beliefs similar to her own, with and without GLBT taboos; and meet with members of an organization for families of GLBT individuals.

In therapy, cultural and social messages about being gay would be explored, as would the societal expectations for Jackie as a woman. What would it mean to live openly as a lesbian within her cultural context? What would it mean for her to live a heterosexual lifestyle? To live privately as a lesbian? To live as a single and celibate woman? Did she anticipate following the same path as her sisters, or did she envision another life course? What were the expectations of her family and community, and how did Jackie anticipate they would enforce them? How did she view herself vis-à-vis these gender and social roles? How did they shape her values, her self-image, and her self-appraisal?

Karen and I proposed that Karen would initiate this session by referring back to her own comments in the previous session and by requesting feedback about Jackie's perceptions of and feelings about their interaction. Karen and I both felt that Karen's expressed concern about her lack of sensitivity to issues central to Jackie's value system would reestablish trust and a working alliance.

Karen also identified that she was uncomfortable with Jackie's disregard for her partner Beth's feelings. Karen pointed out that Jackie seemed to approach or avoid the relationship solely on the basis of her own needs and conflicts and had not recognized the impact this had on Beth. I concurred that it was important for Jackie to explore her sexual orientation within a framework of personal ethical responsibility that included not exploiting Beth or other potential partners, female or male. Together, Karen and I planned a way to present Jackie with this perspective in a way that was neither judgmental nor punitive.

I reiterated that Karen needed to remove her own biases from her therapy with Jackie. Karen and I developed a plan for Karen to continue to monitor the imposition of her values and biases on the therapy and for her to seek outside resources to gain additional information about evangelical religious perspectives, life in rural cultures, and the advantages and disadvantages of coming out. I disclosed some of my own process to identify and monitor my own biases and stereotypes and attempt to keep them from interfering with the client's direction and self-determination.

This example focuses on one session early in the supervisory process. I was able to address a number of sensitive issues because of the receptiveness and experience level of this particular supervisee. I attempted to evaluate the supervisee's readiness for an open, mutually reflexive dialog early in supervision. The willingness to openly explore difficult issues, such as one's bias in therapy, occurs in an environment of mutual trust, where the supervisor has assumed a nonpunitive and respectful stance toward the supervisee's use of self-reflection. I have found that with many supervisees, their openness to exploring their own biases occurs in stages. I have proposed a four-stage model of supervision, aimed at promoting self-examination and openness while developing increasing awareness and competence in providing gender- and culturally sensitive therapy. The process (a) begins with a more didactic and directive exploration of the socially constructed aspects of client's "problem," such as reading about GLBT therapeutic approaches; (b) moves to exploring in supervision the client's social location and the manifestations, origins, and impact of specific oppressions pertaining to the client at the societal level; then as the supervisee seems more confident about treatment and aware of his or her role in a broader cultural context, the process (c) begins to address the supervisee's own misconceptions, biases, privilege, and prejudices at a personal level as they arise in the therapy and supervision; and then (d) expands to include social action and community involvement (Porter, 1995).

In the following example, the introduction of diversity variables into the supervisory equation is illustrated. The supervisee is female, Latina, moved to the United States from Venezuela for college and graduate school, and is upper middle class. She has attended a highly research-focused graduate school and comes to internship with excellent research training and much less direct clinical experience. The supervisor is female, White, and moved from the Midwest in her 20s. The client family is African American.

AN EXAMPLE OF THE APPROACH

Supervisor: [Within the first supervisory sessions after discussion of mutual goals and tasks.] I'd like us to think about how you and I differ from each other, and each of us differs from the client, and how this will affect the treatment and our supervision. Is this something you typically think about? [Introducing the topic and setting the stage.]

Supervisee: I would like very much to do that, as I know that those differences are significant, but I have never had a supervisor who has talked about that as a specific factor. I have always thought it is critical, have done readings on it, but it has not directly come up in supervision.

Supervisor: Okay, let's think about different factors. We could use Falicov's [1998] framework to start. Ecological context might be a good way to begin. I am Caucasian, live in a middle-class neighborhood, a house, and am surrounded by English speakers in my neighborhood. I feel pretty dominant there. So there are issues of privilege, socioeconomic status, and dominance.

Supervisee: Well, I moved here from Venezuela, as you know, when I was 17. I live in an apartment near campus, near the frat houses. I only see my parents about once a year, and that has been very hard. Most of the other grad students are Caucasian or Asian, and so there hasn't been so much opportunity to talk about this at all. I don't know about my new client, so this is something I can bring up early in treatment, to explore differences between us, and how that affects them. I am a little worried about seeing an African American client, as I haven't had much experience and I'm worried whether they will feel comfortable with me. I am usually assigned only

Latinos because I'm Spanish speaking. As for the client, what I can tell from the phone screening, the family lives in the part of the city that has the highest number of drive-by shootings. They are African American, and the mother is raising four children ranging in age from 7 to 14. They're coming in 'cause the school referred the 14-year-old for angry, oppositional behavior, truancy, and failing grades. He is in a school-based program for youth at risk for dropping out.

Supervisor: So there are big differences among us in socioeconomic status, ethnicity, and race. We will need to focus on this in the treatment. I'm wondering how you are going to deal with both your feelings about working with this client [and racial group] and with introducing the topic to them.

Supervisee: I'm thinking I'd like to do that kind of the same way you just did . . . pointing out that I'd like us to talk about how we are different, and what that's like. [This early discussion lays groundwork for consideration of differences and similarities, and differing worldviews.]

Supervisor: A second area is family life cycle. I am mother of sons, and they are college graduates or soon to be. I am married.

Supervisee: Well, I am a daughter, and my parents are still in Venezuela, and we only see each other infrequently but talk often. I would like to marry and have children, but that is down the road. From what I can see, the family is the single mom and her children. I'll need to see what extended family there is and how they fit in; also, whether there is a father in the picture, and I see the four kids have two different last names, so I need to understand that.

Supervisor: Okay, so this raises questions about differing perspectives as each of us is at a very different place in the life cycle. We need to factor that into our considerations. Next is migration, acculturation. I will tell you that I moved here from the Midwest, and still am a Midwesterner at heart. I've lived in California for over 30 years now . . . but I am conservative, family values-wise.

Supervisee: I've been in California since I was 17, and now I am 25, and I feel that I am pretty acculturated. Although I speak Spanish to my family, I mainly speak English to everyone else, outside of therapy clients. I find myself really acculturated and think only infrequently about where I came from. I'd like to find out whether this family moved from somewhere else and how long they've been in California, and their journey, if there is one, to get here.

Supervisor: The last area we'll consider at this point is religion/spirituality. For me, spirituality is an important part of my identity, but I am not very observant.

Supervisee: I am a lapsed Catholic, but I know a lot about Catholicism, having gone to all Catholic schools till college. There is not indication about the family's religion or spirituality, but that might be very important to know and understand.

Supervisee: [Next supervision hour.] The first session was pretty intense. Mrs. Sharp was angry about her son's school performance, embarrassed he hasn't been going to school, and mad that he doesn't go to church with her. She told me right out that she wished she had a Black therapist, preferably a woman, who could understand her. So that really laid the issue right out on the table. I asked her what it was like for her to have me, and she said, "You could be my daughter!" We hadn't discussed age! Just life cycle, but I just asked what that would be like, and she said she was okay with it but just wanted to see if I could figure out how to get Jerome, her son, in line. And that maybe it's good I'm Hispanic because he seems to have lots of friends like that. Jerome was withdrawn while the mom was in the room, but once she left said he was happy he had someone who maybe could understand him because he hangs with mostly "homies." And that he wouldn't go to church with her if his life depended on it.

Supervisor: How are you feeling about how that went?

Supervisee: I am very worried about Jerome, think the mom is so angry she can't talk to him, and I guess hasn't been able to for years. The family moved here from Alabama about 2 years ago, and things have been going downhill ever since. He didn't want to move. . . . But I am feeling good about the way I introduced some aspects of the diversity issue, and that laying it out felt so right. Now to see where to go from here!

Supervisee: [Several weeks later.] Things are going well. I am feeling very positive. Mrs. Sharp told me that she really wondered if I could understand what it was like to be Black in this country. Jerome was picked up by the police last week. He had gotten a new bike from his uncle the week before and the police were sure it was stolen, so they took him to the station, handcuffed, and Mrs. Sharp had to go with her brother, and the sales receipt, to prove it wasn't stolen. We talked about it first just the two of us and then with Jerome. I wonder what else I could have done to deal with that—it is oppression and White privilege, and to them, I seem privileged. It is so amazing to me, as I have never felt that kind of privilege, at least not since

I have been living in the U.S. Also, I realized that for me, law enforcement has incredibly positive valence; for them, they represent oppression and all the wrongs that have been done to them. That is a big difference in worldview! The whole bicycle episode was very traumatic for Jerome, but he thinks it might be good in a funny way. It helped him understand his mother's fear, and it helped him to see what the consequences could be if he did something seriously wrong. It really brought him close to Mrs. Sharp . . . they talked to each other for the first time, and he's going to go to the church group . . . one time only, to try it. We just have to figure out how to make the connection last.

SUMMARY

The approaches to supervision described in this chapter differ in the extent to which the supervisor is directive, self-disclosing, and expository. However, all three approaches focus on encouraging supervisees to engage in self-examination and perspective taking to understand and appreciate (a) their own and their clients' culturally based beliefs, views, attitudes, and values; (b) the cultural influences in the transactions among the supervisor, supervisee, and client(s); and (c) the contexts or ecologies of the supervisor, supervisee, and client(s). Through the examples given, supervisors may gain strategies for incorporating culture and diversity into supervision. Supervisors have the responsibility for diversity competence in terms of knowledge, skills, attitudes, and values. Rather than viewing culture as something to add on or to be addressed once and then ignored, the supervisor must initiate conversation, integrate into conceptualization and treatment, have significant self-awareness and humility, and be able to conduct difficult conversations about culture without violating boundaries (i.e., extended questioning in areas not related to the client or process of supervision). The knowledge and skills of supervisees may be more sophisticated than that of their supervisors, introducing a greater complexity in the power differential. However, omitting or devaluing culture and individual differences strains or ruptures the supervisory relationship and plays out in the therapy the supervisee conducts with the client. The inclusion of culture and diversity in conceptualization and all aspects of treatment is synonymous with good clinical practice and is an ethical standard (APA, 2002).

REFERENCES

American Psychological Association. (2002). Ethical principles of psychologists and code of conduct. *American Psychologist, 57*, 1060–1073.

American Psychological Association. (2003). Guidelines on multicultural education, training, research, practice, and organizational change for psychologists. *American Psychologist, 58*, 377–402.

American Psychological Association, Division 44/Committee on Lesbian, Gay, & Bisexual Concerns Task Force. (2000). Guidelines for psychotherapy with lesbian, gay, and bisexual clients. *American Psychologist, 55*, 1440–1451.

Burkard, A. W., Johnson, A. J., Madson, M. B., Bruitt, N. T., Contreras-Tadych, D. A., Kozlowski, J. M., et al. (2006). Supervisor cultural responsiveness and unresponsiveness in cross-cultural supervision. *Journal of Counseling Psychology, 53*, 288–301.

Cammaert, L. P., & Larsen, C. C. (1988). Feminist frameworks of psychotherapy. In M. A. Dutton-Douglas & L. A. Walker (Eds.), *Feminist psychotherapies: Integration of therapeutic and feminist systems* (pp. 12–36). Norwood, NJ: Ablex Publishing.

Falender, C. A., & Shafranske, E. P. (2004). *Clinical supervision: A competency-based approach.* Washington DC: American Psychological Association.

Falicov, C. J. (1998). *Latino families in therapy.* New York: Guilford Press.

Hansen, N. D., Randazzo, K. V., Schwartz, A., Marshall, M., Kalis, D., Frazier, R., et al. (2006). Do we practice what we preach? An exploratory survey of multicultural psychotherapy competencies. *Professional Psychology: Research and Practice, 37*, 66–74.

Koss-Chioino, J. D., & Vargas, L. A. (1999). *Working with Latino youth: Culture, development, and context.* San Francisco: Jossey-Bass

Larsen, C. C., & Rave, E. J. (1995). Context of feminist therapy ethics. In E. J. Rave & C. C. Larsen (Eds.), *Ethical decision-making in feminist therapy* (pp. 1–17). New York: Guilford Press.

Lerman, H., & Porter, N. (Eds.). (1990). *Feminist ethics in psychotherapy.* New York: Springer Publishing Company.

Marsella, A. J. (1998). Toward a "global-community psychology": Meeting the needs of a changing world. *American Psychologist, 53*, 1282–1291.

Porter, N. (1995). Supervision of psychotherapists: Integrating anti-racist, feminist, and multicultural perspectives. In H. Landrine (Ed.), *Bringing cultural diversity to feminist psychology: Theory, research, and practice* (pp. 163–175). Washington, DC: American Psychological Association.

Porter, N. (2005.). Location, location, location: Contributions of contemporary feminist theorists to therapy theory and practice. *Women and Therapy, 28*, 143–160.

Porter, N., & Vasquez, M. (1997). Covision: Feminist supervision, process, and collaboration. In J. Worell & N. G. Johnson (Eds.), *Shaping the future of feminist psychology: Education, research, and practice* (pp. 155–171). Washington DC: American Psychological Association.

Vargas, L. A. (2004, July–August). *Elusive concept of culture: Implications to psychology practice and policy* [Presidential address, Division 37]. Presented at the 112th Annual Convention of the American Psychological Association, Honolulu, HI.

7

A RELATIONAL APPROACH TO SUPERVISION: ADDRESSING RUPTURES IN THE ALLIANCE

JEREMY D. SAFRAN, J. CHRISTOPHER MURAN,
CHRISTOPHER STEVENS, AND MICHAEL ROTHMAN

Establishing, sustaining, and repairing ruptures in the therapeutic alliance are among the most important competencies in psychotherapy. For the novice psychotherapist, strain within the therapeutic alliance usually arouses feelings of insecurity and may undermine the trainee's developing, yet precarious, sense of confidence. Alliance strains and ruptures pose unique challenges for the clinical supervisor as well, who must safeguard client welfare while facilitating the supervisee's professional development (Falender & Shafranske, 2004, p. 6). The types of skills required for the therapist to be able to constructively negotiate alliance ruptures are complex, multifaceted inner and interpersonal skills. They require a basic capacity for self-acceptance (or at least an ability to work toward it), a willingness to engage in an ongoing process of self-exploration, and a capacity to engage in a genuine dialogue with the client. The quality and style of the supervisory process thus play a critical role in the development of these skills.

Portions of this chapter are from *Negotiating the Therapeutic Alliance: A Relational Treatment Guide*, by J. D. Safran and J. C. Muran, 2000, New York: Guilford Press. Copyright 2000 by Guilford Press. Adapted with permission.

In this chapter, we discuss how our supervision model prepares therapists to address ruptures in the therapeutic alliance. We begin by outlining our model of the rupture resolution process. Next we outline general principles of supervision. We then outline some of the basic features of our group supervision model. We conclude with a transcript illustrating the supervisory process.

RESOLVING RUPTURES IN THE THERAPEUTIC ALLIANCE

The therapeutic alliance is one of the key mutative factors in psychotherapy (Horvath & Symonds, 1991; Martin, Garske, & Davis, 2000), and learning how to explore and repair therapeutic alliance ruptures should be an important focus of supervision. For more than 15 years, we have been encouraging therapists to pay careful attention to the therapeutic relationship and to the ongoing relational "pushes and pulls" that occur between the client and the therapist. We believe that inherent in all relationships, including therapy, is a negotiation between the subjectivities of each person. Within the context of psychotherapy, these negotiations are often most explicit in the form of ruptures or therapeutic impasses. We have identified and classified the types of therapeutic ruptures that we believe are germane to the therapeutic process and, on the basis of our research findings, have developed a model of the rupture resolution process (Muran, Safran, Samstag, & Winston, 2005; Safran, 1993a, 1993b; Safran, Crocker, McMain, & Murray, 1990; Safran & Muran, 1996, 2000; Safran, Muran, Samstag, & Stevens, 2002; Safran, Muran, Samstag, & Winston, 2005; Safran & Segal, 1990; Samstag, Muran, & Safran, 2004).

Our goal in focusing on and working with ruptures is not simply to repair them so that work can continue with a revitalized alliance. Rather, the aims are to help clients develop a fuller understanding of how they construe events and how that construal impacts their interaction with others, and to provide them with a new experience of relating. Ideally, this will help them to become more comfortable with their own emotional states and needs, and to develop greater flexibility in expressing those feelings and needs, with an improved expectation of maintaining relatedness with important others.

Elsewhere (Safran & Muran, 2000), we have found it useful to distinguish *withdrawal ruptures* from *confrontation ruptures*, and we have developed specific resolution models for each type of rupture. For our purposes here, however, we have abstracted a more general model consisting of five basic positions describing the therapist–client dyadic interaction: (a) identifying the rupture maker, (b) recognizing and disembedding from the relational matrix, (c) exploring the client's construal, (d) exploring the avoidance of aggression–vulnerability, and (e) emergence of the underlying wish or need.

For heuristic purposes, these are presented as a consecutive series of separate and distinct positions. In practice, however, work with ruptures often moves back and forth through different stages. As a result, it is essential for the therapist to be focused on the moment-to-moment dyadic interactions instead of relying on the theoretical stepwise progression we describe here.

Position 1: Identifying the Rupture Marker

Ruptures begin when during the course of therapeutic work, the client notices some action of the therapist that confirms his or her dysfunctional or pathogenic expectations about relationships. The client reacts by either confronting or withdrawing from the therapist. This often triggers a defensive or angry reaction from the therapist, which in turn, confirms the client's expectations. Whether the client's initial perception was realistic or distorted, at this point, both the therapist and client are engaged in a cycle of reaction and counterreaction

Position 2: Recognizing and Disembedding From the Relational Matrix

The first step in beginning the resolution process is for the therapist to recognize that he or she is embedded in a relational cycle with the client. When a client begins to openly criticize or blame the therapist or abruptly withdraws by becoming silent in sessions, repeatedly missing visits, or coming late to sessions, it can be easy to recognize that the normal negotiation process has broken down. Other ruptures, however, can be much more subtle and difficult to detect. This is especially true when clients try to conceal their anger or dissatisfaction. In cases like this, it may only be by noting his or her own subjective experience (e.g., feeling frustrated, spaced out, confused, or angry) that the therapist is able to recognize that the negotiation process has been compromised.

In this way, maintaining an ongoing sense of awareness of their own emotional reactions allows therapists to detect strains in the relationship and begin to identify client behaviors that are pulling for a complementary response. Once the rupture has been detected and the therapist realizes that both he or she and the client are caught in a cycle, the disembedding process, in which both the therapist and the client attempt to step back and communicate about what is going on, can begin. This process involves the therapist metacommunicating his or her observations about the cycle to the client (communicating about the communication process). No matter how the rupture began, the therapist must recognize, and be able to talk about, his or her own contribution to the cycle. This prevents the client from feeling blamed and gives him or her important feedback about how he or she is affecting others. It can also serve as a model for the idea that expressing feelings, even uncomfortable ones, can lead to closeness rather than increase alienation and can open up further exploration.

Position 3: Exploring the Client's Construal

The goal in this stage is to unpack and explore the client's construal of events. The focus here should remain on the interaction in the moment. The goal is to provide the client with the experience of working his or her way out of those cycles with another person, not simply to come to greater understanding of these cycles. To do this, the therapist needs to help the client to unpack his or her understanding of what happened to precipitate the rupture.

Position 4: Avoidance of Vulnerability–Aggression

Although exploring the client's experience of the rupture may lead to a resolution, talking about these feelings can often generate considerable anxiety and may trigger avoidance of underlying feelings. As a result, an ongoing awareness of the emotional shifts in both client and therapist is critical, and the focus needs to be kept on what is happening in the moment. As clients become anxious, the focus needs to shift to the current anxiety, and the exploration needs to shift between both the feelings and the avoidance. This can help clients to better understand, and more comfortably express, a wider range of feeling states. It is not uncommon for ruptures to be partially resolved and then to reappear in slightly different form as the underlying schema is reactivated later in therapy.

Position 5: Expressing the Underlying Wish or Need

Clients often believe that their underlying wishes or needs are unacceptable or will go unmet, leading them to express them in a qualified or indirect way, which may pull for complementary feelings of frustration, confusion, or irritation from the therapist. If the therapist is not aware of his or her own feelings and responses, this may perpetuate a new enactment of the cycle. Providing the therapist can continue to be mindful of his or her own responses, continued work can lead to the examination of the underlying wish or need. As the exploration continues, and the therapist continues to validate the client's emotional responses, the client can gradually become more comfortable with his or her underlying feelings and needs, and more capable of expressing them directly without feeling that doing so will endanger his or her ability to relate to others. At the same time, the client begins to understand that all of his or her wants and needs cannot be met and that the feelings of sadness and disappointment that result can be tolerated and accepted. Learning to facilitate such a process, which in our view is an essential clinical competency, is initially learned and practiced within clinical supervision.

Supervision is directed at helping therapists develop a particular stance, including an awareness of, and ability to work with, their own feelings and reactions. To do this, we believe that training needs to go beyond a didactic presentation of the model and a set of techniques. To help therapists develop the ability to integrate procedural knowledge and self-awareness (which is necessary to respond to clients in a flexible and creative way), it is essential that training have a substantial experiential component and emphasize the process of personal growth for therapists. Below are a number of principles that facilitate the development of this type of focus and awareness. First, we talk about general principles, and then we describe the specific structure and exercises of a typical group supervision session.

General Principles

There are some basic principles that guide our approach to supervision and that help define the stance taken by the supervisors and are encouraged in trainees. They include a strong emphasis on an experiential focus and the relational context of supervision, the use of supervisors as models, and openness to diversity issues.

Explicitly Establishing an Experiential Focus

The process of establishing an experiential focus often involves a partial shift away from many traditional ways of thinking about doing therapy that emphasize the development of a case formulation and the implementation of interpretations guided by this formulation. Although case formulations can be extremely helpful, they can also lead to premature formulations that foreclose experience.

It can be useful to begin the supervision process by explicitly presenting a rationale for an experiential emphasis to training. Typically, we begin by discussing the dangers of assimilating new experience to preconceptions and emphasizing the value of striving to develop what the Zen master Shunru Suzuki (1970) referred to as a "beginner's mind" (i.e., a state of mind that is conducive to new learning and discovery). We encourage trainees to attempt to relate to videotapes of other trainees' therapy sessions at a more experiential, rather than a conceptual, level and to give feedback of a more experiential nature. Over time, a group culture develops that is more experiential in nature and a more natural flow back and forth between experiential and conceptual levels emerges. At first, however, the disciplined and intensive focus on the experiential may feel somewhat constraining.

Self-Exploration

Our approach places an overarching emphasis on helping therapists to find their own unique solutions to their problems rather than providing our own formulations or suggestions for intervention (although this can be helpful as well). Therefore, we focus on helping therapists to develop a way to talk with their clients about what is going on in the moment in a way that is unique to the moment and their experience of it. The supervisor's task is to help trainees develop the ability to attend to their own experience of the moment and use it as a basis for intervening.

Because this kind of self-exploration can be threatening, especially given the complexity of the dual relationship between trainees and supervisors (supervisors have both an evaluative and a semitherapeutic relationship with trainees), it is important to pay considerable attention to establishing an adequate supervisory alliance. The first step is to begin the work by explicitly discussing the role that self-exploration plays in training. Like the establishment of the therapeutic alliance, the development of a supervisory alliance involves the negotiation of relevant tasks and goals. When working in a group context, we begin by speaking about the fact that self-exploration will play a central role in supervision, and we make it clear that we anticipate that some therapists may feel less comfortable with this emphasis than others.

At the same time, we make it clear that it is also critical for therapists to respect their own needs for privacy. We thus emphasize that it is important for trainees to be able to take responsibility for halting the exploratory process when they feel uncomfortable with going further. In turn, we strive to be responsive to trainees' feedback that we are pushing too hard. We have found that as therapists come to experience us as trustworthy and respectful of their needs for privacy and come to recognize our commitment to this, they find it easier to take risks and to explore vulnerable areas.

The Relational Context of Supervision

Just as we believe that each therapeutic interaction needs to be taken on its own terms, we feel that supervision has to be tailor-made to the needs of the trainee. Trainees need to maintain their self-esteem, and supervisors need to balance the need for support versus new information or confrontation in a given moment. One way we have found particularly helpful is to have trainees choose the specific issue or theme that they want to work on. If trainees are able to choose the focus, it facilitates the agreement on supervisory goals and helps improve the supervisory alliance.

It is critical for supervisors to monitor the quality of the supervisory relationship in the same ongoing way that therapists monitor the quality of the alliance in therapy. When there is an adequate alliance, the supervisory relationship can move to the background and does not need to be explicitly addressed. When, however, strains or tensions emerge, the exploration of the supervisory relationship should assume priority over other forms of supervision.

The traditional parallel process model (Ekstein & Wallerstein, 1958; Searles, 1955) is used by many supervisors as a way to talk about the dynamics of the supervisory process and explain conflicts and defenses that may be unwittingly enacted. Although the framework can be useful, it can also provide supervisors and trainees with a way of defensively removing themselves from the relational equation. By conceptualizing a supervisory impasse as a parallel to an impasse in the case being supervised, the supervisor can disown responsibility for is or her contribution to the interaction. This is not the best way of modeling the process of acceptance of responsibility to the trainee.

For this reason, we tend to apply the parallel process framework to supervision sparingly. Instead, we prefer to explore supervisory impasses in the same way we think about therapeutic ruptures. This involves a collaborative exploration of both partners' contribution to the impasse. Sometimes there are parallels between ruptures in both supervisory and therapeutic relationships, and sometimes there are not. Regardless of whether working through a supervisory impasse helps to understand the particular strains in a case being supervised, the process of working through supervisory impasses provides therapists with valuable experiential learning about the process of working through relational impasses.

Supervisors as Models

Seeing their supervisors in action can be a valuable learning experience for trainees. The supervisor, modeling his or her therapeutic work, can stop and answer questions regarding his or her internal processes at critical points. When supervisors present their own videotaped material, trainees can ask the supervisors questions about their own thoughts and feelings. Although this process places supervisors in a somewhat exposed and vulnerable position, it highlights the fact that ruptures are an inevitable and valuable part of the therapeutic process, not something that can be avoided with sufficient training or experience. It allows trainees to see what the supervisor's work is really like, rather than some idealized version of it. When trainees see their supervisors struggling to help their clients and alternating between moments of skillfulness and confusion, they can begin to develop a greater sense of self-acceptance toward themselves in their own struggles as therapists.

Trainees also get to see their supervisors in action when they help trainees to engage in the process of self-exploration in either individual or group supervision. The dual nature of the supervisory relationship limits the depth of this type of exploratory work to some extent, but it also provides the opportunity for supervisors to use the process to make didactic points and to ask trainees if they have questions or observations. The interweaving of exploratory and didactic work can create a rich learning experience. It can also allow supervisors to modulate the intensity of the exploratory work by introducing a certain degree of intellectual distance when the exploratory process moves beyond what they think will feel safe in a training context.

Diversity Issues

We believe that diversity issues, including those regarding race, gender, sexual orientation, and cultural background, need to be focused on in the context of the particular therapist–client dyad. Knowledge about other cultures can be extremely helpful to clinicians. Sometimes, however, generalizations made on this basis can be used defensively to avoid the anxiety raised by tensions around these issues and can lead to clinicians making premature and inadequate clinical formulations. We believe that focusing on the elements of the model described in this chapter—therapist self-awareness, a focus on experience, and tracking of the continually shifting tensions of the moment—allows therapists to become aware of, and to begin a dialogue about, the particular issues of diversity that become salient for a specific dyad. Sue (1998), describing the elements necessary for developing cultural competency, emphasized the importance of nonspecific factors such as (a) *scientific mindedness*, that is, the ability to form hypotheses that avoid premature conclusions about culturally different clients and the ability to test these hypotheses creatively and (b) *dynamic sizing*, that is, the ability to know when to generalize and be inclusive and when to individualize and be exclusive. We believe that the approach described in this chapter can help to facilitate the development of these skills.

Structure of Group Supervision Sessions

There is a structure and several basic elements that we find useful to include in most sessions: starting with a mindfulness induction exercise, choosing a case to present and orienting the case presentation, playing an audiotaped or videotaped segment of the session, defining the rupture event, doing an experiential exercise, and finally, debriefing the group and the presenting trainee.

Mindfulness Induction Exercise

The practice of mindfulness plays a significant role in the therapeutic process. Structured mindfulness exercises at the beginning of each supervision session can help supervisees to develop an awareness of, and openness to, their own experience rather than focus on their intellectual understanding.

Such exercises also help trainees sharpen their abilities to become participant observers.

To begin each session, trainees are given some simple mindfulness exercises, such as carefully attending to the sensory experience of eating a raisin (Kabat-Zinn, 1991), focusing on their bodies for a few moments in an attempt to become aware of any physical sensations that emerge and to note when they find their mind wandering, or attending to the breath (following the inhalations and exhalations with attention). These exercises set the tone for each session by focusing trainees' awareness on the present and helping them adopt a sense of nonjudgmental awareness of their own sensory and emotional states.

Over time, this type of mindfulness work helps trainees increase their awareness of subtle feelings, thoughts, and fantasies that emerge when working with their client, which provide important information about what is occurring in the relationship. One of the most valuable by-products of this kind of mindfulness work is a gradual development of a more tolerant and accepting stance toward a full range of internal experiences. In fact, we conceptualize therapeutic metacommunication as type of mindfulness in action, insofar as it involves reflecting on experience in a relational context as it emerges in the here and now, in an attentive, nonjudgmental fashion (Safran, 2002; Safran & Muran, 2000).

Orienting the Case Presentation

Following the mindfulness exercise, the attention is shifted toward a specific case that a trainee will present. We strive to establish a culture of acceptance that privileges the presentation of difficult moments. As discussed, it is important that moments of confusion and not knowing come to be as valued as moments of clarity and skillfulness. As a result, we want trainees to focus their presentations on moments when they felt most stuck and confused. As described above, this can make presenting especially anxiety provoking. Because of this, we grant trainees control over what they want to focus on and encourage them to monitor and limit their level of exposure. After he or she chooses a focus, we ask the trainee to present case material including, when possible, an audiotaped or videotaped segment.

Audiotaping and Videotaping

Using audiotaped or videotaped recordings of sessions in supervision can be a simple and powerful way for supervisors to get a look at what actually takes place in sessions. It allows therapists to gain some distance from their own work and adopt an outside perspective. This process can help them to disembed from whatever relational matrices are being played out.

We have found it useful to use audiotapes and videotapes in several ways, listed next.

1. Although we have found that allowing the trainee a chance to preface or set up the segment they want to present can provide a useful orientation to the group and provide the trainee with a desirable sense of control, we also encourage playing the segment without any introduction. This increases the emphasis on attending to new perceptions and experiences rather than on conceptualizing what is going on. We also tend to err on the side of playing more tape rather than less. This tends to reduce the tendency for group members to interrupt with their observations in a competitive fashion without understanding the larger context and the complexity of the situation.

2. Tapes are stopped at moments when therapists appear unknowingly engaged in enactments, and the therapists are asked to try to reconstruct their feelings at the time. This can help them to notice feelings that they were unaware of and allow them to begin to disembed. The supervisor stops the tape and says to the therapist, "Any sense of what you were feeling in that moment?"

3. Group members are encouraged to provide therapists with subjective feedback about the impact that the client has on them, for example, "Watching the client here, I notice myself beginning to feel tuned out." Supervisors imagine that they are in the therapeutic situation and "think aloud" about the kind of unobservable internal processes that they go through watching the client, including feelings, thoughts, intuitions, internal struggles, and observations (e.g., the look on the client's face or a change in his or her voice tone). This gives less-experienced therapists a glimpse of the covert processes of a more experienced therapist.

Watching recorded material can feel especially exposing to the therapist being observed. During the use of recorded material, it is important for the supervisor to use an empathic, exploratory approach to help therapists to begin to articulate semi-inchoate feelings and experiences. To do this, therapists are encouraged to go beyond simple, one-word responses and to explore the more subtle forms of their experience. The initial task, on viewing the video, is to define the rupture event. The task is to help the therapist become aware that he or she is embedded in the relational matrix with the client and to help him or her with the processes of exploration and disembedding. A relevant moment is chosen and used as a jumping-off point for designing an experiential exercise to allow both the presenting trainee and the group to begin to explore.

Awareness-Oriented Role Plays

Awareness-oriented role plays can help ground the training process at an experiential level and promote self-awareness in trainees. These consist of having therapists role play a segment of a session that has been problematic, either with the assistance of a training group member who plays the role of either the client or therapist or plays both roles themselves (alternating back and forth between the role of therapist and client). As with the other interventions discussed, although this may be of some use to practice with different ways of intervening, the focus here is on the exploration of feelings.

Because the goal is to facilitate awareness, therapists start with whatever they remember from the impasse, but they are encouraged not to worry about perfectly recreating what actually transpired in the session. These role plays take on a life of their own and provide valuable learning experiences even when they end up departing considerably from the original situation. The supervisor may encourage the therapist either to respond (either as the therapist or the client) in a way that feels emotionally plausible in the moment or to try to talk about what he or she is feeling. The goal of directing the therapist's attention inward at specific moments is to help the therapist become aware of feelings that are unconsciously influencing the interaction with the client.

Alternatively, different supervision group members can take turns playing the role of therapist and client in a moment of impasse. In this way, all of the group members can be actively engaged in the experiential learning process, and the kind of one-upmanship common to group supervision settings and case conferences can be reduced. Finally, other group members are able to struggle experientially with the dilemma of the presenting therapist. This often increases empathy for the therapist's dilemma, promotes an atmosphere of trust and mutuality, and facilitates the type of genuine self-exploration that is most helpful when therapists are caught in a difficult therapeutic impasse. Finally, by engaging in role plays as their clients, therapists can often notice client communications and emotions that for some reason they had not previously been aware of, for example, how hostile or scared the client was.

Debriefing

Each session is concluded by debriefing the group. During this stage, we gather final impressions and check in with the trainee who presented to see where he or she is vis-à-vis the group and then the case.

AN EXAMPLE OF THE APPROACH

In this section, we illustrate how our supervisory approach is put into practice. Much of our supervisory work has been done within the context of group supervision, and we will share an example from a supervision group that was conducted by two of us (the first and second authors) with a group of psychology interns. As we mentioned above, we use videotaped sessions for supervision. The supervision session presented below was audiotaped. What follows below is an annotated and somewhat edited (due to space constraints) version of a transcribed account of what took place in a supervision group. We selected this segment of supervision because we believe it captures a number of important aspects of our work.

As we have been discussing throughout this chapter, we place a strong emphasis on helping our supervisees cultivate an awareness of their own internal processes when confronted with ruptures in their treatments. This provides them with greater flexibility when confronted with an impasse, so they can more easily disembed from it and engage in a dialogue about the rupture. We use a number of techniques from the gestalt therapy tradition to facilitate this improved awareness, including empty-chair exercises and role plays.

In this supervision session, a trainee (who we will call Simon) presented a case that he was feeling stuck with. He stated that his client questioned some of the fundamental premises of the therapy and that he was not sure how to handle it. The client was a 40-year-old single woman, currently living alone, who was having difficulty establishing and maintaining a romantic relationship. She had a tendency to disown her own needs and to feel uncomfortable showing vulnerable feelings. As she talked about the recent death of her cat, she began to cry and then began to defend against her sadness.

> Simon: She began to cry and then tried to get away from the crying very quickly. She moved to a more affectively neutral part of the story and began to talk in a chatty way about friends' explanations for why the cat died and so on. When I tried to explore what leads her to avoid the sad feelings, she started to question the method of what we're doing, and that's really what I'm stuck with. I think she pushed some buttons in me.

> Supervisor: Why don't you play a little segment of the session so the group can get a more nuanced sense of what's going on?

Videotaped Session Segment

> Simon: Let's talk about how come you moved away from the sadness. Is it some sort of numbing? A way to numb yourself and then go on with the story? I don't mean to call it a story. It's something you get comfort from, but I think we're both sitting here and wondering why it happened. What do you think it's about? Why do you choose to tell that part of the story?

> Client: I think it's a way of getting away from the pain.

Simon:	It's a way of numbing yourself?
Client:	I mean, you know, just about every week I come here, and I cry. I wonder if things will ever get solved.
Simon:	So you're not sure that crying has . . .
Client:	I feel I've been depressed for most of my life, and I've cried a lot. I mean, what does that say? What does that solve? What does it do except make you feel a little better because it's a physical release. You know . . . part of my expectations of this therapy . . . I go back to that.
Simon:	What do you mean?
Client:	I don't know . . . more feedback from you . . . I don't know if we agree about what's important.
Simon:	What's missing for you?
Client:	Feedback.
Simon:	About what in particular?
Client:	What do you see? What do you think about all this? I don't know. . . . You're the psychologist. [End of segment.]

In the segment above, the client initially presented with a withdrawal rupture, pulling away from her affect and engaging in storytelling. As Simon attempts to explore the process, the client begins to challenge the treatment and shifts to a confrontation rupture. The supervisor instructs Simon to stop the videotape at this point, as he imagines it might provide a good entrée into Simon's experience of having his "buttons pushed" and probes for his experience.

Supervisor:	Okay, Simon, why don't you stop the tape here. [Pauses.] Any sense of what you're feeling at this moment?
Simon:	I don't know. Confused.
Susan:	Couldn't it be useful at this point to comment on the way in which she goes on the attack to defend against her vulnerability?
Supervisor:	Perhaps. But I think it's important in these situations to remember that with hindsight, it can be easy to see how you might have dealt with it. But the issue is that when you're in the situation, you're embedded. You can't see beyond it. I know that when I'm the therapist, when I'm stuck, I'm stuck. And it's often only in retrospect that I can gain some sense of what's going on. What I'm going to suggest is this now. Rather than keeping the focus on Simon, I'd like to

give other people the opportunity to start doing some work . . . at least in role play form. I'm wondering if I can have two volunteers? One to play the client and one to play Simon?

Geena: I'll play the client.

Howard: I'll play Simon.

Simon is not able to put his feelings into words, and at this point, one of the trainees (Susan) attempts to be helpful by suggesting a particular technical strategy that involves interpreting the client's defenses. However, the supervisor chooses to stay at the experiential level in an effort to help Simon become more fully aware of his own feelings that may be contributing to the impasse. Sensing that Simon is somewhat stuck, however, and that there is some impatience in the group, he encourages more group involvement at an experiential level, by structuring a role play exercise.

Supervisor: Okay. So here we have an impasse. The client is pressuring the therapist and saying in a sense, "I'm not getting what I want." And the therapist's task is to try to comment on the interaction in a way that facilitates the therapeutic process. The trick is to try to find some way of talking about what's going on in a way that doesn't mobilize further defensiveness on the client's part. You're the therapist [pointing to Howard], and you're the client [pointing to Geena]. So can the two of you reenact a little bit of what we saw in the tape? Howard, I'd like you, as the therapist, with the benefit of hindsight, to try to use your experience to metacommunicate with your client about what's going on. And Geena, I think it will be important for you in the client's role to try to get some sense of what it feels like getting this kind of feedback from Howard and to respond in a fashion that is informed by the way you're really feeling in role. So if it feels like a criticism or an insult or whatever, you'll try to respond on that basis.

As Geena and Howard enact the impasse between Simon and his client, they find themselves growing increasingly frustrated, and Howard breaks the exercise to enlist help from the group.

Howard [as therapist]:   So, you don't see how expanding developing a greater awareness of . . .

Geena [as client]:   I don't see how my becoming more aware will help. That's for you to tell me.

Howard:	[To the group.] I don't know what I would do in this situation.
Supervisor:	What's happening for you right now?
Howard:	I'm feeling nailed to the wall. But I'm afraid that if I say that to her, it will just alienate her.
Simon:	Yeah. I know that feeling.
Supervisor:	So why don't you try metacommunicating about your dilemma to her?

The supervisor uses this as an opportunity to explore the feelings that are emerging within different people in the group. Howard articulates his experience of feeling "nailed to the wall," and this contribution frees up Simon to sharpen his awareness of his own experience. Howard is then encouraged to experiment with using this experience as a starting point for metacommunication.

Howard [as therapist]:	[To Geena as client.] I feel a little bit like I'm being nailed to the wall. I'm feeling like I don't know how to answer your question. I want to stay with you on this, but I'm not quite sure I know what to say.
Geena [as client]:	Well, I'd be interested in hearing from your point of view, what you think is important in therapy and what you hope to accomplish. [Long pause . . . Howard looks frustrated.]
Supervisor:	[To Howard.] What's happening for you now?
Howard:	I'm feeling really stuck. I tried to negotiate a way for myself to sort of be in the room, but it feels like she comes back at me with a rapid fire question, and I'm stuck again. And I don't want it to be a situation where we keep going back and forth in this way.
Supervisor:	It's a real bind. You've tried to talk with her about what's going on, and she's put the pressure back on you again. So where do you go from here? Right?
Howard:	Right.
Simon:	I didn't metacommunicate as much as Howard did, but my sense is that if I had, the same interaction would have happened and I would have gotten nailed again.

Supervisor:	My suggestion is that in this type of situation, you just continue to comment on the process.
Howard:	Comment on the process?
Supervisor:	Yeah. For example, let's imagine that it keeps going back and forth for awhile. I could imagine myself saying something like "I keep trying to put the ball in your court, and you keep trying to put it back into mine."

The supervisor uses this as an opportunity to help trainees begin to develop an understanding of the importance of continuing to play the role of the participant observer by noting and commenting on whatever emerges in the moment, rather than becoming fixated on their initial understanding of the situation. The next effort to resume role playing was met with some resistance, as supervisees were experiencing the rupture as insurmountable. This was ultimately helpful for Simon, as he was able to feel supported in his frustration. He agreed to try again as the therapist in a role play, and he and Nicole (as client) end up in a similar place in which the client persists in expressing discomfort with progress made in the treatment.

Simon [as therapist]:	Right . . . What are you feeling right now?
Nicole [as client]:	Another feeling question. I'm feeling like this just isn't getting me anywhere.
Simon:	[Shrugs and gestures to group as if to say, "I'm stuck." Silence for a moment, and then everyone laughs.]
Supervisor:	[To Simon.] What are you experiencing?
Simon:	I don't know. I just don't have a comeback.
Supervisor:	Okay. So you're at a loss.
Simon:	Yeah.
Supervisor:	Okay. So can you work from this point? "I'm at a loss . . . " or whatever . . . in other words . . . try to put into words the feeling of the gesture you made to the group.
Simon:	Okay. I don't want to say, "I'm at a loss." But let me see . . .
Supervisor:	Why not?
Simon:	Well . . . okay. I'll try it.
Supervisor:	You don't have to try it . . . but I'm just curious to find out what your reservations are.

Simon:	Well . . . I think of saying, "I don't know," and my heart starts beating.
Supervisor:	Can you say a little more?
Simon:	Well . . . it's like my competency is on the line. I guess it feels like that a lot with her.
Supervisor:	So it's not okay with you not to have the answers right now?
Simon:	I guess not.

Through the role play, Simon accesses an experience of being at a loss. When the supervisor encourages him to use this experience as a point of departure for metacommunication, Simon begins to appear anxious, and he is about to push through this anxiety in an act of compliance. The supervisor stops him and instead uses the opportunity to begin to explore an internal conflict that may be contributing to the therapeutic impasse.

Supervisor:	Okay . . . I'm going to suggest an experiment. It sounds like there's an internal split. It's not just that you feel at a loss but also that there's a part of you that finds that unacceptable. Does that fit?
Simon:	Yeah.
Supervisor:	Okay. So can you sit in this chair [pulls up an empty chair] and play the part of yourself that finds it unacceptable? [Simon moves to empty chair.] . . . In other words, tell the part of you that feels at a loss [gestures to empty chair] that it's not acceptable.
Simon:	[Speaking to empty chair.] You should have the answers. What's wrong with you? [Pauses.]
Supervisor:	Can you switch to the other chair and respond?
Simon:	[Switching to other chair.] I don't know. I guess I'm feeling stuck.
Supervisor:	Can you switch chairs and speak as the other side?
Simon:	[Switching chairs.] That's not good enough. You should have the answers.
Supervisor:	Switch, please.
Simon:	[Switching chairs.] Well, I don't, and that's all there is to it [gesturing with hand].
Supervisor:	What's the feeling that goes with the gesture?

Simon:	It's like "Back off. I can't be where I'm not."
Supervisor:	Switch chairs, please.
Simon:	[Switches chairs and looks at the empty chair thoughtfully.]
Supervisor:	What's happening for you?
Simon:	Well . . . that makes sense. I feel a sense of letting go.
Supervisor:	Okay. So now I'm going to suggest as an experiment that you try talking about your feeling of being stuck to your client and see how it feels. Imagine that she's sitting in the empty chair [gesturing to it] and try talking with her about your experience.
Simon:	[To empty chair.] You know . . . I'm feeling kind of stuck right now. I'd like to say something that's helpful to you, but I just can't seem to find the right thing to say. [Long pause.]
Supervisor:	What does that feel like?
Simon:	It actually feels okay. It feels like a relief.
Supervisor:	Okay. Now there's no guarantee as to how your client would respond if you said that . . . but it seems like an important place to come to internally.
Simon:	Yeah. I agree.

The supervisor uses an empty-chair exercise to help Simon explore the way in which his intolerance of his own feelings of helplessness contributes to the impasse. Because of this intolerance, he is more likely to get into a struggle with the client in an attempt to manage his own feelings of discomfort. By separating out parts of himself that feel helpless and the part that criticizes these parts, he becomes more aware of his own internal conflict and achieves an experiential awareness of the impact of being the object of his own self-criticism. This initiates a process of self-acceptance. This process begins when the part of the self that has been the object of self-criticism asserts itself and defends itself against the self criticism ("Back off. I can't be where I'm not."). It continues with a softening of the part of the self that is being critical ("Well . . . that makes sense. I feel a sense of letting go."). This type of internal shift will not be permanent, but it does provide him with a momentary taste of what it is like to be more self-accepting on this issue.

We have found that the devotion of supervision time to opening therapists' awareness of their multitude of experiences is the heart of the work. By having Simon engage in and observe role plays, he was able to reach a new level of understanding about how he feels when he is challenged by his client. Ultimately, he felt a sense of relief and a decreased sense of paralysis, as he accessed his sense of helplessness and became more accepting of it. This allowed him to stay more present and attuned to his client, and he became much more adept at managing her challenges.

We hope that this case has been illustrative of our supervision model and philosophy. The emphasis is on helping trainees to develop an experientially grounded sense of their own contribution to impasses and to articulate semi-inchoate experience that is relevant to understanding what is taking place in the therapy. Our focus is on helping therapists explore their own dissociated feelings to facilitate the process of disembedding from impasses that are often emotionally complex and charged in nature. Mindfulness exercises, videotaped material, and role-playing exercises are extremely helpful in facilitating the supervisees' level of connection to their own internal experiences. Consistent with our belief that ruptures are relational experiences, we think it is critical for supervisors to facilitate therapists' deepening of awareness into both (a) the ways they experience, and perhaps contribute to, the rupture and (b) how they might negotiate or metacommunicate about this situation.

Although we find group supervision to be extremely helpful, our model can also be used quite effectively in individual supervision. In individual supervision, we use mindfulness exercises, various role plays, and empty-chair exercises and continue the focus on the therapist's experience over and above the interpretation of the client's experience. Although our rupture resolution model was originally designed in the context of relationally oriented psychotherapy, therapeutic alliance ruptures are a transtheoretical phenomenon. The relationally oriented model of supervision outlined in the chapter can thus be adapted for use in the context of a range of different treatment modalities. In addition, such training provides both a perspective and a foundation of skills and experiences to resolve ruptures, should they occur within the supervisory relationship.

FUTURE DIRECTIONS FOR RESEARCH

We currently have a number of research initiatives under way to investigate various aspects of our supervision model. One study that is currently taking place is examining whether cognitive therapists who undergo rupture resolution training in the fashion outlined in this chapter show an improvement in their ability to resolve ruptures in the therapeutic alliance. A second study is examining therapist individual difference variables that mediate the effectiveness of this training. For example, do therapists who (prior to supervision) are able to reflect on their experience with their clients in a nondefensive fashion show a greater improvement in therapeutic skills as a consequence of supervision than therapists who are more defensive? Do therapists' own relational schemas or attachment styles mediate their ability to benefit from our supervision approach? Is there a relationship between therapists' abilities to reflect on both their clients' and their own states of mind, on the one hand, and the benefit they derive from supervision, on the other? Other potentially fruitful research directions may involve dismantling studies. For example, do therapists who are trained in the fashion described in this chapter improve their skills more than therapists who simply receive mindfulness training? How critical are the more experiential aspects of the supervision model? Research of this type will play a critical role in further refining our ability to help therapists through the process of supervision develop the complex cognitive, affective, and interpersonal skills necessary to work with challenging clients.

REFERENCES

Ekstein, R., & Wallerstein, R. (1958). *The teaching and learning of psychotherapy*. New York: International Universities Press.

Falender, C. A., & Shafranske, E. P. (2004). *Clinical supervision: A competency-based approach*. Washington, DC: American Psychological Association.

Horvath, A. O., & Symonds, B. D. (1991). Relation between working alliance and outcome in psychotherapy: A meta-analysis. *Journal of Counseling Psychology, 38*, 139–149.

Kabat-Zinn, J. (1991). *Full catastrophe living*. New York: Delta.

Martin, D., Garske, J., & Davis, K. (2000). Relation of the therapeutic alliance with outcome and other variables: A meta-analytic review. *Journal of Consulting and Clinical Psychology, 68*, 438–450.

Muran, J. C., Safran, J. D., Samstag, L. W., & Winston, A. (2005). Evaluating an alliance-focused treatment for personality disorders. *Psychotherapy, 42*, 512–531.

Safran, J. D. (1993a). Breaches in the therapeutic alliance: An arena for negotiating authentic relatedness. *Psychotherapy: Theory, Research, and Practice, 30*, 11–24.

Safran, J. D. (1993b). The therapeutic alliance as a transtheoretical phenomenon: Definitional and conceptual issues. *Journal of Psychotherapy Integration, 3*, 33–49.

Safran, J. D. (2002). Brief relational psychoanalytic treatment. *Psychoanalytic Dialogues, 12*, 171–196.

Safran, J. D., Crocker, P., McMain, S., & Murray, P. (1990). Therapeutic alliance rupture as a therapy event for empirical investigation. *Psychotherapy: Theory, Research, and Practice, 27*, 154–165.

Safran, J. D., & Muran, J. C. (1996). The resolution of ruptures in the therapeutic alliance. *Journal of Consulting and Clinical Psychology, 64*, 447–458.

Safran, J. D., & Muran, J. C. (2000). *Negotiating the therapeutic alliance: A relational treatment guide*. New York: Guilford Press.

Safran, J. D., Muran, J. C., & Samstag, L. W. (1994). Resolving therapeutic alliance ruptures: A task analytic investigation. In A. O. Horvath & L. S. Greenberg

(Eds.), *The working alliance: Theory, research, and practice* (pp. 225–255). New York: Wiley.

Safran, J. D., Muran, J. C., Samstag, L. W., & Stevens, C. (2002). Repairing alliance ruptures. In J. C. Norcross (Ed.), *Psychotherapy relationships that work* (pp. 235–244). New York: Oxford University Press.

Safran, J. D., Muran, J. D., Samstag, L. W., & Winston, A. (2005). Evaluating an alliance-focused treatment for potential treatment failures. *Psychotherapy, 42,* 512–531.

Safran, J. D., & Segal, Z. V. (1996). *Interpersonal process in cognitive therapy* (2nd ed.). Northvale, NJ: Jason Aronson.

Samstag, L. W., Muran, J. C., & Safran, J. D. (2004). Defining and identifying alliance ruptures. In D. Charma (Ed.), *Core concepts in brief dynamic psychotherapy* (pp. 187–214). Mahwah, NJ: Erlbaum.

Searles, H. (1955). The informational value of the supervisor's emotional experience. *Psychiatry, 18,* 135–146.

Sue, S. (1998). In search of cultural competence in psychotherapy and counseling. *American Psychologist, 53,* 440–448.

Suzuki, S. (1970). *Zen mind, beginner's mind.* New York: Weatherhill.

8

ADDRESSING ETHICAL AND LEGAL ISSUES IN CLINICAL SUPERVISION

GERALD P. KOOCHER, EDWARD P. SHAFRANSKE,
AND CAROL A. FALENDER

The training of mental health practitioners presents a unique set of challenges. In addition to facilitating the development of technical competence in trainees, supervisors must carefully monitor the psychotherapeutic process to ensure the provision of accepted standards of client care. This task inevitably involves a delicate balance between providing opportunities to the supervisee to engage directly in clinical decision making and practice, affording a measure of autonomy to the trainee, and simultaneously ensuring safety by maintaining oversight and quality control of all clinical services. Although one can glibly note that supervisors owe their primary responsibility to the client, conflicts may nevertheless arise when fulfilling the ethical obligations inherent in treatment and in training. Further, as in all professional involvement, ethics and law remain ever-present and shape the nature, process, and focus of clinical supervision.

In this chapter, we illustrate how ethical and legal issues usually arise in the supervisory process, suggest strategies to engage supervisees in actively grappling with these issues, and describe how to mold and define supervision practice by attending to legal and ethical parameters. Consistent with Falender and Shafranske (2004), consideration of ethics and law goes beyond the narrow discussion of specific clinical problems or situations and begins with the essential values that inform the supervisory relationship. Through the expression of principles such as beneficience, fidelity, integrity, justice, and respect for all persons (American Psychological Association [APA] Ethics Code, 2002; see also the APA Web site version at http://www.apa.org/ethics/) within the supervisory relationship, together with the application of laws (Association of State and Provincial Psychology Boards, 1998), our supervisees observe the real-world integration of law and ethics into practice. In this way, we encouraged them to internalize and to practice professional standards.

APPROPRIATE FOCI OF CLINICAL SUPERVISION

The ethical practice of clinical supervision requires understanding its functions and the multiple (and at times conflicted) roles performed by the supervisor. We as mental health practitioners must carefully consider the relationship itself, because we belong to one of the few professions in which supervisors routinely engage in discussions of a subordinate's inner life as well as disclose at times aspects of their own personal and professional experiences as part of clinical training. Supervision inevitably requires a measure of self-disclosure, as doing so assists supervisees (and supervisors) to improve technique, develop empathic understanding, and acquire insight into oneself and one's clients and supervisees. In addition to monitoring technical competencies, supervisory practice encompasses the universe of factors drawn from the supervisee's background (professional and personal) that directly influence clinical practice.

Different clinical activities and theoretical systems require varying levels of self-disclosure. The APA Ethics Code (APA, 2002) takes account of this in Section 7.04 under the heading "Student Disclosures of Personal Information." Examples of generally inappropriate lines of inquiry include sexual history; history of abuse and neglect; psychological treatment; and relationships with parents, peers, and spouses or significant others. Exceptions fall into two categories: first, if the program has clearly put the trainee on written notice about a potential need to address these matters, and second, if the trainee's own behavior raises questions of competence or threats related to these topics. Essentially, the Ethics Code focuses on consent and safety. A supervisor dealing with neuropsychological assessment or classroom behavior management would have little need to discuss such issues. However, candidates at psychoanalytic institutes would routinely expect to engage in discussions of this nature. In addition, when case-specific issues evoke emotional reactions, one should certainly address personal contributory factors.

The key considerations when a supervisor addresses a trainee's personal world involve consent, respect, and appropriate incorporation in the evaluation process. The trainee deserves an explanation of why the supervisor has raised the issues and should have the right to defer detailed discussions of the issues to personal psychotherapy. The supervisor should focus on how the trainee can best address the needs of the client(s), notwithstanding the trainee's own issues. When evaluating the trainee, the supervisor should address the trainee's professionalism, openness to feedback, and clinical work but should not inject any sensitive data or personal disclosures made by the trainee into the content of written evaluation materials.

Clinical supervision involves observing, monitoring, assessing, evaluating, instructing, training, mutual problem solving, supporting, modeling, and mentoring, to name but a few responsibilities (Bernard & Goodyear, 2004; Falender & Shafranske, 2004). Although each function involves ethical and legal principles, in this chapter we focus on selected domains: monitoring the work of the supervisee, legal responsibility, ethical issues and practices, clinical competence, and personal functioning. These different functions can and do overlap in many instances, but each requires a degree of special attention to ensure adequate coverage.

Monitoring

Several aspects of the monitoring function of the supervisor radiate through the other foci of supervision; however, chief among these is the basic responsibility for knowledge of cases assigned to the supervisee, and evaluation and decision making regarding the degree of supervision and oversight needed for each case. This determination occurs in light of the specific clinical competencies required to address the psychological difficulties presented in each case and the supervisee's level of competence in performing such recommended interventions and procedures. If something goes wrong, a key legal standard will involve what the supervisor knew or should have known in the particular circumstance, regarding both the supervisee's skill level and the clinical needs of the client. Failure to monitor performance is a significant ethical violation in supervision (Ladany, Lehrman-Waterman, Molinaro, & Wolgast, 1999).

Legal Responsibility

In all cases, the specific laws of the jurisdiction in which the professional works with the client takes place will apply to both supervisor and supervisee. Generally speaking, the doctrine of *respondeat superior* makes the supervisor legally responsible for the cases of those whose professional work he or she oversees. The term originated with the Latin for "let the master answer," which holds that employers or supervisors have responsibility for the actions of those they hire or supervise in the course of their employment (see, e.g., http://dictionary.law.com/ for other legal terminology definitions). The supervisor has both direct liability for providing adequate supervision and vicarious liability for the acts or omissions of their supervisees.

Ethical Knowledge and Behavior

Supervisors should have knowledge of the ethical standards of the profession and should consistently model appropriate behavior. Rather than treating ethics as an add-on or adjunctive piece of behavior, supervisors bear responsibility to fully integrate ethical principles. One excellent model for conceptualizing the supervisee process of ethical integration is the acculturation-strategies framework (Handelsman, Gottlieb, & Knapp, 2005). In this context, *ethical acculturation* can be viewed as a developmental process in which supervisees enter training with their own morals, value traditions, and beliefs and confront new ethical principles, rules, and responsibilities within the clinical setting, some of which may prove inconsistent with their prior ways of responding. Included in this process is the development of respect for the values and beliefs of others, which may in fact be at variance with one's own personal values and commitments. Part of the supervisory process is teaching that ethical behavior is complex and not easily resolved, and that it is the process of identifying and thinking through ethical dilemmas that is critical to professional functioning. Knowledge of multiple problem-solving paradigms is a significant part of the process in which ethical practice is instilled into the discourse of supervision and, ultimately, is infused the supervisee's decision-making strategies and practice.

Clinical Competence

Clinical competence in supervision flows like traffic on a superhighway. The supervisor should demonstrate not only competence in ethics, professional practice, and the content domain of the supervision (e.g., psychotherapy, psychodiagnostic testing, consultation) but also expertise in the practice of supervision itself. Multiple competencies are involved in the flow of supervision, including the ability to "change lanes" to respond to changing situations in client care and training (e.g., shifting from a focus on case management to evaluating performance or to demonstrating a skill). Because education and training in supervision are relatively new in the field, some aspects of supervisory competence may require focused development on the part of the supervisor, for instance, knowledge of supervision models, research, and best practices. It is commonly acknowledged that many supervisors grow as a result of good supervision, suffer from not-so-good supervision, or become skilled and sensitive supervisors in part because of their experiences of poor supervision. Also, many of us have benefited by the experience of working with supervisees collaboratively to discover effective practices and to thereby learn competencies along the way. The take-away point is that competence in providing supervision does not remain static and benefits from substantial effort, training, and openness to learn from both successes and failures.

Personal Functioning

The APA Ethics Code (2002; Section 2.06) stresses the importance on remaining attuned to any personal problems or conflicts that might bear on our work. The Ethics Code specifically encourages us to avoid initiating activities when a substantial likelihood exists that our personal problems may prevent us from performing our work competently. Supervisors may reasonably inquire into the personal lives of their supervisees to the extent necessary to address apparent personal problems that become manifest of the job (APA Ethics Code, Section 7.04). Informed consent must be given to trainees before admission to the program, should there be an expectation of personal exploration in supervision (APA Ethics Code, Section 7.04). When a supervisor becomes aware of personal problems that may interfere with fulfilling professional responsibilities, the individual should consider obtaining professional consultation or assistance, and determine whether to limit, suspend, or terminate any work-related duties. These obligations apply equally to supervisors and supervisees.

MULTIPLE ROLES

The supervisor, by necessity, functions in multiple roles simultaneously, including those of teacher; mentor; facilitator of self-awareness and personal exploration; evaluator; gatekeeper; administrator; and model of ethical, legal, and professional practice standards. Such complex overlapping roles are inevitable, yet they require sensitivity so as not to constitute an ethical problem. The APA Ethics Code (2002; Section 3.05) describes multiple relationships as occurring when a psychologist holds a professional role with a person and simultaneously: (a) holds another role with the same person, (b) has a relationship with a person closely associated with or related to the person with whom the psychologist has the professional relationship, or (c) promises to enter into another relationship in the future with the person or with another closely associated with or related to the person. Functioning in multiple roles is not, prima facie, an ethical breach. Rather, the determining factor involves whether entering into a multiple relationship might reasonably be expected to impair the psychologist's objectivity, competence, or effectiveness in performing their professional duties, or otherwise risk exploitation or harm to the person with whom the professional relationship exists. The Ethics Code also explicitly notes that multiple relationships unlikely to cause impairment, risk exploitation, or harm are not unethical. In the case of supervision, multiple roles must in fact be performed to fulfill the obligations to the client, the trainee, the profession, and society. Burian and Slimp's (2000) decision tree described in the To Go or Not to Go narrative provides an excellent frame for determining whether a multiple relationship in internship is ethical.

The APA Ethics Code (APA, 2002; Section 3.08) cautions against exploitative relationships with people over whom we have supervisory, evaluative, or other authority such as clients, students, supervisees, research participants, and employees. Examples of multiple relationships between supervisor and supervisee with potential for exploitation include a supervisor who develops a social relationship with an intern, hires an intern as a babysitter, or provides psychotherapy. Supervisors must be sensitive to avoiding exploitation of their own supervisees and to ensuring that trainees not exploit clients.

Supervisory roles should not be blended with intimate social roles. Psychologists do not engage in sexual relationships with students or supervisees who are in their department, agency, or training center or over whom they have or are likely to have evaluative authority (APA Ethics Code; APA, 2002; Section 7.07). This expansion in the 2002 Ethics Code includes not only those who have evaluative authority or direct supervisors but also those who are colleagues. All too frequently, a colleague will become blinded by their emotions, particularly when they have problems in their personal lives. Sexual attraction, normative between therapist and client, and even perhaps between trainee and supervisor, should be viewed as a significant indicator of need for consultation or for personal therapy. Inappropriate supervisor behavior is hugely problematic for the supervisee because of the power differential and the reality that that supervisor will evaluate performance.

RECONCILING THE POWER DIFFERENTIAL, EVALUATION, AND GATEKEEPING

Recognizing and respecting the power differential between supervisor and supervisee is critical to negotiating and maintaining an effective relationship. In many ways, the supervisor can become a kind of professional parent figure, with all the issues of role differentiation, management of countertransference, approval seeking, and quests for autonomy that such a relationship implies. The process of informed consent must be highly articulated with elaborate descriptions of criteria for successful completion, consequences for less than that, and steps that will be enacted to alert trainees as to evaluation issues. This evaluative, power responsibility may span many years after the internship or training period, as supervisors are called on for letters of recommendation and verification or evaluation for licensure, hospital privileges, and employment.

A key challenge involves helping the supervisee to share vulnerabilities, including feelings about what might have gone wrong and right in the work under discussion. Feelings of emotional distress, insecurity, and other personal vulnerabilities triggered in work with clients may constitute appropriate topics for discussion in supervision. The delicate balance here involves a distinction between the roles of a supervisor and a psychotherapist, as the discussion should maintain focus on the client–therapist or therapist–supervisee–supervisor relationships.

Because human memory is fallible and messages involving criticism may trigger an emotional response, it is often wise to document oral feedback. In addition, inviting the student to think about the feedback and reopen the discussion at a later date may also prove useful for individuals, providing time for a thoughtful response. Some supervisors express fears of being sued by a former supervisee should they report a negative evaluation that results in a poor grade or termination from a training program. Use of a competency-based approach (Falender & Shafranske, 2004)—which entails integrated contracting, development of a supervisory alliance, thoughtful evaluation, timely feedback, and good documentation of problems and remediation efforts—will reduce the likelihood of such an occurrence. In essence, following good ethical practices constitutes solid risk management in terms of subsequent hazards.

CONFLICTS BETWEEN ETHICAL STANDARDS AND RISK MANAGEMENT

Although trainees expect treatment in line with the same ethical standards they use with their clients, they at times feel ethically violated in several areas, in part because discussion of one's own vulnerabilities routinely occurs during supervision. We encourage trainees to seek counseling or therapy as needed. However, students who have sought counseling for psychological distress, often depression, have at times have been reported to the administration and, in several cases, experienced suspensions from school (Capriccioso, 2006). One could argue that severing the relationship with the university may increase the risk to the student, ending treatment and increasing hopelessness and lack of control. The legal issues focus on whether a special relationship exists and whether institutional personnel might have foreseen the student's risky action (e.g., danger to self). The university perspectives have evolved in response to case law *Schieszler v. Ferrum College* (2002) (also; Laverne F. Schieszler v. Ferrum College) and *Shin v. MIT* (2005), dealing with the existence of a special relationship between student and the college or university. A key factor involves whether a foreseeable risk of harm, a duty of care, and ultimately, a duty to protect apply. These case law decisions raise issues of confidentiality, in that the counseling center disclosed serious mental health diagnoses to administrators who then moved to suspend the student. Behnke (Capriccioso, 2006) stated that providing broad rights to disclose a client's condition could result in a decrease in students seeking help. However, from the risk management perspective of the university, these cases serve as reminders "to be proactive in their handling of potentially suicidal students as a best practice to avoid liability" (Armstrong, 2005, p. 1).

In such instances, both supervisors and trainees must clearly understand confidentiality issues related to both the Family Education Rights and Privacy Act (FERPA; 1974) and Health Insurance Portability and Accountability Act (HIPAA; 1996). FERPA protects educational records including student grades and educational records, and HIPAA covers personal health information (PHI). Records from a college counseling service or student health service may fit either or both categories, depending on their nature and context. One important distinction between these two acts is that HIPAA violations focus on individuals who disclose PHI, whereas FERPA does not provide for claims against individuals, only institutions. Those responsible for supervising trainees in school, college, or university settings should make certain that the consent to treatment and release of information documents in use at their institution provides sufficient latitude to intervene effectively in emergency situations.

In another ethical and legal situation, trainees in placement or internship have between a one-in-six and a one-in-nine chance of treating a client who commits suicide (Kleespies, Smith, & Becker, 1990). Trainees may not have an option of discussing the suicide or processing their feelings, sense of responsibility, or other aspects of the case, because the administration may fear a lawsuit and worry that such disclosures would enhance the plaintiff's case. In reality, suicide is one of the most frequent causes of litigation against mental health professionals (Bennett et al., 2007). In Spiegelman and Werth (2005), trainees who experienced either a client committing suicide or a serious attempt described their experience and the lack of support, supervision, or debriefing. Ultimately, the task involves balancing the rights and welfare of the trainee against the risk management of the institution.

RISKY INDIVIDUALS

Caution and vigilance remain critical to good supervision, both as part of the monitoring function of the supervisor and in helping supervisees think in a thoughtful and farsighted manner about potential consequences of actions or inaction. For example, helping supervisees anticipate worst-case scenarios of particular courses of action or interventions can help instill a sense of self-confidence by virtue of knowing what to do if problems should occur. Similarly, keeping trainees apprised of back-up plans and ways to make contact after hours also boosts their sense of security. The key in focusing on vigilance and caution involves maintaining a thoughtful, supportive, and proactive manner with a supervisor who feels more like a safety net than a grand inquisitor. This approach is particularly important when working with individuals who pose risks within the training process (Harrar, VandeCreek, & Knapp, 1990; Katsavdakis, Gabbard, & Athey, 2004). Paying special attention to recognizing and intervening early with risky individuals also minimizes hazards in the supervisory process (Brenner, 2006; Enochs & Etzbach, 2004).

Once again, one should remember that risky individuals may crop up on either side of the supervision equation. The characteristics of both supervisees and supervisors who pose ethical and practical hazards have remarkable similarities. Those who will pose the greatest risks are emotionally unstable or labile; have high levels of arrogance or narcissism; have highly critical, sarcastic, or hostile interpersonal styles; or are inclined toward impulsivity or procrastination (Brenner, 2006). Watching for such traits and either coaching the party or reassigning them is a wise decision (Enochs & Etzbach, 2004). In addition, creating clear policies and procedures for supervision and offering training for novice supervisors will reduce hazards. The key involves recognizing the people and situations most likely to trigger unfortunate emotional responses and designing systems to minimize tensions (Koocher & Keith-Spiegel, 2008).

Another important consideration involves obligations to the profession and public with respect to people enrolled in training programs who become identified as risky individuals. If we do not believe that trainees have the knowledge and skills needed to safely and beneficially serve the public, we have a professional and ethical obligation not to issue misleading credentials, grades, or other statements of qualification. A decision to issue a failing grade in a clinical course, to deny satisfactory internship completion credentials, or to decline a recommendation to a licensing board should never come as a surprise to a student. Rather, such actions should only occur following a well-documented attempt to afford the student the opportunity to meet appropriate standards of clinical skill and professionalism (Koocher & Keith-Spiegel, 2008).

SEXUAL HARASSMENT

Unwelcome sexual advances are all too common in some workplaces. Although requests for sexual favors or physical conduct of a sexual nature that forces submission as an explicit or implicit condition of employment or academic standing clearly constitutes ethical misconduct, more subtle situations can also raise concerns. Any situation or conduct that creates a hostile, intimidating, or offensive learning or work environment could be deemed harassing. This fact leaves some room for misunderstanding, for example, when a supervisor and supervisee are addressing sensitive matters with transference and countertransference issues. In such instances, a supervisor should approach matters cautiously, especially if it seems that a trainee may have particular sensitivities making it difficult to address or explore some necessary issues with a client or in supervision.

Supervisors who massage backs or grope and fondle supervisees should know that such behavior constitutes an ethical violation and is highly problematic. Court decisions have made it clear that unwelcome sexual advances or comments may be deemed abusive and that a hostile work environment can also be deemed abusive (see, e.g., *Harris v. Forklift Systems, Inc.*, 1993; *Meritor Savings Bank v. Vinson*, 1986).

In some situations, what seems like an innocent supportive or congratulatory hug to the giver may feel inappropriate to the recipient. Surveys have found that 25 percent to 90 percent of women have reported feeling some degree of sexual victimization in the workplace, although this mostly goes unreported (Rubin & Borgers, 1990). Management often tends to deny or minimize such complaints, with comments such as "It never happened" (denial); "She misunderstood" (minimized); "It wasn't intentional" (minimized); or "She came on to me" (blaming).

When a supervisee expresses any discomfort with the supervisor's behavior in this regard, a respectful acknowledgement of the concern and effort to obtain consultation from colleagues is a wise course of action. Acknowledging the expressed discomfort and engaging a third party shows respect for the sensitive person and broadens the contextual discussion in a way that can often defuse the tensions of the moment. In a survey of experienced supervisors, de Mayo (2000) found that most (55%) respondents reported receiving no supervisee reports of sexual harassment experiences by clients, but a significant percentage (45%) reported one or more incidents of a supervisee reporting sexual harassment by a client. Reports ranged from persistent inappropriate sexual comments to physical actual sexual assaults. Supervisors' responses ranged from supervisory discussions to active interventions. The vast majority of supervisors (74%) mentioned talking with the supervisee about the incident in supervision, typically processing the supervisee's feelings about the incident, validating his or her response to the client, clarifying the manner in which a therapist might process the event with the client, and strategizing with the supervisee about how to establish and maintain firm boundaries to prevent a recurrence of the problematic behavior. Clinical supervisors can help prepare trainees for such potentially harassing situations by providing them with both a conceptual framework to understand the phenomenon of sexual harassment and specific strategies to manage these situations. By encouraging trainees to disclosure such issues in supervision, the supervisor can better set a tone for open and collaborative supervision and promote learning about how to resolve such matters effectively, safely, and therapeutically.

ISSUES IN GROUP SUPERVISION

Supervising trainees in groups can provide for efficient supervision. Group peer supervision can also help experienced clinicians avoid feeling isolated and gain broader perspective on their cases. However, such situations have some inherent ethical hazards. The use of group supervision to save supervisory time might result in shoddy coverage. Excessive use of group supervision can reduce the individual attention each trainee gets and may lead to inadequate supervisory oversight. Depending on differential needs and case load sizes, the benefits of shared wisdom and peers' support may be outweighed by feelings of relative neglect on the part of some trainees or by letting a weaker trainee fall off the supervisor's radar screen. Group settings may also inhibit some disclosures by trainees, especially if they are worried about criticism, embarrassment, or loss of esteem among their peers as a result of raising their concerns. Group supervision models may also generally reduce confidentiality assurances and alter legal privilege. For example, when a former client filed suit against a licensed psychotherapist for a perceived treatment error, the therapist had to acknowledge at deposition that he had discussed the case in anonymous sanitized form during a monthly peer consultation group with other licensed professionals. Each of the other colleagues was then subpoenaed for deposition to learn what comments and advice they had offered in the case (Koocher & Keith-Spiegel, 2008). Although all members of the group were independent practitioners and fully licensed, some feared they might fall subject to a risk from vicarious liability on the basis of advice they gave, which their colleague may have followed. Such a risk would actually be quite low among independently licensed practitioners, in contrast to cases in which a licensed person supervises an unlicensed person. Nonetheless, the matter deserves careful thought in structuring such groups, as a similar situation could occur in a training setting.

Clients may also have a right to know about, and withhold, consent to having their cases discussed in such contexts, assuming that the data presented might enable the others in the supervision group to identify the client. This tends not to be a problem when the supervision occurs within a single agency or institution responsible for client care or in contexts in which the client knows that his or her clinician is in training and has a supervisor who hears about the case regularly.

LETTERS OF REFERENCE

Letters of reference raise many interesting ethical issues and can pose a range of risks. The importance of such letters and the weight assigned to their content vary widely. On the one hand, if the letter offers effusive praise, includes supportive data, and comes from a respected colleague, it will likely have a positive effect on the candidate's chances. On the other hand, faint praise can be damning, and critical comments of any sort can tend to torpedo a candidate's chances. Although we may want to help advance our students' and colleagues' careers, we also owe a responsibility to the recipients of our letters not to lie or put clients at risk by endorsing unqualified or ethically challenged candidates.

How can supervisors and supervisees negotiate writing ethical reference letters without worrying about legal problems? Supervisees can begin the process by asking supervisors, before listing them as references, whether they feel comfortable in providing a "strong positive letter." If the supervisor balks or hesitates, the wise supervisee will look elsewhere for a reference. The primary concern of most supervisors involves avoiding defamation in written (i.e., libel) or oral (i.e., slander) forms. Defamation occurs when a person knowingly makes false statements causing another person to suffer harm (i.e., damages). The truth constitutes a defense against claims of defamation; however, opinion can vary widely across individuals. When writing letters of reference or giving oral recommendations, do not assume perpetual confidentiality; rather, anticipate that the candidate will at some point see your letter. Make your comments honest, direct, and focused on behavioral indicators and objective evidence, avoiding opinion or innuendo.

If supervisors do not believe they can write a strong letter, discuss this problem with the candidate or just say No. In situations in which a supervisor's experiences with the supervisee are mixed, one can draft a letter, show it to the supervisee, and ask whether they would like it sent. In some cases, supervisees may feel satisfied with a letter discussing both strengths and weaknesses openly.

If the former supervisee needs an official attestation of graduation, completion of a number of supervised hours, or you must write a letter in an official capacity (i.e., as a training director) attesting to a factual matter (e.g., "The candidate completed his PhD degree requirements."), the letter can focus only on the facts necessary. Providing such confirmation is not the same as writing a positive endorsement. It would not be ethically appropriate to withhold confirmation of factual confirmation of legitimate accomplishments simply because one had other concerns about a former supervisee.

EXAMPLES OF THE APPROACH

The three vignettes that follow originated in actual clinical supervision contexts and provide useful illustrations involving diversity, sexual harassment, self-disclosure, monitoring, and feedback issues. Alteration of critical details protects the identities of the parties.

Confronting Racism in Supervision

Paul, an African American psychology intern with a White supervisor, has begun treating a 7-year-old boy of Irish American heritage whose parents brought him to the clinic seeking treatment for school failure and enuresis. During the second session, the boy sets up a row of toy soldiers and knocks them down one by one alternately shouting out, "bam," "pow," and "kill that n*****," while making sidelong glances at Paul. Paul reported this to his supervisor at the next session, noting that he attempted to address the boy's implicit anger while ignoring the blatantly racist comments.

The supervisor invited Paul to consider his own feelings about the manner in which the child used "kill the n*****" in the session, and Paul acknowledged feeling angry and paralyzed about how to respond. The supervisor validated the appropriateness of Paul's anger and praised his restraint in the moment but asked Paul to think through with him how to address the issue in the next session with the boy. Paul was able to think about whether the "anger" he ascribed to the client was more accurately a reflection of his own feelings and what the child might have been testing out with the clearly provocative behavior. Paul was encouraged to address the issue directly with the child during the next session by noting that he had been thinking about the prior events and wanted the boy to understand that using words like the "n*****" word is hurtful and offensive. Paul was able to stress that he wanted to help the boy do better in school and solve his bed-wetting problem but that the name calling would get in the way. Paul wondered aloud whether he and the boy could work together without such words. The child agreed and apologized, and the relationship went forward productively. The therapist felt encouraged and supported by the ethically appropriate intervention of the supervisor to recognize and directly address the inappropriate conduct he had felt he somehow should avoid.

A key element in this case involves ethically appropriate ways to address racism and racial differences in supervision (Herlihy & Watson, 2003; Johnson, 2002). The Black trainee clearly felt comfortable enough to raise the child client's racist comments with his Caucasian supervisor. The supervisor recognized the importance of inviting the trainee to recognize and name the feelings he experienced in relation to the client's behavior, to confirm the inappropriateness of the remarks, and to help the trainee formulate a strategy to address the behavior in subsequent sessions. In situations such as this one, the support of the supervisor in recognizing the personal feelings and well-being of the supervisee becomes as important as helping the trainee to implement an intervention. Unfortunately, this situation was not the first, nor will it be the last, confrontation with racism the trainee will experience in his career. In this situation the young man had a supervisor who served both as a professional guide and a personal ally in confronting the problem.

The Deceptive Trainee

One of Amy's, the trainee's, 6-year-old clients with acute myelocytic leukemia has relapsed and seemed certain to die within the next 6 months, but Amy's fellowship was to end in 9 more weeks. The supervisor indicated he would take on the case as a transfer and encouraged Amy to begin termination work. For the next several weeks, Amy discussed the progress of termination in her weekly supervision sessions. After her departure from the training program, the supervisor went to visit the child, who asked, "Where's Amy?" The trainee had never told the child she was leaving and had fabricated her discussion about the termination process in her reporting to her supervisor and in her progress notes. The supervisor contacted Amy at her new worksite to express grave concern and some anger at her lack of professionalism and frank lying. Amy tearfully reported that she has suffered some troubling personal loss experiences and could not bear to reawaken them by raising her departure with the child or discussing her feelings with the supervisor.

This situation illustrates a significant interaction problem between a supervisor who may have become too complacent and a trainee whose personal issues got in the way of appropriate professional conduct (Johnson, 2002; Sutter, McPherson, & Geeseman, 2002). On the one hand, the supervisee lied and caused some emotional distress to her client as a result. The lie involved misleading her supervisor, writing false content in a medical record, and showing a lack of responsiveness to the client's welfare. We do not know why she felt unable to tell the supervisor of her emotional distress or difficulty in raising termination issues with the client. Ideally, if she had done so, the supervisor might have collaborated with her in working through the problem or finding a constructive alternative. The supervisor may also have become too complacent in monitoring the work of the trainee. For example, he might have suggested a joint session including the trainee and the client to discuss the impending transfer. Such a step would be wise and respectful client care, and it would have directly prevented the problem that occurred.

This incident also leads to the question of how the supervisor ought to deal with the now-departed supervisee and handle reference requests regarding her. One obvious step would involve recommending that the former supervisee seek professional help in understanding her emotional problems and in preventing them from interfering in work with future clients. The supervisor may also want to have a frank conversation with Amy about whether she misled him regarding any other clinical matters. If the supervisor had already written feedback or reference letters to Amy's university or potential employers, the supervisor needs to consider whether to send an addendum mentioning the incident. Similarly, how should future inquiries regarding Amy's training by licensing boards, insurance carrier approval panels, or potential employers be handled? Whether to disclose this particular incident will depend on the supervisor's analysis of the seriousness of the problem, whether the behavior constitutes an isolated incident or more significant pattern, and the degree of confidence the supervisor has about the likelihood that a danger to future clients exists.

The Harassing Supervisor

Melissa, a young, petite, single intern approached the training director with concerns about the behavior of a testing supervisor, a married man, 30 years older than she is, who has persistently asked personal questions about her social life and invited her on social outings. These events had occurred amid "joking" sexual innuendo within the first 6 weeks of the internship program. The training director immediately validated Melissa's feelings of discomfort by designating the supervisor's behavior as inappropriate. He offered her three alternative courses of action.

The first option would involve simply reassigning Melissa to a different supervisor and having the training director counsel the supervisor about the inappropriateness of his conduct. This would only be done, he explained, with her permission. If she did not wish the supervisor to know she has spoken up, she could also have the option of reassignment to a new supervisor based on a contrived excuse (thus sparing her any potential discomfort about confrontation with the offender). The training director also offered a third option, making it clear that he placed no preference on Melissa's choice. The third option would involve coaching Melissa on dealing directly with the supervisor to correct his behavior, if she wished to continue working with him on the rotation.

When Melissa asked about the third option, the training director suggested that when the supervisor next offered a personal or intrusive inquiry, she very intentionally alter her posture (e.g., by pushing back her chair slightly) and the intensity of her voice a bit and say, "Dr. Smith, I very much want to continue learning about psychodiagnostic assessment from you but would prefer that we keep our work together focused on the professional issues at hand." The training director believed that this clear signal would lead the supervisor to alter his behavior and help Melissa take control of a situation in which she had felt somewhat meek and powerless. The training director indicated that if this strategy did not work, he would recommend reassigning her and assured her that no negative evaluative comments from the offending supervisor would become a part of her record. Melissa felt empowered by the option and wanted to try it, with the training director acting as a protective background coach.

The strategy proved effective and Dr. Smith reverted to an appropriate supervisory role. Some years later, Melissa told the training director that the intervention had been one of her most powerful professional learning experiences and had served her well in other situations.

In this situation, the training director did not attempt to avoid or trivialize the concerns Melissa expressed. He also recognized that a range of options existed and actively engaged the supervisee in discussing these, with special attention to her needs and comfort level. He provided appropriate protections and backup, along with contingency planning, should the initial steps prove insufficient. In many ways, Smith was able to turn a tense situation into a valuable mentoring experience for Melissa.

The nature of the harassment in this case involved innuendo and subtle verbal pressures (as opposed to threatening or assaultive acts), and the offender responded appropriately to the intervention. In this instance, an informal intervention, which never involved a need to counsel or discipline the offender, succeeded. If the nature of the harassment had risen to a more serious level, formal action might have been required.

To Go or Not to Go

Central to supervision is the use of problem-solving frameworks for ethical dilemmas. Consider the following supervision issue.

Supervisee: Before we start with my cases, I wanted to ask you a question. Remember how we were talking about the play that is sold out at the Globe Theatre? Well, by a weird coincidence, my mother gave me two tickets that she had bought but found she can't use. I know you love plays, and I remember you were sad you couldn't get seats, so I wonder if you might like these orchestra seats? It's funny, I was feeling really uncomfortable asking you this—and I feel awkward now!

Supervisor: Well, first, thank you so much for your thoughtful offer. That is a very generous thought, and you are right, I do love plays! I am particularly interested in your discomfort and wonder if we could work through this, as an example of some of the difficult situations that arise in supervision. As supervisor, I am sorely tempted to accept, but also, like you, feeling that there is more to this. Let's apply a few problem-solving frames and see what we discover.

Supervisee: Okay. Sounds like an interesting idea.

Supervisor: First let's try Koocher and Keith-Spiegel's [1998] ethical problem-solving framework derived from Tymchuck [1986] and Haas and Malouf [1989]. First we must determine if the matter is an ethical one. As the matter is one involving a possible multiple relationship for us, I think the answer would be yes. Do you agree?

Supervisee: Yes, I think that is what I was feeling strange about.

Supervisor: Inserting a step suggested by Barret, Kitchener, and Burris [2001], let's stop and consider the emotional impact on each of us of the dilemma. As I am definitely unable to get any seats to that play, much less good seats, given that the play is sold out, it is totally unattainable to me. I really want to go and at the same time am saddened by the consideration that going may be a bad idea. I am grateful to you for offering, knowing that I enjoy plays. So I feel sadness—and appreciation. What about you?

Supervisee: Well, I am thinking about the multiple relationship aspect and feel a little worried that you might view me negatively just for having offered the tickets in the first place . . . or be mad at me for bringing it up. If I hadn't, you wouldn't even be thinking about the play. So I'm feeling worried about how this could affect our supervisory relationship.

Supervisor: Okay, I really appreciate your candor! It is so important to remember that being forthright about situations like this and feelings is the thing I value highly! So that is something we have to continue to think about. Next, let's consult the available ethical guidelines that might apply to provide a possible mechanism for resolution. From the Ethics Code 3.05 (APA, 2002), "a psychologist refrains from entering into a multiple relationship if the multiple relationship could reasonable be expected to impair the psychologist's objectivity, competence, or effectiveness in performing his or her functions as a psychologist, or otherwise risks exploitation or harm to the person with whom the professional relationship exists." So, if there is any danger of exploitation or whether accepting the tickets might inhibit my ability to proceed objectively, as in feedback and evaluation of your performance. . . . Anything else to add?

Supervisee: I think that covers it well.

Supervisor: Let's consider all sources that might influence the kind of decision one might make. Possible sources to consider, besides the ethical codes, are the other trainees and the impact the gift might have upon them, colleagues who might be affected in their judgment of you for giving and of me for accepting. I think it could be viewed as if we had some type of special relationship, which might affect my partiality or objectivity. Next we locate and consult with a trusted colleague. The individual we select reviews multiple relationships—let me call one. [Conversation for a few minutes while supervisor explains situation to colleague on speakerphone.] Okay, she basically says that she would not feel comfortable accepting such a valuable gift from a trainee, and that the mere fact that the supervisor is applying the ethical decision-making framework might be indicative of feeling uncomfortable about it, and that for her it is not a good idea at all. It could influence her objectivity and really interfere if she needed to give the trainee constructive feedback down the road. Back to the ethical problem-solving framework, next, evaluating the rights, responsibilities, and vulnerability of all affected parties leads one to think of your, the supervisee's, right to autonomy and to have a supervisor who behaves ethically, maintaining responsibility for the supervision and the relationship, and ensuring that another complexity of the power differential (with the supervisee a vulnerable party) not be introduced. Generating alternative decisions include accepting the tickets or graciously refusing the offer. The consequences of accepting the ticket might have been changing the dynamic of the supervision relationship and introducing a friendship or a situation in which the supervisee is "owed" something by the supervisor.

Supervisee: That is really interesting. Puts it all in perspective. I lean towards giving the tickets back to my mother. What do you think?

Supervisor: I agree, but just for the experience, should we look at two other frameworks to see if they lead us the same way?

Supervisee: Yes, I'd like to.

Supervisor: A second approach is to use the multiple-relationship risk management questions by Gottlieb, Robinson, and Younggren (2007) and Younggren and Gottlieb (2004). The first question is whether this second relationship is necessary, and if not, whether one could avoid it. What do you think?

Supervisee: I would say, it is totally avoidable and definitely not necessary to have the second relationship in this situation.

Supervisor: One can also ask could it potentially cause harm to you, the supervisee? The answer to this might be yes, in that you might suffer from observing less than ethical consideration and behavior, and from potentially not receiving accurate feedback or evaluation because of me feeling as if I owe you something, thus compromising your training experience. The third approach is use of the Burian and Slimp's (2000) decision tree. Let's consider whether the internship multiple relationships is for personal development of the trainee or of the supervisor. In this instance, it would be for personal development of the supervisor and thus is a clear "no."

Supervisee: Interesting. I like all three, and really it is good to use more than one because it provides different perspectives. I feel like that was incredibly useful. I hope you are not upset with me for offering.

Supervisor: Actually, I think it was a great learning experience for us both. I am particularly impressed with your candor and willingness to be open about your feelings and to work through this with me.

The use of ethical problem-solving frameworks models the importance of ethical thinking and adherence to codes while helping the supervisee, and the supervisor, grapple with difficult issues that frequently arise in supervision. It also provides prototypes for them to use in practice and in their future supervision experience.

Role Conflict

The supervisee has a very difficult case and is feeling that it is not going very well. Her supervisor is supportive, but the supervisee is fearful that if she were to explain to him how overwhelmed she is feeling by this case, he would evaluate her negatively. She broaches the subject gingerly.

Supervisee: I wondered if we could spend a little extra time on the Brown case today?

Supervisor: Sure. I'm working on the evaluation your school sent and am highlighting that you are making great progress in being autonomous.

Supervisee: Thanks . . . the problem is that this week. . . . The husband mentioned to me that he is going to leave his wife, told me not to tell her, and I'm worried. . . . I have some ideas what to do, but I'd like some help here

Supervisor: Well, remember how we talked last week about needing for you to be more autonomous. Let's let you work that out.

Supervisee: [Reluctantly.] Okay.

In this instance, the supervisee is fearful of evaluation—fearful that if she discloses the extent of her worry about the case, her supervisor will view her negatively. The supervisor unwittingly decreases disclosure by the supervisee and violates the ethical principle of "do no harm" as he does not put client care above supervisee development. A different example of this is the very knowledgeable trainee who is fearful to pursue discussion of such issues because the supervisor may evaluate him or her negatively as it shifts the power differential.

CONCLUSION

As we have seen, ethical issues emerge throughout therapeutic and supervisory processes. The very nature of supervision in the practice of psychotherapy forces us to explore matters that would not normally come up in more typical work situations. Effective supervision requires degrees of openness, non-defensiveness, and respectful critical thinking that challenge the best of us. Beyond simply obtaining rote knowledge of legal and ethical principles, psychologists are required to apply such guidelines within complex contexts. Through study, supervision and consultation, and faithful attention and application of ethics and law, clinicians ensure the highest standards of practice to the benefit of their clients and supervisees.

REFERENCES

American Psychological Association. (1993). Guidelines for providers of psychological services to ethnic, linguistic, and culturally diverse populations. *American Psychologist, 48*, 45–48.

American Psychological Association. (2002). Ethical principles of psychologists and code of conduct. *American Psychologist, 57*, 1060–1073.

Armstrong, J. R. (2005). *Education law update*. Retrieved from http://cache.zoom info.com/CachedPage/?archive_id=0&page_id=1341853070&page_url=%2f %2fwww.psgglaw.com%2fEducation%2520Law%2520Update%2520October %25202005%Final.htm&page_last_updated=12%2f3%2f2005+5%3a39%3a46 +AM&firstName=Jeffrey&lastName=Armstrong

Barret, B., Kitchener, K. S., & Burris, S. (2001). A decision model for ethical dilemmas in HIV-related psychotherapy and its application in the case of Jerry. In J. R. Anderson & R. L. Barret (Eds.), *Ethics in HIV-related psychotherapy: Clinical decision making in complex cases* (pp. 133–154). Washington, DC: American Psychological Association.

Bennett, B. E., Bricklin, P. M., Harris, E. A., Knapp, S., VandeCreek, L., & Younggren, J. N. (2007). *Assessing and managing risk in psychological practice: An individualized approach*. Rockville, MD: American Psychological Association Insurance Trust.

Bernard, J. M., & Goodyear, R. K. (2004). *Fundamentals of clinical supervision* (3rd ed.). Needham Heights, MA: Allyn & Bacon.

Brenner, A. M. (2006). The role of personal psychodynamic psychotherapy in becoming a competent psychiatrist. *Harvard Review of Psychiatry, 14*, 268–272.

Burian, B. K., & Slimp, A. O. (2000). Social dual-role relationships during internship: A decision-making model. *Professional Psychology: Research and Practice, 31*, 332–338.

Capriccioso, R. (2006, March 13). Counseling crisis. *Inside Higher Education*. Retrieved from http://www.insidehighered.com/news/2006/ 03/13/counseling de Mayo, R. A. (2000). Clients' sexual behavior and sexual harassment: A survey of clinical supervisors. *Professional Psychology: Research and Practice, 31,* 706–709.

Department of Health and Human Services. (2005). *Code of federal regulations, Title 45, Part 46: Protection of human subjects.* Retrieved December 3, 2007, from http://www.hhs.gov/ohrp/humansubjects/guidance/45cfr46.htm

Enochs, W. K., & Etzbach, C. A. (2004). Impaired student counselors: Ethical and legal considerations for the family. *Family Journal: Counseling and Therapy for Couples and Families, 12,* 396–400.

Falender, C. A., & Shafranske, E. P. (2004). *Clinical supervision: A competency-based approach.* Washington, DC: American Psychological Association.

Family Education Rights and Privacy Act, 34 C.F.R. 99(1974).

Gottlieb, M. C., Robinson, K., & Younggren, J. N. (2007). Multiple relations in supervision: Guidance for administrators, supervisors, and students. *Professional Psychology: Research and Practice, 38,* 241–247.

Haas, L. J., & Malouf, J. L. (1989). *Keeping up the good work: A practitioner's guide to mental health ethics.* Sarasota, FL: Professional Resource Press.

Handelsman, M. M., Gottlieb, M. C., & Knapp. S. (2005). Training ethical psychologists: An acculturation model. *Professional Psychology: Research and Practice, 36,* 59–65.

Harrar, W. R., VandeCreek, L., & Knapp, S. (1990). Ethical and legal aspects of clinical supervision. *Professional Psychology: Research and Practice, 21,* 37–41.

Harris v. Forklift Systems, Inc., 510 U.S. 17, 114 S. Ct. 367 (1993).

Health Insurance Portability and Accountability Act of 1996, Pub. L. No. 104–191.

Herlihy, B., & Watson, Z. E. (2003). Ethical issues and multicultural competence in counseling. In F. D. Harper, & J. McFadden (Eds.), *Culture and counseling: New approaches* (pp. 363–378). Needham Heights, MA: Allyn & Bacon.

Johnson, W. B. (2002). The intentional mentor: Strategies and guidelines for the practice of mentoring. *Professional Psychology: Research and Practice, 33,* 88–96.

Katsavdakis, K., Gabbard, G. O., & Athey, G. I. (2004). Profiles of impaired health professionals. *The Bulletin of the Menninger Clinic, 68,* 60–72.

Kleespies, P. M., Smith, M. R., & Becker, B. R. (1990). Psychology interns as client-suicide survivors: Incidence, impact, and recovery. *Professional Psychology: Research and Practice, 21,* 257–263.

Koocher, G. P., & Keith-Spiegel, P. (1998). *Ethics in psychology: Professional standards and cases* (2nd ed.). New York: Oxford University Press.

Koocher, G. P., & Keith-Spiegel, P. (2008). *Ethics in psychology and the mental health professions: Standards and cases* (3rd ed.). New York: Oxford University Press.

Ladany, N., Lehrman-Waterman, D., Molinaro, M., & Wolgast, B. (1999). Psychotherapy supervisor ethical practices: Adherence to guidelines, the supervisory working alliance, and supervisee satisfaction. *The Counseling Psychologist, 27,* 443–475.

Laverne F. Schieszler v. Ferrum College, No. 7:02CV00131 (W.D. Va. 1993).

Meritor Savings Bank v. Vinson, 477 U.S. 57 (1986).

Rubin, L. J., & Borgers, S. B. (1990). Sexual harassment in universities during the 1980s. *Sex Roles, 23,* 397–411.

Schieszler v. Ferrum College, et al., 236 F Supp 2d 602 (W.D. Va. 2002).

Shin v. Massachusetts Institute of Technology, et al., 19 Mass L Rep 570 (Middlesex Super Ct 2005).

Spiegelman, J. S., & Werth, J. L. (2005). Don't forget about me: The experiences of therapists-in-training after a client has attempted or died by suicide. *Women & Therapy, 28,* 35–57.

Sutter, E., McPherson, R. H., & Geeseman, R. (2002). Contracting for supervision. *Professional Psychology: Research and Practice, 33,* 495–498.

Tymchuck, A. J. (1986). Guidelines for ethical decision-making. *Canadian Psychology, 27,* 36–43.

Younggren, J. N., & Gottlieb, N. C. (2004). Managing risk when handling multiple relationships. *Professional Psychology: Research and Practice, 35,* 255–260.

9

MULTISYSTEMIC APPROACHES TO SUPERVISION: TALES OF WOE (CULTURAL NONCONNECT) IN SUPERVISION AND UNDERSTANDING THE FIT

PHILLIPPE B. CUNNINGHAM AND JEFF RANDALL

Mental health professionals have been widely criticized for their lack of success with ethnic minority populations. One treatment model, multisystemic therapy (MST; Henggeler & Borduin, 1990; Henggeler, Schoenwald, Borduin, Rowland, & Cunningham, 1998; Henggeler, Schoenwald, Rowland, & Cunningham, 2002), has demonstrated success in treating serious and chronic juvenile delinquents, many of whom have been ethnic minority children (Cunningham & Foster, 2005). The success of MST has not been moderated by demographic characteristics such as age, race, class, gender, or arrest history (see Henggeler, Melton, & Smith, 1992). Supported by 14 published clinical trials, MST has been identified by federal agencies (e.g., National Institute on Drug Abuse, 1999), leading reviewers (e.g., Weisz, 2004), consumer groups (e.g., National Alliance for the Mentally Ill, 2003), and policy groups (e.g., Annie E. Casey Foundation, GAINS Center, Points of Light Foundation) as an effective treatment.

Several features of MST are critical to its success: addressing known risk factors, providing services in natural settings, integrating evidence-based therapies (e.g., behavior therapy, cognitive behavior therapy, pragmatic family therapy), and recognizing the key role of caregivers in long-term outcomes. However, one of the most important features of MST is the use of a multifaceted quality assurance protocol to support treatment fidelity (Henggeler & Schoenwald, 1998; Henggeler, Schoenwald, Liao, Letourneau, & Edwards, 2002). An integral part of the MST quality assurance system is clinical supervision (Henggeler & Schoenwald, 1998), as evidence has supported the linkage between MST supervision and therapist adherence (Henggeler et al., 2002).

In this chapter, MST clinical supervision serves as the clinical backdrop for describing how MST supervision helps MST therapists work with ethnic minority families. Beginning with a brief review of the theoretical basis of MST treatment and supervision and MST treatment principles, we focus on applying MST supervision practices to address the issue of cultural nonconnect.

CONCEPTUAL BASIS OF MST TREATMENT AND SUPERVISION

MST is based on the theory of social ecology (Bronfenbrenner, 1979). From this perspective, individuals are nested within complex, but interdependent, social systems that can have direct and/or indirect influences on their behavior (Bronfenbrenner, 1979). Applying a social ecological framework to clinical supervision would suggest that a therapist working with clients from different cultural backgrounds is embedded within a clinical team, embedded within an organization, embedded within a service system. Each of these components has their own unique cultural influences that can influence therapist–client interactions. Similarly, the social ecology of the family, with its own unique culture, can also influence therapist–client interactions. In short, there is a series of bidirectional interactions that ultimately influence therapist–client interactions (Falender & Shafranske, 2004).

Using therapist difficulty establishing a therapeutic alliance (i.e., engaging a client in treatment) as an example, researchers have shown that the development of the therapeutic alliance is associated with characteristics of the individual client (e.g., level of motivation, openness, involvement, psychopathology), therapist (e.g., empathy, directiveness), client–therapist interactions (e.g., complementary interactions), and pretherapy relational skills (e.g., interpersonal qualities, availability, responsiveness; Hubble, Duncan, & Miller, 1999). These relationships can be depicted graphically using, in the vernacular of MST, a fit circle (see Figure 9.1). A *fit circle* is part of MST assessment that is an ongoing reiterative process throughout the course of treatment that focuses on identifying the combination of social ecological factors that influence behavior or interactions. A fit circle, then, is a method of graphically depicting hypotheses (which are subject to continuous testing and revisions) about how certain factors or combinations of factors are causative with a particular problem. As shown in Figure 9.1, poor engagement can be reasonably hypothesized to be the result of a combination of factors. One factor may be that the caregiver has limited motivation for treatment and is

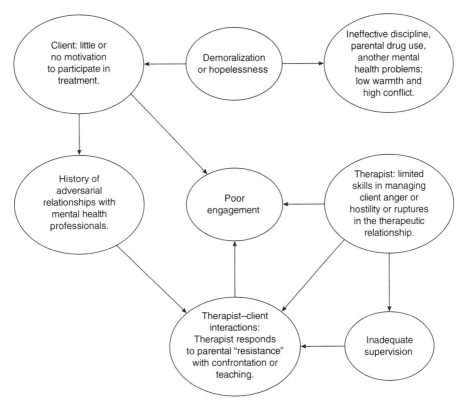

Figure 9.1. Example of a fit assessment for poor engagement.

demoralized as a result of previous failed experiences trying to manage his or her child's behavior (lack of parental knowledge and skills), negative experiences with mental health professionals, and coercive interactions with mental health professionals. Another factor might be that the therapist has limited experience managing difficult interactions with hostile or angry clients, or that the therapist leaves supervision unclear about how to manage current difficulties or feeling blamed for the lack of movement in a case.

Nine Treatment Principles and the MST Analytic Process

MST is specified by nine treatment principles (see Exhibit 9.1) that define the parameters for design and implementation of clinical and supervisory interventions.

MST Analytic Process

The MST supervisory process begins with a careful, reasoned analysis of the social context and its influence on client–therapist behavior (i.e., fit

EXHIBIT 9.1
Multisystemic Therapy Treatment Principles

Principle 1: The primary purpose of assessment is to understand the fit between the identified problems and their broader systemic context.

Principle 2: Therapeutic contacts should emphasize the positive and should use systemic strengths as levers for change.

Principle 3: Interventions should be designed to promote responsible behavior and decrease irresponsible behavior among family members.

Principle 4: Interventions should be present focused and action oriented, targeting specific and well-defined problems.

Principle 5: Interventions should target sequences of behavior within and between multiple systems that maintain identified problems.

Principle 6: Interventions should be developmentally appropriate and fit the developmental needs of the youth.

Principle 7: Interventions should be designed to require daily or weekly effort by family members.

Principle 8: Intervention effectiveness is evaluated continuously from multiple perspectives, with providers assuming accountability for overcoming barriers to successful outcomes.

Principle 9: Interventions should be designed to promote treatment generalization and long-term maintenance of therapeutic change by empowering caregivers to address family members' needs across multiple systemic contexts.

assessment). From the moment of referral to the end of treatment, MST supervisors and therapists gather data from multiple sources regarding the most salient drivers (i.e., fit factors) of referral problems. Hypotheses regarding these drivers are developed and tested throughout MST interventions. This deductive and repetitive approach is encompassed within the MST analytical process (aka, "MST Do-Loop"; Henggeler et al., 1998; Henggeler & Schoenwald, 1998) depicted in Figure 9.2. Supervisors use the MST analytical process continuously with therapists to develop, prioritize, implement, measure, and evaluate interventions. The MST principles and the analytic process provide the underpinnings of MST supervision.

This analytic process also has an important benefit in a cross-cultural counseling context. Because MST therapists are required to gather data and to develop and test hypotheses regarding their clients' behavior—what S. Sue (1998) calls being "scientifically minded"—MST therapists can avoid negative stereotyping and ethnocentric biases (S. Sue, 1998).

MST Supervision

The MST model of supervision evolved from the efficacy research in MST clinical trials (see, e.g., Henggeler, Melton, Brondino, Scherer, & Hanley, 1997; Henggeler, Pickrel, & Brondino, 1999). Using the analytic process as a guide, MST supervisors help their therapists identify and select specific interventions to attain desired clinical outcomes. MST supervisors use empirically supported

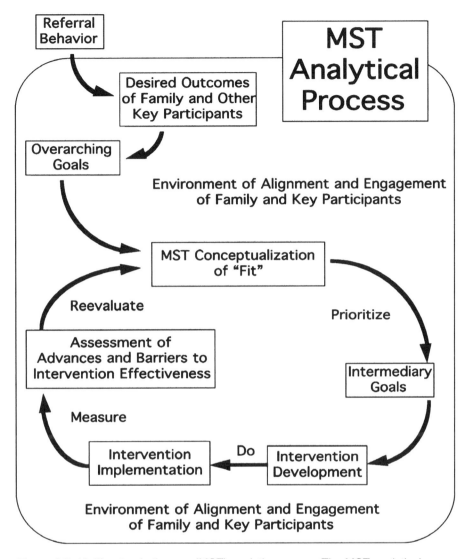

Figure 9.2. Multisystemic therapy (MST) analytic process. The MST analytical process is used by MST supervisors and therapists to help them understand complex phenomena for clinical decision making.

skill acquisition procedures to teach therapists evidence-based interventions (e.g., expert modeling, guided practice, behavioral rehearsal, corrective feedback, positive reinforcement [praise]). Skill acquisition procedures are particularly helpful with novice therapists who want and expect greater amounts of structure, support, and encouragement from supervisors (Falender & Shafranske, 2004; Goodyear & Bernard, 1998; Holloway & Neufeldt, 1995; Johnson & Stewart, 2000).

The goal of MST supervision is to help each MST therapist learn to effectively change the social ecology of youths and families in ways that lead to sustainable positive outcomes (Henggeler et al., 1998). To achieve this goal, supervision must be responsive to both the therapist's needs and strengths and to the clinical needs and strengths of each family.

MST supervision is conducted weekly in a small-group format (for a description, see Henggeler & Schoenwald, 1998) and lasts about approximately 2 hours. However, the motto of MST treatment and supervision is doing whatever it takes to achieve favorable client outcomes. Thus, MST supervision can occur several times a day if needed, and similar to MST therapists, MST supervisors are available 24 hours a day, 7 days a week.

Although individual supervision is not the norm in MST (Henggeler & Schoenwald, 1998), it is warranted when a therapist needs to develop specific competencies and skills or address personal barriers to clinical effectiveness. Therapists are encouraged to request individual supervision when they experience difficulties with a particular family. On the basis of our work with youth who abuse substances (Randall, Henggeler, Cunningham, Rowland, & Swenson, 2001), individual supervision might be indicated when, despite consistent feedback in group supervision, a therapist persists in (a) suggesting that clients are not motivated for treatment, (b) describing clients in judgmental or pejorative language, (c) resisting alternative hypotheses to explain client behavior, (d) describing cases without the requisite precision, (e) relying on clinical stereotypes over hypothesis testing, (f) failing to address treatment barriers, or (g) failing to carry out group supervision recommendations. The following case example highlights how cultural factors can disrupt treatment success. However, a basic assumption of MST supervision is that impasses in treatment (e.g., failure to establish a therapeutic alliance, ruptures in the alliance), whether based on a cultural nonconnect or some other social ecological factor, can be understandable (via the analytical process) and managed like any other behavior.

CULTURAL NONCONNECT

Regardless of race, a common therapist barrier to establishing a therapeutic alliance or managing ruptures in the alliance is a lack of understanding and appreciation for cultural or values-based differences (Cunningham & Henggeler, 1999; Henggeler & Schoenwald, 1998). For example, a middle-class female therapist may have difficulty with a very poor inner-city mother who is more interested in her son getting a job to contribute to the family income and not becoming a father versus getting the child to go to school. Therapists who have difficulties empathizing with a caregiver—often the result of a lack of cultural understanding—will lead to a poor therapeutic relationship that lacks trust, collaboration, and ultimately unfavorable outcomes. The following case example highlights the impact cultural nonconnect can have on treatment success. This case is provided to illustrate how a European American therapist's expectations regarding the therapeutic relationship with an African American client may represent a cultural nonconnect resulting in the therapist perceiving the client as appearing angry and resistant and the therapist feeling frustrated.

AN EXAMPLE OF THE APPROACH

Anne, a European American therapist with more than 20 years experience working with adolescents who abuse substances, has been working with a 43-year-old African American mother and her 16-year-old son for 6 weeks. The youth was referred to the MST program for substance abuse and dependence. Over the course of several weeks in group supervision, Anne has reported that despite her best efforts, the caregiver was not engaged in treatment (from an MST perspective, service providers are responsible for engagement, even though client factors may play a role in engagement). Furthermore, Anne noted that when she arrives at the family's home for sessions, the caregiver often presents as angry or hostile. Using the analytic process, the supervisor asked, "What is the fit of the mother's behavior?" Anne responded somewhat defensively, "No matter what I do, I really think this mother just doesn't want services. She just isn't motivated, as she has her own needs that supersede those of her child." Anne further noted that "I know the value of working with the parent (a core MST value) to help the child, but during my last visit to the family's home, this was the first time in 6 years that I told a parent that I felt the case could move faster if I met only with the youth at school."

As an old African adage states, "Until lions have their own historians, tales of hunting will always glorify the hunter." Anne's use of such harsh and critical language to characterize the caregiver (e.g., "unmotivated," "not interested in services"), even if true, will not facilitate the development of the therapeutic alliance (i.e., engagement). There are, of course, other hypotheses, those based on more proximal factors that could account for the mother's angry and hostile demeanor besides "not wanting services." Unfortunately, Anne, who was angry with this mother, was at a loss to come up with these other hypotheses as a result of not applying the analytic process—it is hard to think clearly when you are angry with someone.

Anne's struggle with this caregiver was a general difficulty engaging what she called a "resistant" client. *Resistance* is a term frowned on in the vernacular of MST, as it suggests that the basis for a lack of engagement resides with the client (not to mention its pejorative and judgmental conveyance). Anne's struggle with this client is not unique; such struggles often occur among therapists working with "deep-end families"—those families who consume substantial service system dollars. For example, Patterson and Forgatch (1985) showed that therapist behavior during treatment sessions reliably predicted parental resistance, which altered therapist behavior. According to their "struggle-and-working-through" hypothesis, resistance should increase from the beginning of treatment (when therapists are teaching parenting skills) to midtreatment (when demands for behavior change are greatest) and then level off or decrease (as parents apply new skills and achieve some success) by termination (Patterson & Chamberlain, 1994). Measures of this struggle-and-working-through process predict treatment success. Conversely, the failure to struggle and work through (e.g., low levels of resistance, increasing and consistently high levels of resistance) predicts treatment failure (Stoolmiller, Duncan, Bank, & Patterson, 1993). As such, irrespective of the unique cultures that each part of the therapist–client dyad brings to the clinical enterprise, it should be characterized at some point by struggle. When a therapist responds to client resistance with more teaching as opposed to support, resistance increases (Patterson & Chamberlain, 1994). Unfortunately, when therapists struggle to engage ethnic minority clients in treatment, the assumption is often that the therapist is not culturally competent. Such assumptions may serve to further polarize the dyad, as the therapist may become increasingly more likely to blame the victim over his or her repeated failed interventions (for a discussion of this topic, see Cunningham & Henggeler, 1999). We argue that at these difficult moments in treatment, the supervisory focus should be to understand the fit of the current difficulty and to develop interventions derived from this assessment. We believe that such a focus will lead to more clinically competent, as well as culturally competent, therapists.

The fit analysis (see Figure 9.1) suggests that Anne's difficulty in engaging this parent was primarily the result of her lack of experience and skill managing severe negative affect with African American adults, coupled with the caregiver's characteristics (i.e., demoralization, history of adversarial interactions with mental health professionals). There are, however, cultural factors at work that may not be as obvious. From a European American counseling perspective, clients entering treatment "ought to" be willing to listen to, and learn from, the therapist, and when there are therapeutic impasses, the client must be willing to discuss these "openly and honestly" (i.e., demonstrating commitment to participate in the therapeutic endeavor, collaborating with the therapist in the work involved). This cultural perspective was operative with Anne, who when asked in group supervision if there was anything she may have done to "anger the mother," responded "No, I asked her how therapy was going and she said everything was fine." Given the sociohistorical context of the South and the well-documented likelihood of evasive responding by African Americans to European Americans in positions of authority (e.g., see D. W. Sue & Sue, 1990), this cultural perspective may have been operating with Anne and this caregiver. For example, to avoid the severe consequences associated with upsetting Whites, Blacks would, historically, placate

Whites by feigning agreement (i.e., "Yes Sir" or "Yes Ma'am"), when in fact they wanted to disagree. Why feign agreement? A Black person living in the South who responded openly and honestly to Whites would have risked condemnation, if not physical violence.

Managing Cultural Nonconnect

Another basic assumption of MST supervision is that each therapist is a hard-working professional who is doing his or her best. Consequently, when treatment is not going well, it is assumed that the needs of the client exceed the competencies of the therapist. It follows, then, that supervisors should not blame therapists for failures but should remain scientifically minded by using the MST analytic process to maintain a solution focus—identifying and addressing barriers to success when a therapist struggles with a client—and to focus on skill development. Therapists never learn anything new from clients who follow their advice without questions. Families that therapists struggle with actually help them to learn new skills and competencies. In this context, new learning can occur in supervision only when a therapist must confront (i.e., is not allowed to avoid or escape) his or her most difficult clinical exigencies and where skill acquisition is a focus.

Anne's description of her sessions with this "resistant" client in supervision provides a glimpse of what she wants to gain from supervision: "I don't want to work with this parent because it is much too hard, and I want you to understand my suffering and not force me to do something I don't want to do." Anne's behavior, however, does not mean that she is consciously deciding to "fire" this caregiver from treatment. On the contrary, Anne's response is a normal reaction of any hardworking, caring professional who is invested in the health and welfare of children. Working with "resistant" clients can be quite demoralizing and aversive for therapists. This is especially true of MST therapists because (a) they often work with chronic and serious juvenile delinquents or youth with conduct disorders and their caregivers and (b) they are held accountable for engaging the caregiver in treatment. A natural "human response" to any aversive stimulus (in this case an angry and hostile mother) is either escape or avoidance. The impact of tales of woe in supervision often elicit care and concern from colleagues (rather than confrontation, as it is hard to kick someone when they are down) in that they justify the therapist's position (escape or avoidance) and ultimately negatively reinforce such behavior in supervision. Hence, Anne's "tales of hunting" in supervision often paint herself as a noble warrior trying desperately to succeed, despite the overwhelming odds of working with "someone who does not want to get better." In a cross-cultural counseling context, this is even more pronounced as the participants (i.e., therapist and client) may lack similarity, a factor known to enhance the therapeutic relationship (Cormier & Cormier, 1998). A more insidious problem associated with this dynamic in supervision (i.e., negative reinforcement of escape–avoidance behavior), however, is that as long as Anne is able to opt out of working with a "resistant" or difficult client, she will never develop the skills and competencies needed to effectively work in a cross-cultural context. Although supervision must be supportive and provide specific skill training and competencies, it must also negate escape–avoidance behavior through exposure.

For Anne, at this juncture, individual supervision was required. The goals of individual supervision for Anne were to (a) normalize her response to this caregiver, (b) reinforce her use of the MST analytic process, (c) reframe her conceptualization of the mother's behavior, and (d) teach her specific skills in managing her own responses to and interactions with this caregiver.

Normalization

One immediate benefit from supervision is *normalization*, the process of depathologizing the therapist's experience or attempts to cope with working with a difficult-to-treat client. It is essential that the supervisor counter the oftentimes internal dialogues that therapists have when treatment is not going well, such as "I am an incompetent therapist because I can't engage this mother in treatment," with statements such as "Any therapist working with this mother would have difficulty." That is, the supervisor must communicate that it is a normal reaction to struggle in this situation, and it does not make one a bad therapist.

At the beginning of individual supervision with Anne, the supervisor provided her with a rationale for the individual supervision session and, at the same time, tried to normalize her experience: "Anne, it seems to me that you are struggling to engage this mother in treatment. You have been working really hard to engage this mother, but nothing seems to be working with her. Any therapist working with this mother would be frustrated."

Reinforce the Use of the MST Analytic Process

After providing the rationale, the supervisor conducts a fit analysis of Anne's response to the mother, and vice versa. Examining Anne's case in light of Figure 9.1 suggests that her difficulty in engaging this caregiver was primarily the result of her lack of experience and skill in managing severe negative affect, coupled with a combination of caregiver characteristics (i.e., demoralization, history of adversarial interactions with mental health professionals). Cultural factors, however, may be operative but not as obvious. From Anne's perspective (that of a European American counselor), a client's verbalizations in treatment "ought to" represent reality. This cultural perspective was operative with Anne; when asked if there was anything she may have done to "anger this mother," her response was "No, I asked her how therapy was going and she said everything was fine." As mentioned above, the mother's response may be more related to Anne being a European American than it is an accurate appraisal of therapy. This question then became the focal point of the fit analysis.

As noted earlier, Blacks (or others who are not in a position of power) may feign agreement for reasons other than an accurate reflection of their opinion. There are, however, self-presentational concerns that may arise when a person fears that he or she may appear as unreasonable. When Anne asked this African American mother the best time to meet (MST therapists are required to meet at a time and place convenient for clients), the mother responded that between 1:00 p.m. and 2:00 p.m., "when I am getting up and ready for work" (this mother often worked two consecutive shifts, 3:00 p.m. to 11:00 p.m., and 12:00 a.m. to 8:00 a.m.) would be best. From the perspective of the mother's schedule, the best time to meet would be between shifts, not when she is getting off from a 16-hour workday. Again, why would this mother not tell Anne that the best time to meet would be between 11:00 p.m. and midnight? There are two possible explanations. First, the therapist framed the question poorly by asking for the best time to meet with the mother as opposed to walking her through her typical day, which would have made workable meeting times, such as 11:00 p.m., more obvious to the therapist. Second, the mother is attempting to tell the therapist what she thinks the therapist wants to hear, which is a cultural nonconnect. Because of the mother's history of being blamed by mental health professionals for the behavior of her son, she might be quite sensitive about appearing unreasonable to Anne. It is more reasonable to suggest that counseling sessions be held in the early afternoon, as opposed to 11:00 p.m. If the counseling session is scheduled for 11:00 p.m., the therapist would not expect the youth to attend the session, which is appropriate given that a main focus of MST is to empower caregivers.

But, what would explain the caregiver's open hostility toward Anne? Here again the analytic process can be used. Making the mother's anger and hostility directed toward Anne the focal point of this fit analysis, several factors were considered. First, emotional expression is culturally determined. Anne and this mother express emotions differently. This mother was loud, would yell and curse at the youth, and would yell and curse when discussing the youth with Anne. According to Anne, the mother stated on several occasions, "I am a direct person who always speaks her mind." Anne, however, was soft-spoken and believed in handling interpersonal problems through "reasoned action" and negotiation. Second, a more likely driver of the mother's anger and hostility directed toward Anne is that people in general are notoriously cranky in the morning. For this mother, the worst possible time to engage in interpersonal interactions is when she is getting off from a double shift that included a midnight shift.

A wonderful outcome often associated with conducting a fit analysis (see Figure 9.2) is that it seeks to understand difficult interpersonal interactions with a client, and it forces a therapist to consider the interaction from the client's perspective, a process that likely increases empathy with the client. As noted by Cunningham and Henggeler (1999), therapist empathy increases clients' trust and feelings of being understood and is often seen by clients as their most helpful experience in therapy. By having Anne put herself in the mother's shoes, she began to appreciate that this mother was hard working and wanted the best for her child but that time and circumstances were working against her. Thus, when the supervisor began reframing the mother's behavior, Anne was open to viewing this mother in a more positive light.

Reframe the Mother's Behavior

Following the fit analysis, the session shifted to reframing Anne's and the mother's behavior. At this juncture in supervision, Anne was asked to think about the mother's strengths thus far in the therapeutic relationship. Anne quickly noted that the mother attends all therapy sessions even though she is tired from working two jobs. The supervisor also noted that the mother obviously cared about her son and was looking for ways to better manage his behavior, even though it was quite different from what Anne recommended (e.g., she recommended reinforcing contingencies, and the mother suggested spanking). Anne acknowledged that there were signs that the mother cared about her son (attending sessions, history of trying different things, working multiple low-wage jobs to provide for him). These thoughts led Anne to realize that the mother's style of interaction with her son and the therapist's style of interaction with the youth, although different, had similar goals (e.g., saving the boy). To assist Anne in reframing her thoughts about the mother, her supervisor summarized the supervision session by stating, "You and this mother are strong women who care desperately about this kid but have very different styles of expressing feelings, managing interpersonal conflict, as well as different priorities of treatment."

Skill Acquisition

Once Anne's frustration in working with this mother was addressed by using normalization and reframing, the next goal of individual supervision was to equip Anne with basic clinical skills associated with developing the therapeutic alliance (e.g., warmth, genuineness, reflective listening, etc). Anne and her supervisor agreed that two steps were required to move treatment forward: (a) engage this mother in treatment and (b) manage her own anxiety or anger when interacting with clients, generally, and with this mother, particularly. To engage the mother in treatment, Anne and her supervisor agreed that she should schedule a time to meet with the mother between shifts and take responsibility for, and apologize for, the tension that had come to characterize their work together. To accomplish the latter, therapists of all experience levels often want to know, But what do I do and what do I say? Consequently, part of this supervision session focused on writing a script for Anne (words and phrases) to use and then to role play, using this script with the supervisor acting as Anne and Anne acting as the mother (i.e., expert modeling). To manage her own emotional reactions to the mother, Anne and the supervisor agreed to use several strategies, diaphragmatic breathing and coping statements—on the basis of the reframes from above—that Anne found useful in other contexts. These strategies were incorporated into the role plays.

Outcome of Supervision

Supervision recommendations that rely solely on therapists verbal reports without observing (through in vivo, audiotape recordings of sessions) are null and void—think of the "tales of hunting" proverb. Consequently, Anne's supervisor asked her to record the next session she had with the mother. In this next session, Anne was able to follow the script and convey to the mother:

> I know you care deeply about your son and try to provide him the best home possible, by working several jobs and seldom taking time for yourself. I have failed to help you obtain the treatment goals you and I decided on when you and I began treatment. I apologize for failing, not focusing on your treatment goals.

During this meeting, the mother discussed how frustrated she had become with her son and how at times she wished she never had him, which compounded her feelings of guilt and shame. The mother became as vulnerable as Anne and began crying and apologizing for the way she had been acting with Anne. It was as if Anne was able to perceive the mother's internal frame of reference with accuracy and understanding. Once Anne was able to engage this mother in treatment, the mother was more open to the parenting strategies that Anne was trying to teach her. The youth is attending school regularly and is substance free.

CONCLUSION

Supervision is a complex process that requires skilled supervisors to assist therapists in confronting and addressing difficult clinical exigencies. Cultural nonconnect is a unique set of factors that often occurs when therapists provide therapy in a cross-cultural context. Although challenging, cultural nonconnect can be addressed by staying scientifically minded—in the case of MST, using the analytic process. We suggest using a similar type of fit assessment in supervision to evaluate the role that social ecological factors, including cultural factors, may play in treatment by paying particular attention to interactions between therapists and their clients. It is easy in supervision to label a lack of treatment progress as client or therapist resistance. However, we feel strongly that clients and therapists are doing their best but need new tools. For MST therapists to be held accountable for treatment outcome, supervisors must provide them with the skills and competencies they need.

REFERENCES

Bronfenbrenner, U. (1979). *The ecology of human development: Experiments by design and nature*. Cambridge, MA: Harvard University Press.

Cormier, S., & Cormier, B. (1998). *Interviewing strategies for helpers: Fundamental skills and cognitive behavioral interventions*. Pacific Grove, CA: Brooks/Cole.

Cunningham, P. B., & Foster, S. L. (2005). Operationalizing cultural competence: One programmatic effort. *Child and Family Policy and Practice Review, 1*, 12–15.

Cunningham, P. B., & Henggeler, S. W. (1999). Engaging multiproblem families in treatment: Lessons learned throughout the development of multisystemic therapy. *Family Process, 38*, 265–281.

Falender, C. A., & Shafranske, E. P. (2004). *Clinical supervision: A competency-based approach*. Washington, DC: American Psychological Association.

Goodyear, R. K., & Bernard, J. M. (1998). Clinical supervision: Lessons from the literature. *Counselor Education and Supervision, 38*, 6–22.

Henggeler, S. W., & Borduin, C. M. (1990). *Family therapy and beyond: A multisystemic approach to treating the behavior problems of children and adolescents*. Pacific Grove, CA: Brooks/Cole.

Henggeler, S. W., Melton, G. B., Brondino, M. J., Scherer, D. G., & Hanley, J. H. (1997). Multisystemic therapy with violent and chronic juvenile offenders and their families: The role of treatment fidelity in successful dissemination. *Journal of Consulting and Clinical Psychology, 65*, 821–833.

Henggeler, S. W., Melton, G. B., & Smith, L. A. (1992). Family preservation using multisystemic therapy: An effective alternative to incarcerating serious juvenile offenders. *Journal of Consulting and Clinical Psychology, 60*, 953–961.

Henggeler, S. W., Pickrel, S. G., & Brondino, M. J. (1999). Multisystemic treatment of substance-abusing and dependent delinquents: Outcomes, treatment fidelity, and transportability. *Mental Health Services Research, 1*, 171–184.

Henggeler, S. W., & Schoenwald, S. K. (1998). *The MST supervisory manual: Promoting quality assurance at the clinical level*. Charleston, SC: MST Services.

Henggeler, S. W., Schoenwald, S. K., Borduin, C. M., Rowland, M. D., & Cunningham, P. B. (1998). *Multisystemic treatment of antisocial behavior in children and adolescents.* New York: Guilford Press.

Henggeler, S. W., Schoenwald, S. K., Liao, J. G., Letourneau, E. J., & Edwards, D. L. (2002). Transporting efficacious treatments to field settings: The link between supervisory practices and therapist fidelity to MST programs. *Journal of Child and Adolescent Psychology, 31,* 155–167.

Henggeler, S. W., Schoenwald, S. K., Rowland, M. D., & Cunningham, P. B. (2002). *Serious emotional disturbance in children and adolescents.* New York: Guilford Press.

Holloway, E. L., & Neufeldt, S. A. (1995). Supervision: Its contribution to treatment efficacy. *Journal of Consulting and Clinical Psychology, 63,* 207–213.

Hubble, M. A., Duncan, B. L., & Miller, S. D. (1999). *The heart and soul of change: What works in therapy.* Washington, DC: American Psychological Association.

Johnson, E. A., & Stewart, D. W. (2000). Clinical supervision in Canadian academic and service settings: The importance of education, training, and workplace support for supervisor development. *Canadian Psychology, 41,* 124–130.

National Alliance for the Mentally Ill (2003, Fall). An update on evidence-based practices in children's mental health. *NAMI Beginnings,* 3–7.

National Institute on Drug Abuse. (1999). *Principles of drug addiction treatment: A research-based guide.* NIH Publication No. 99–4180.

Patterson, G. R., & Chamberlain, P. (1994). A functional analysis of resistance during parent training therapy. *Clinical Psychology: Science & Practice, 1,* 53–70.

Patterson, G. R., & Forgatch, M. S. (1985). Therapist behavior as a determinant of client noncompliance: A paradox for the behavior modifier. *Journal of Consulting and Clinical Psychology, 53,* 846–851.

Randall, J., Henggeler, S. W., Cunningham, P. B., Rowland, M. D., & Swenson, C. C. (2001). Adapting multisystemic therapy to treat adolescent substance abuse more effectively. *Cognitive and Behavioral Practice, 8,* 359–366.

Stoolmiller, M., Duncan, T., Bank, L., & Patterson, G. R. (1993). Some problems and solutions in the study of change: Significant patterns in client resistance. *Journal of Consulting and Clinical Psychology, 61,* 920–928.

Sue, D. W., & Sue, D. (1999). Counseling the culturally different: Theory and practice (3rd ed.). New York: Wiley.

Sue, S. (1998). In search of cultural competence in psychotherapy and counseling. *American Psychologist, 53,* 440–448.

Weisz, J. R. (2004). *Psychotherapy for children and adolescents: Evidence-based treatments and case examples.* Cambridge, England: Cambridge University Press.

10

SUPERVISORY ISSUES IN CLINICAL HEALTH PSYCHOLOGY

CYNTHIA BELAR

After years of development in its scientific knowledge base and the application of that knowledge to practice, clinical health psychology was formally recognized as a specialty in professional psychology by the American Board of Professional Psychology in 1991 and the American Psychological Association (APA) in 1997.

> The specialty of clinical health psychology applies scientific knowledge of the interrelationships among behavioral, emotional, cognitive, social, and biological components in health and disease to the promotion and maintenance of health; the prevention, treatment, and rehabilitation of illness and disability; and the improvement of the health care system. The distinct focus of clinical health psychology is on physical health problems. The specialty is dedicated to the development of knowledge regarding the interface between behavior and health, and to the delivery of high-quality services based on that knowledge to individuals, families, and health care systems (APA, 1997). Fundamental to the specialty is the biopsychosocial

This chapter was prepared in Cynthia Belar's personal capacity and does not reflect the policies and positions of the American Psychological Association.

model of human behavior, knowledge of the relationships between behavior and health, and the ability to work in a broad array of health care settings with other health care disciplines. (Belar, 1997, p. 411).

A key feature of clinical health psychology is its breadth in terms of knowledge base, procedures, problems addressed, and populations served (Belar, 2003). No one health psychologist can be trained in each and every area of practice. Thus, for purposes of this chapter, I focus on supervision related to work with adult medical surgical patients in medical settings, the area in which I have had the most experience, beginning with my own internship at Duke University Medical Center in 1973.

After completing my internship, I began my career as a faculty member at the University of Florida Health Science Center, where the then named "Department of Clinical Psychology" administered both an APA-accredited clinical psychology doctoral program and an APA-accredited clinical psychology internship. Soon after my arrival, I began developing what was then called "medical psychology" education and training opportunities through formal coursework, independent study, clinical practica, and research training. I also established the Medical Psychology Consultation Service and the Pain and Stress Management Laboratory as part of the Shands Teaching Hospital and Clinics patient care system. My focus in *Training the Clinical Psychology Student in Behavioral Medicine* (Belar, 1980) was on what was transportable from traditional clinical training, what needed to be added, and what needed to be subtracted when preparing students to provide behavioral medicine services.

Since then, the preparation of health service providers in psychology has steadily evolved from a primary focus on psychology as a mental health profession to that of psychology as a health profession, of which mental health is a subset. We as psychologists have been witnessing what many of us predicted—a true figure–ground reversal in which mental health as the universal domain of professional education and training is viewed as a subset of the broader health domain for which psychologists are trained to provide important services. By 1990, health psychology and behavioral medicine had already become the modal content area in doctoral education and training programs in clinical psychology (Sayette & Mayne, 1990).

Yet despite this growth, little, if any, has been written about the distinctive supervisory issues that arise in preparing trainees to practice clinical health psychology. The purpose of this chapter is to focus on those issues, using examples for illustrative purposes. Although supervision occurs across a wide variety of settings, problems, and activities, to highlight distinctive features in clinical health psychology, the frame of reference I use is comparison with traditional mental health services and settings, where the bulk of clinical supervision in professional psychology has been conducted to date. The focus is on work with adult medical surgical patients, with more emphasis on hospital-based services than outpatient settings. I would also like to highlight that my comments are based primarily on my own professional experiences rather than any body of research on supervision in clinical health psychology. It is admittedly a firsthand account and is thus subject to inherent biases.

An underlying assumption to supervision in clinical health psychology is that prior to actually conducting it, supervisors are competent to practice in this area themselves—a basic ethical principle. It is also important to note that although supervision in clinical health psychology has some distinctive features and challenges, the basic supervisory process as so clearly explicated in *Clinical Supervision: A Competency-Based Approach* (Falender & Shafranske, 2004) is not distinctly different.

SUPERVISORY ISSUES ASSOCIATED WITH SETTINGS

When patients come to a clinician's office for services, supervision opportunities abound. There are opportunities for direct participation and observation, including synchronous approaches (e.g., "bug in the ear") and postsession audiotaped and videotaped review. Many clinical health psychology services are provided in a similar manner and thus offer similar opportunities for the supervisory process.

However, many hospital-based consultation and treatment services pose logistical challenges for supervision. Many patients are seen on the floors in either specialized units such as burn, bone marrow transplant, dialysis or intensive care, or in their hospital rooms, often with roommates present. Collateral professional activities are conducted at the nurses' station or in multidisciplinary team meetings. Although technology is available that would enable portable recording systems and even telemonitoring of these professional services, such systems are not in widespread use for hospital-based clinical training, and they do not seem practical at this time. Where technology is most often used is in providing immediate communications access to the supervisor by the trainee.

The importance of immediacy of supervision cannot be overstated in hospital-based care. In a traditional care model or even outpatient clinical health psychology service, a trainee may have a session and then obtain supervision during a regularly scheduled weekly session. However, when a hospitalized patient is seen, there must be at least a brief chart entry at the time of service, and in the case of a consultation, a full report on the chart is often required within 24 hours. In the meantime, there may be the need for numerous contacts with other disciplines regarding the patient, contacts that have direct implications for the medical and nursing care rendered. In short, the next steps in the delivery of health care services cannot wait for a weekly scheduled supervisory hour. The supervisor must be on site and available to supervise the service delivered, as well as to meet face-to-face with the patient and to sign off on relevant documents. Face-to-face meetings with the licensed care provider is a requirement for billing under many insurance plans and is often a component of the Patients Bill of Rights provided to patients on entry to the hospital.

In my own view, there is no substitute for direct, in vivo supervision in the early stages of training for hospital-based consultations. Unless a trainee has demonstrated experience and basic readiness for this area of practice, I will have the trainee accompany me on the first several cases and watch what I do. Although I encourage participation, there is no pressure to say anything. We talk later about what, why, and how. Over the course of training, trainees take increasingly more responsibility for the interview, case conceptualization, communications with other professionals, and charting. At the point that I have confidence in the basic clinical skills, professional behavior, self-awareness of limitations, and oral and written communications of the trainee, I will allow him or her to conduct the service outside of my presence. However, I will always be reachable for supervision, and I will sign off on what he or she charts within a short period of time.

What makes for readiness to provide a hospital-based consultation? In addition to basic clinical skills, readiness includes understanding the rules and regulations of the setting with respect to issues such as privileges, charting, dress, identification, infection control procedures, and so on. For example, trainees need to be able to decipher medical abbreviations and know how to make entries into a medical chart with the appropriate format, ink color, and so on. Increasingly they will need to work with an electronic recorder.

They need to know universal precautions and the symbols for various infection control procedures, which vary across the hospital, depending on the unit or individual patient. They need to know how to check for these on ward or room entry and how to follow the directions relevant to their dress or behavior. For example, requirements for patient contact or ward entry can include gown, hair covering, foot covers, handwashing, mask, or combinations thereof.

Readiness also includes the ability to translate psychological concepts and findings into language that has meaning for other health care professionals, language that is free of psychological jargon and that has direct implications for the behavior of others. Indeed, a key feature of readiness is understanding how to work with other health care professionals, the supervision of which is a distinct focus of clinical health psychology supervision.

Formal rules and regulations govern how entries are made in medical charts. Consultation reports are placed on the chart when completed, but the section titled "Progress Notes" provides a running diary of services rendered and is an important means of communication among staff. Thus, supervision of charting itself involves careful attention to a graduated series of increasingly independent experiences. In the initial stages, I sit at the nurse's station and discuss our entry with the trainee. The next stage is to have the trainee make the entry, with my immediate supervision and sign off. When the trainee is seeing the patient outside of my presence, an entry at the time of consultation at a minimum would state something along the lines of

> 0930h. Consultation. Chart reviewed, patient seen 1 hour for interview and psychological assessment. Full report to follow.
> —*Joseph Smith, Intern, Clinical and Health Psychology*

Trainees will be encouraged to provide more information regarding preliminary findings and recommendations as they demonstrate more competence, and at some point they will be able to provide a full consultation report at the time of service. However, as a supervisor, I am concerned that formal chart entries be made only when I have some confidence that I will not need to make subsequent changes, because all changes I do make will be observable to all in the legal medical record. Although any error can (and must) be corrected in a chart, I prefer to avoid the potential for student embarrassment and bias from other professional staff that might result from any misinterpretation of chart entries.

One supervisor I knew did not like to round once or twice each day to review entries and sign off, so he would ask trainees to bring a blank progress note page to him for signature and to then return it to the chart. Because progress notes are not to contain blank lines, trainees would have to strike through whatever space was left after the previous progress note, so that their note would be the next in the timed entry format, as well as strike through the rest of their unused double-sided page. Although technically correct, those charts were filled with pages with blank line strikethroughs, and they may have conveyed a less than positive message to other professional staff concerning the supervision being provided by psychology.

Another issue in supervising hospital-based services is the need to pay special attention to the environmental context of the service provided. A trainee providing services in an outpatient clinic usually works within the context of a rather stable set of environmental stimuli, a context that is often not discussed in supervision unless there are issues related to process (e.g., seating arrangements in a family session, one-way mirrors) or unusual events (e.g., a fire drill). Such stability in the environment cannot be assumed for hospital-based services. In fact, an integral part of the supervisory process involves asking the trainee to assess the impact of context on their own clinical observations, interventions, and case conceptualizations.

During the provision of hospital-based services, staff and other patients are often in the immediate vicinity, especially in burn units and intensive care units. I always inquire about issues related to both real and perceived privacy in the interactions. I may also ask the trainee about recent events on the unit, the nature of the roommate and visitors, and so on. Context and chance events can stimulate hope and social support, or they can provide additional stressors for the patient. Many patients will see signs of illness they have not experienced before. The supervisory process needs to include directed attention to the immediate context of service, which can be changing and unpredictable.

SUPERVISORY ISSUES ASSOCIATED WITH INTERDISCIPLINARY WORK

Virtually all clinical health psychology services require interaction with other health care disciplines. Hospital-based services demand significant amounts of such collaboration. Although students may have a general understanding of the professions of medicine and nursing, the differences in disciplinary cultures and subcultures, and their implications for professional relationships and patient care, are a frequent topic in supervision.

Health care remains dominated by the medical profession. Although there are real instances of professional chauvinism, students may also read disciplinary slights into situations that are common in all consultee–consultant interactions—even within medicine and its various specialties. In addition, because of perceived differences in power hierarchies, students may quickly assume a defensive stance in interactions, and they may attempt to enlist the supervisor in defending the profession. Using the format of Kadushin (1968) in describing supervision "games," the scenario here is "You're more powerful here; help me and the profession out." The intern, for example, might complain to the supervisor, "The resident doesn't listen to me or take my recommendations seriously. Since you are such an expert in this area, maybe it would help if you had a talk with her." The supervisor, thinking that this is yet another chance to educate physicians or wanting to increase the power position in a particular situation may be enticed to go head to head with the resident. However, such a strategy could also undermine the role of intern in relation to the resident and may have implications for the role of the supervisor in regards to the attending physician.

I consult with many residents in the course of caring for patients, and I have great respect for their expertise and authority in patient care. However, if there are actual problems with a resident's relationship with my supervisee that cannot be handled through the supervisee, I will contact the resident's supervisor.

In my experience, some of the students most prone to perceiving slights from those perceived as more powerful are themselves more prone to dismissing the contributions of nondoctoral personnel to health care. Developing interdisciplinary competencies does not just apply to working with medicine but with all of the disciplines involved in care, with the same respect and understanding for their contributions. I believe it is important for the supervisor to not only model that value but also actively inquire about these issues in the supervisory process of individual patient care. A useful strategy in working with psychology trainees is to encourage their empathy for the roles, functions, and stressors of the other health professionals involved, as well as the patient.

Supervisors need to be alert to the complex dynamics involved in interdisciplinary team situations, and they need to continually work with supervisees to sort out how much of what is transpiring is a systems issue, a professional issue, or an individual issue of the trainee or other professionals involved. This is not simple, but it is much easier to do when working with a trainee over an extended period of time and when knowledgeable about the other professionals involved. Issues related to frustration tolerance are certain to arise in this area of practice. If they do not surface spontaneously in supervision, one needs to be sure to inquire. A risk to be alert to is the potential for trainee overidentification with medicine in an effort to fit in, which in the worst stereotypic way can result in a patronizing objectification of patients to whom things are done. Such an approach is not consistent with a psychological model or a biopsychosocial model for either psychology or medicine.

Although competence in working with other disciplines has always been fundamental to clinical health psychology, this competence is now recognized as fundamental to the entire health care system. Consistent with the Institute of Medicine's (IOM; 2001) report *Crossing the Quality Chasm: A New Health System for the 21st Century*, the Health Professions Education Summit in June 2002 reaffirmed competence in interdisciplinary teams as a core competency for quality health care in the 21st century (IOM, 2002). Yet unanswered is when and how best to train for such competence. Some advocate that it be from Day 1 of professional education and training; others say after a solid disciplinary identity has been established. Although each approach has its advantages and disadvantages, there is no substantive evidence for one approach over the either. However, I believe that in the supervisory process, attention to the interplay between disciplinary identity and interdisciplinary functioning needs to be explicitly addressed.

SUPERVISORY ISSUES ASSOCIATED WITH PROBLEMS ADDRESSED AND POPULATIONS SERVED

As more fully described elsewhere, there are at least nine categories of problems addressed in clinical health psychology practice (Belar, 1980, 2003; Belar, Deardorff, & Kelly, 1987):

1. psychological factors secondary to disease, injury, or disability;
2. somatic presentations of psychological dysfunction;
3. psychophysiological disorders;
4. physical symptoms or conditions responsive to behavioral interventions;

5. somatic complications of disease or injury associated with behavioral factors;
6. psychological presentation of organic disease;
7. psychological and behavioral aspects of stressful medical procedures;
8. behavioral risk factors for disease, injury, or disability; and
9. problems of health care providers and health care systems.

The specific populations served by clinical health psychology reflect the life span and

> include (but are not limited to) persons with asthma, pain, organ failure, physical disability, irritable bowel syndrome, headache, hemophilia, Raynaud's disease, diabetes, premenstrual syndrome, pregnancy, infertility, arthritis, terminal illness, cardiovascular disease, cancer, acquired immune deficiency syndrome, sickle cell disease, injury, obesity, dental disease, osteoporosis, stroke, hypertension, as well as those individuals at risk for these problems and those who desire to develop or maintain a healthy lifestyle. Patients' family members and health care providers are also recipients of clinical health psychology services. (APA, 1997, p. 1)

A distinctive feature of such practice is that many patients are physically ill, and this may be of concern to trainees. One advanced trainee told me that she did not like working with medical patients because they had "real" problems that her anxiety disorder patients did not. I wondered what that meant in terms of her attitude toward both mental health problems and the psychological components of medical problems. Contemporary U.S. has many stereotypes and related "-isms" regarding mental health problem and care. In addition, mind–body dualism is as alive and well among many mental health professionals as it is with medical personnel. These areas need exploration in supervision.

It is also important to remember that trainees beginning their work in clinical health psychology may have had little experience with issues such as death, dying, disfigurement, and chronic pain. They may even have had little interaction with the health care system, especially at the tertiary care level. Many are unprepared to see and experience the consequences of illness, the efforts to heal, and the results of medical–surgical interventions. A period of acclimatization is often needed to facilitate coping and adaptation to the sight of blood, debilitating illness, smells, and hearing patients' concerns about death. Pictures and videos in medical libraries can facilitate some visual desensitization, but there are always issues that arise (even for the most experienced clinicians). I believe that these issues should be anticipated and addressed proactively in a supportive but matter-of-fact manner. When I witnessed my first surgery, I was advised of the symptoms of an impending faint and to "fall backward rather than forward" on top of the patient on the table. I was determined to tough it out but wise enough to move away and use some relaxation techniques when I experienced the onset of tunnel vision. I did not faint, and I was always thankful to the wise surgeon whose expectations of my reactivity normalized the experience and facilitated not only my coping but also my subsequent learning.

In the case above, the patient was unconscious, but I recall another event as an intern when I was so distracted by a facially disfigured patient in the next bed that I had difficulty focusing on my interview. I have worked with many trainees who have been troubled by their experiences, and one who was actually hospital phobic. We as clinicians remember that patients can be negatively impacted by the reactions of others and that we must first do no harm. Supervision regarding many of these issues needs to occur prior to the patient contact, not after. We need to understand our trainee's readiness to deal with such matters and their own health belief models—yet another reason I prefer the in vivo approach with beginning trainees.

Preparation for clinical work can be designed using methods similar to how patients are prepared for stressful medical procedures. When strong emotions are aroused in a clinical session, the supervisor can advise the use of the same strategies as those applied in the course of any clinical contact. The clinician's feelings can be used to both inform and guide the process (*I'm wondering what you are thinking about how others might react to your colostomy? How has your husband reacted to your mastectomy?*). One's own reactions can also clue one as to what important issues are being avoided (*Since your pelvic exenteration, have you discussed with your surgeon the options available regarding sexual intimacy? Do you anticipate any change in your relationship with your sister-in-law if she is the biological mother of your child?*) Whatever preparation we provide for trainees, however, we can be sure that they will have experiences that threaten their own sense of control, bodily integrity, and mortality and that these issues will arise in supervision. Our trainees will also experience losses and will need to grieve their patients. We can also be sure that they will have experiences that are completely unexpected. A student on his very first practicum involving patient contact was greeted by a most welcoming patient who immediately threw off his bedsheet to expose his naked torso and the catheter running into his penis. He kept pointing to his penis and repeatedly asked for us to adjust his catheter to make it more comfortable.

SUPERVISORY ISSUES ASSOCIATED WITH PROCEDURES USED

As described more fully in other texts (e.g., Belar & Deardorff, 1995; Boll, Johnson, Perry, & Rozensky, 2002), a wide variety of procedures are applied in the practice of clinical health psychology. Assessments and interventions can be targeted at the level of the patient, his or her family, health care provider, and social system. Multicultural competence is a must. In my opinion, most of the supervisory issues encountered with respect to the use of particular methods are similar to those in more traditional mental health services, although there are some areas of distinctive focus. Issues regarding the trainee's own health belief model and values often arise. In addition, religion can play an important role in the acceptability of various medical treatments (e.g., transfusion, donor egg in vitro fertilization, abortion) and thus pose issues for trainees themselves in providing related services.

In providing consultations, the trainees must often learn about the nature of the medical problem involved prior to conducting the service. Supervision needs to include training in self-assessment for readiness to provide the service and in how to rapidly obtain the information required. Continual training in self-assessment is critical in supervision, as it is fundamental to lifelong learning and professional development. Learning how to learn and how to assess the limits of one's competence are critical to graduate education and training. Belar et al. (2001) have developed a template in the form of a series of questions that can be used to assess readiness (see Exhibit 10.1).

Without knowledge of the medical condition, significant errors can occur. One intern with considerable experience with organ transplantation, including kidney, heart, and bone marrow, had difficulty with a case involving lung transplant. She reported concern that the patient seemed much more anxious than her other patients but seemed to be denying it. On further examination and review, it became obvious that the intern was basing her impression of anxiety on some slight trembling in the voice and hands and the patient's breathing pattern—all symptoms of either her medical problem or side effects of prescribed medication.

Another distinctive feature of hospital-based services is that consultation requests for psychology are usually made by physicians or nursing staff rather than the patient himself or herself. When an outpatient referral is made, patients can vote with their feet and not show up if they do not want to follow through. As inpatients, when a psychology consult is called, the provider shows up in the patient's room, usually unannounced and needs to ensure privacy when a roommate may be present. Changing locations is sometimes possible. Whispering behind pulled curtains is more often the case. Many patients welcome the consultation; others are reluctant; and still others are downright hostile. Negative reactions are frequent enough that this is another area that requires supervision prior to the patient contact so that trainees accustomed to the help-seeking framework in patient interactions are not surprised. They need an opportunity to develop appropriate tools to establish a good working relationship and to deal appropriately with issues of informed consent and privacy. Only recently did I learn that these tools might be misinterpreted by some. A 2nd-year practicum student told me how

EXHIBIT 10.1
Template for Self-Assessment in Clinical Health Psychology

1. Do I have knowledge of the biological bases of health and disease as related to this problem? How is this related to the biological bases of behavior?
2. Do I have knowledge of the cognitive–affective bases of health and disease as related to this problem? How is this related to the cognitive–affective bases of behavior?
3. Do I have knowledge of the social bases of health and disease as related to this problem? How is this related to the social bases of behavior?
4. Do I have knowledge of the developmental and individual bases of health and disease as related to this problem? How is this related to developmental and individual bases of behavior?
5. Do I have knowledge of the interactions among biological, affective, cognitive, social, and developmental components (e.g., psychophysiological aspects)? Do I understand the relationships between this problem and the patient and his or her environment (including family, health care system, and sociocultural environment)?
6. Do I have knowledge and skills of the empirically supported clinical assessment methods for this problem and how assessment might be affected by information in areas described by Questions 1–5?
7. Do I have knowledge of, and skill in implementing, the empirically supported interventions relevant to this problem? Do I have knowledge of how the proposed psychological intervention might impact physiological processes and vice versa?
8. Do I have knowledge of the roles and functions of other health care professionals relevant to this patient's problem? Do I have skills to communicate and collaborate with them?
9. Do I understand the sociopolitical features of the health care delivery system that can impact this problem?
10. Am I aware of the health policy issues relevant to this problem?
11. Am I aware of the distinctive ethical issues related to practice with this problem?
12. Am I aware of the distinctive legal issues related to practice with this problem?
13. Am I aware of the special professional issues associated with practice with this problem?

Note. From "Self-Assessment in Clinical Health Psychology: A Model for Ethical Expansion of Practice," by C. D. Belar et al., 2001, *Professional Psychology: Research and Practice, 32,* p. 137. Copyright 2001 by the American Psychological Association.

much he enjoyed coming onto the wards with me because in these experiences he just got to talk with people rather than conduct formal interviews as he did in the outpatient clinic. I was appalled: What I had developed as skills in relating to unprepared patients and obtaining the required information in the least threatening manner was seen as chitchat by a novice?

I have always worked from a model of supervisees being thoroughly trained in basic clinical skills prior to working in health psychology, but as more of these experiences are integrated earlier in training, how does the trainee know when shortcuts are being taken, when seeming informality is masking a carefully executed professional strategy, and so on? This issue still troubles me, as would be expected, given my own heritage in training. When

I was in my 20s, my college-age clients were required to call me "Mrs.,"which I thought was overly formal. Yet, it forced me to deal with the perceived and real power differential in professional relationships, issues that might have been easily avoided without that stimulus. On a related theme, I have always found it harder to do briefer interviews than long ones, or to write shorter reports than long ones. If students in training only write abstracts, how do I know they are capable of the full study? Sometimes I have required two reports, one that gives a thorough case conceptualization for educational purposes and another one more appropriate to the medical chart. I am sure there are other ways to address these issues in supervision; it is an area about which I remain concerned for training in clinical health psychology.

One issue that arises frequently in supervision is that related to touch. Many of us psychologists were trained that touch between psychologist and the adult patient was forbidden, other than perhaps a professional handshake or accepting the spontaneous hug of appreciation. In the 1970s, however, with the growth of applied psychophysiology, we found ourselves scrubbing skin and applying electrodes to facilitate biofeedback treatments. Although these techniques have advanced tremendously over the years, with greatly increased efficiency, there is still touch involved. Many psychology trainees without any prior experience in touching a patient have reactions that need to be addressed.

There are also times when a trainee might touch the shoulder or arm of a patient who is seriously ill—usually as an act of human kindness rather than a deliberate psychological intervention. Although there is a literature on the therapeutic value of touch, in my view the use of touch is one that should always raise awareness of boundary issues. If trainees see me do it, I always bring it to their attention and discuss it.

CONCLUSION

In summary, this chapter has reviewed some of distinctive features of supervision in clinical health psychology. I do not address the issues of forming an alliance in supervisory relationships, building technical competence, formative and summative evaluation, or legal and ethical issues that are the building blocks of good supervision. The focus has been on some of the special issues confronted when working primarily with adult medical–surgical patients in medical settings. There are some distinctive setting-related, problem-related, interdisciplinary and personal issues that can surface in the supervisory process, and in my view, if they do not, they should be addressed explicitly by the supervisor. As professional psychologists are trained in a broader health perspective in the years to come, the framework used for this chapter may become obsolete. I hope so.

REFERENCES

American Psychological Association Council of Representatives. (1997, August). *Archival description of clinical health psychology as a specialty in professional psychology*. Minutes of the Annual Meeting of the Council of Representatives, Chicago, IL.

Belar, C. D. (1980). Training the clinical psychology student in behavioral medicine. *Professional Psychology, 11*, 620–627.

Belar, C. D. (1997). Clinical health psychology: A specialty for the 21st century. *Health Psychology, 16*, 411–416.

Belar, C. D. (2003). Models and concepts. In S. Llewelyn & P. Kennedy (Eds.), *Handbook of clinical health psychology* (pp. 7–19). New York: Wiley.

Belar, C. D., Brown, R., Hersch, L., Hornyak, L., Rozensky, R., Sheridan, E., et al. (2001). Self-assessment in clinical health psychology: A model for the ethical expansion of practice. *Professional Psychology: Research and Practice, 32*, 125–141.

Belar, C. D., & Deardorff, W. W. (1995). *Clinical health psychology in medical settings: A practitioner's guidebook*. Washington, DC: American Psychological Association.

Belar, C. D., Deardorff, W. W., & Kelly, K. E. (1987). *The practice of clinical health psychology*. New York: Pergamon Press.

Boll, T. J., Johnson, S. B., Perry, Jr., N. W., & Rozensky, R. H. (Eds.). (2002). *Handbook of clinical health psychology: Vol. I. Medical disorders and behavioral applications*. Washington, DC: American Psychological Association.

Falender, C. A., & Shafranske, E. P. (2004). *Clinical supervision: A competency-based approach*. Washington, DC: American Psychological Association.

Institute of Medicine. (2001). *Crossing the quality chasm: A new health system for the 21st century*. Washington, DC: National Academy Press.

Institute of Medicine. (2002). *Health professions education: A bridge to quality*. Washington, DC: National Academy Press.

Kadushin, A. (1968). Games people play in supervision. *Social Work, 13*, 23–32.

Sayette, M. A., & Mayne, T. J. (1990). Survey of current clinical research trends in clinical psychology. *American Psychologist, 45*, 1263–1266.

11

EVALUATING AND ENHANCING SUPERVISION: AN EXPERIENTIAL MODEL

DEREK MILNE

Evaluation plays a pivotal role in the supervision process, serving several discrete functions (such as providing corrective feedback and accountability) and linking all other aspects of the educational system. Although much has been done to promote evaluation practice within supervision, some significant challenges remain. A review by Lambert and Ogles (1997), for instance, concluded that to improve matters, evaluative instruments should focus on the trainees' behavior in therapy; consider the supervisees' therapeutic relationship; draw on multiple perspectives; and focus on criterion measures, especially the impact of the trainees' work on the client. In this chapter, I therefore illustrate, in a practical way, how each of these requirements can be addressed. Drawing heavily on my own work (see reference list) in developing an experiential model of supervision (described shortly), I aim to familiarize the reader with a scientifically based method of evaluation, offering suggestions and tools to enhance supervision practice.

I am grateful to Ian A. James for many fruitful years of collaboration over the evaluation of supervision, to Caroline Leck for her stimulating engagement in the local supervision project, and to my other colleagues for their vital collegial support (e.g., in developing the Trainee's Competence Checklist). I am also grateful to Karen Clark, Kathryn Mark, and Barbara Mellors for their help in preparing this chapter.

DEFINITION OF EVALUATION

The term *evaluation* derives from the 18th-century French term meaning the "value from" something (*Concise Oxford English Dictionary*, 2004). Nowadays, it is commonly defined in terms of a judgment regarding the degree to which objectives are achieved and, more generally, "the process of determining the merit, worth, and value of things" (Scriven, 1972, p.17). Other key elements are that evaluations (a) use research methods to determine the effectiveness of interventions, (b) are appropriate to their context, and (c) inform constructive action (Rossi, Lipsey, & Freeman, 2004). Evaluation differs from assessment, therefore, in tending to be more subjective, judgmental, and linked to some publicly defined service outcomes.

In clinical supervision, these outcomes focus on clinical competencies that are defined by professional bodies or training programs and that represent the standards to be achieved by individual trainees or supervisees. During their training, supervisees are typically appraised across a range of these competencies, and their training programs have procedures and evaluation instruments in place to judge their achievement of these objectives. This is in agreement with the view that evaluation concerns "judgments . . . about supervisees' capability for exercising appropriate clinical judgment and their level of clinical proficiency" (Robiner et al., 1997, p. 50).

However, evaluation should also focus on other participants in the supervision system, including the ability of supervisors to achieve their own educational objectives and the success of a training program in developing its supervisors. In an optimal educational system, therefore, evaluation yields information that guides all important elements of that system, facilitating short-term effectiveness and long-term adaptation, leading to ongoing professional development. To bring these points to life, I next summarize an experiential model of clinical supervision and provide examples of this broader definition of evaluation.

AN EXPERIENTIAL THEORY OF SUPERVISION

It has been said that there is nothing as practical as a good theory. This is certainly true in relation to supervision, for which the theoretical work of eminent psychologists such as Lewin, Vygotsky, and Piaget have provided helpful pointers for the supervision enterprise. As summarized by Kolb (1984), these psychologists suggest that supervision can be helpfully construed as the facilitation of learning from experience. Specifically, supervision can be seen as the business of trying to help supervisees to be more aware of their clinical experiences, better able to recall and recount this work, more competent in understanding what has happened, and better able to plan and enact the next steps. It follows that if these are the objectives of supervision, the supervisor's job is, respectively, to heighten awareness of effect, to gather information, to develop the supervisee's understanding, and to guide planning and experiential learning. Within our experiential learning account of supervision, we have chosen to model this as a circumplex (Milne, James, Keegan, & Dudley, 2002; Milne & Westerman, 2001). Figure 11.1 displays this, adding important details regarding what the two parties need to bring to the supervision, placed within a context.

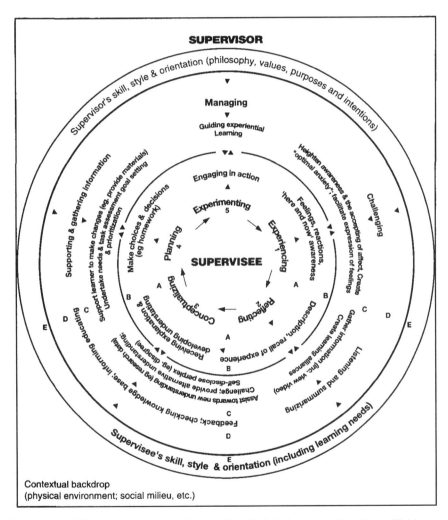

Figure 11.1. The experiential learning model of clinical supervision. From "Evidence-Based Clinical Supervision: Rationale and Illustration," by D. Milne and C. Westerman, 2001, *Clinical Psychology & Psychotherapy, 8,* pp. 444–457. Copyright 2001 by Wiley. Reprinted with permission.

This model provides two fundamental and complementary approaches to the evaluation of supervision, one primarily concerned with the supervisor's performance (a structural approach to evaluation) and the second, with that of the supervisee (a functional approach). Specifically, the outer two circles within the circumplex model (see Figure 11.1) concern competencies and objectives that are the activities of the supervisor, such as managing and challenging the supervisee. These represent structural criteria for evaluating supervision. Under this approach, good supervisors tend to engage frequently in these behaviors, and well-organized workshops are designed to promote and develop these supervision skills. These skills are partly structural because they are the building blocks on which effective supervision is built. However, according to the experiential model, such skills are necessary rather than sufficient for a proper evaluation of supervision.

The evaluation of competent supervision is better indicated by how effectively the supervisor manages the supervisee's experiential learning. For example, did challenging the supervisee lead to the fresh conceptualization (e.g., formulation) of a problem? This more-searching form of evaluation is functional in that the quality or competence of supervision is judged in terms of its effectiveness in promoting such experiential learning in the supervisee. In this sense, Figure 11.1 should be viewed as a set of interlinked wheels, with the outer ones necessary to achieve the short-term objective of experiential learning in the supervisee. If this learning occurs, then the other functions of supervision, such as exercising some quality control over the supervisee's therapy, can be optimized. Another way of putting this is to suggest that the evaluation of supervision should be viewed in a stepwise, systemic way. It can usefully proceed from these "mini-impacts" (McCullough et al., 1991) on the supervisee's learning (facilitated by the supervisor within the supervision session) to the ultimate objectives within professional practice, such as fostering skilled and safe therapy by the trainee. Experiential learning is of course also partly a function of the personalities of the supervisor and the supervisee, and this is why Figure 11.1 notes such contextual influences as the supervisee's orientation and learning history. This model of supervision has been operationalized in the Teachers' Process Evaluation of Training and Supervision (Teachers' PETS) instrument (Milne et al., 2002), described in the section of that same name, subsequently.

FUNCTIONS OF EVALUATION

The literature on clinical supervision is unanimous in viewing evaluation as pivotal to the enterprise (Falender & Shafranske, 2004). Watkins (1997), for instance, noted that "supervision must be evaluative. There is no way that it cannot be so, even though the evaluation can come in different forms" (p. 4).

Furthermore, within the general psychological literature on learning, feedback is seen as "extremely important" (Bransford, Brown, & Cocking, 2000, p. 140). This is because it makes learning visible and affords the opportunity to provide continuous and potentially corrective information back to learners, so that they have the opportunity to develop.

A closely related function of evaluation is that it can also provide the necessary feedback to the supervisor, guiding decisions about what to do next. Careful monitoring of the clinical work of the supervisee cues the supervisor as to what is working and what might need to change in regular supervisory sessions. This might include the use of alternative forms of guiding experiential learning (e.g., less informing and more alliance building) or the other methods set out in the middle ring of Figure 11.1. This is termed the *shaping* function of evaluation in Table 11.1.

Other functions of evaluation include estimating the supervisee's current competence profile (Robiner et al., 1997). As Watkins (1997) observed, such benchmarking or profiling (see Table 11.1) can help to highlight a supervisee's strengths and weaknesses, thereby helping to boost the trainee's confidence and to define an individualized learning contract. As noted in Falender and Shafranske (2004), this kind of educational needs assessment also provides the objectives that should become the basis for both the focus of supervision and its evaluation.

A further function of evaluation is to prompt and direct the selecting (or constructing) of suitable instruments, designed to assess the extent to which these objectives have been achieved. In turn, data from such instruments enables the supervisor to reach summative judgments concerning whether a supervisee has demonstrated the requisite level of competence and so should pass a training program or gain an award.

Falender and Shafranske (2004) also emphasized client outcome as an evaluation focus. Here, evaluation serves the function of linking supervision to its results, a form of outcome evaluation. In this sense, supervision is judged to be effective when it achieves clinical benefits; although, as they note (p. 202), this is an imperfect criterion (because of the profound effect of other factors, such as the client's clinical status—this is one of the reasons a stepwise approach to evaluation is stressed in this chapter). Information on outcome can help to indicate the relative benefits of supervision and to contribute to quality control.

Other functions of evaluation noted in Table 11.1 are to provide data toward clinical accountability (Wampold & Holloway, 1997) and toward the supervisors' continuing professional development (Lambert & Arnold, 1987). This links to a consensus statement by a group of senior practitioners who noted that one of the competencies of effective supervisors was the ability "to encourage and use evaluative feedback from the trainee" (Falender et al., 2004, p. 778). Training programs and other parts of an educational system can similarly benefit from evaluations that furnish corrective information. This is

TABLE 11.1

A Summary of the Main Functions of Evaluation, Together With Some
Illustrative Instruments, With Specific Reference to Supervision

Functions of evaluation	Examples of forms that evaluation takes in clinical supervision
1. *Feedback:* Information to the supervisee on the attainment of objectives; termed "formative evaluation."	Supervisors' rating forms (e.g., TraCC); learning contracts (especially reviewing and redefining learning needs); Helpful Aspects of Supervision Questionnaire.
2. *Gatekeeping:* Judgments about competence and credentialing— fitness for practice and for award; termed "summative evaluation."	Supervisors' ratings of a supervisees' competence, including adherence to a particular therapeutic approach (e.g., Cognitive Therapy Scale—Revised; Blackburn et al., 2001).
3. *Justification:* Accountability evidence, as required to justify actions or decisions.	Internal audits (e.g. Placement Record Form) or external vetting of a trainee system, such as by a professional body like the American Psychological Association.
4. *Formulation:* Providing information within a theoretical model to aid understanding of a supervisory system's functioning.	Evaluate service development to study, for instance, the training of supervisors and supervisees in their work context (see, e.g., Milne, Hanner, Woodward, & Westerman; 2004).
5. *Monitoring:* Longitudinal data, used to follow progress on an individual or system; establishing whether a therapy adheres faithfully to a guideline or specified approach over time.	Clinical outcome data (e.g., Beck Depression or Anxiety Inventories; outcome questionnaire); coping strategies of supervisee or client (see Moos, 1992).
6. *Shaping:* Influences that guide the activities of evaluators, such as supervisees reinforcing the use of a method.	This recognizes that evaluation is a behavior and so may be influenced by all manner of consequences. To illustrate, accrediting bodies may endorse a competency approach within a training program (e.g., TraCC) or supervisees might use the HASQ to discourage excessive challenging by the supervisor.

Note. TraCC = Trainee's Competence Checklist; HASQ = Helpful Aspects of Supervision Questionnaire. See Appendixes A and B, respectively, for copies of the TraCC and HASQ.

referred to as the "formulation" function in Table 11.1, as it can aid comprehension of a system's functioning. A related function is that of monitoring, which might usefully occur at both individual and systems levels (e.g., auditing whether assessment tools are being used by supervisors).

SUMMARY

Perhaps it is not surprising, given these numerous and exacting functions of evaluation (and the relative youth of supervision as a specialization), that the field of supervision is, like a new supervisee, full of development opportunities. For instance, in reviewing such evaluation efforts, Lambert and Ogles (1997) thought that several conclusions and goals were warranted:

1. The most useful measures record specific supervisee behaviors in therapy, using objective tools.
2. The therapeutic relationship is also important, as perceived by the client—Even if weakly related to therapy outcome, the impact of relationship measures in training is substantial (p. 440).
3. Multiple measures of the effectiveness of supervision, from multiple perspectives, is the preferred strategy (Lambert & Ogles, 1997, referred to data about the supervisee from clients and the supervisor, and from trainee self-assessment).
4. The impact of these supervisee behaviors and relationship qualities should be judged in terms of the clinical benefits to clients.
5. Psychometrically sound measures of these criteria should be developed.

The remainder of this chapter provides illustrations addressing these five points. The first four are tackled explicitly in the sections that follow, and the fifth is embedded within them.

POINT 1: ILLUSTRATION OF OBSERVING THE SUPERVISEE

Objective, detailed observation of the learner has a long history, as illustrated by the verbal interaction analysis system used in the classroom (Flanders, 1970). A parallel example from supervision is the Operant Supervisor–Subordinate Taxonomy and Index (OSSTI; Komaki & Citera, 1990). The OSSTI allows one to code some fundamental aspects of the supervisee's interactions within supervision, following a functional analysis approach. However, it is very broad in its focus and is therefore of limited value as a basis for detailed feedback to the supervisee. On the other hand, the OSSTI does look at the relationship between supervisor and supervisee behaviors, a very helpful perspective. This is in contrast to the great majority of supervisee evaluations, which tend to use self-report and rating methods to look at more global constructs, such as styles, orientations, or personal reactions (see Table 24.3 in Lambert & Ogles, 1997, for further examples).

Teachers' PETS

Because of the advantages of direct observation and to provide a tool with an integrative theoretical perspective (and more detailed feedback than available through OSSTI), we developed a new instrument to measure both supervisor and supervisee behaviors (Milne et al., 2002), the Teachers' PETS. This instrument operationalizes the experiential learning model set out above (see Figure 11.1). In terms of its psychometric properties, the items within the instrument were drawn from the various branches of applied psychology, including educational, clinical, community, and sport psychology. This yielded a broad, content-valid list of criteria for defining objectively the activities of the supervisor. Concurrent validity and interrater reliability have also been assessed and have been favorable (e.g., reliability of $K = .84$). As the main focus of this chapter is on the evaluation of the supervisee, the inner two circles within the experiential learning model (see Figure 11.1) are detailed here. Table 11.2 lists the six behaviors, together with their definitions. However, Teachers' PETS also quantifies the supervisor's behavior.

As prescribed in the observation manual (available on request from the author), Teachers' PETS is administered using a momentary time-sampling

TABLE 11.2
Criteria for Evaluating the Supervisee's Experiential Learning,
Drawn From the Observational Instrument Teachers' PETS

Learning mode	Definition
1. Experiencing	Being aware of emotional accompaniments of actions. Showing involvement and engagement in task (in the here and now); for example, tears, smiling, and laughter. Also, expressing an emotion or an attitude to a situation.
2. Reflecting	Considering own perspective (as a learner) or that of own client. Freely expressing own information and ideas (e.g., describing, recalling, clarifying, story telling); self-disclosure. Requesting more information and advice to gain an understanding of the situation.
3. Conceptualizing	Assimilating, accommodating, or integrating information; summarizing defining, or offering an understanding for the trainer; demonstrating an understanding as a result of the trainer's intervention. Defining, reviewing, and reflecting, from the perspective of others (the trainer, other learners, theories and research findings). Responding to questions or requests (e.g., Socratic questioning).
4. Planning	Making decisions, setting goals to go and test out new understanding or methods. Interacting with peers to plan or set goals; making decisions (e.g., homework tasks).
5. Experimenting	Engaging in action: role play exercise, group discussion, watching video, participating in active learning task, etc. Behaviors that develop skills.
6. Other	Can't decide on suitable category (from above); not observable; other behaviors (e.g., social chat, paperwork); off-task behavior.

Note. The experiential learning model of clinical supervision. Teachers' PETS = Teachers' Process Evaluation of Training and Supervision (Teachers' PETS; Milne et al., 2002). From "Evidence-Based Clinical Supervision: Rationale and Illustration," by D. Milne and C. Westerman, 2001, *Clinical Psychology & Psychotherapy, 8*, pp. 444–457. Copyright 2001 by Wiley. Reprinted with permission.

procedure. This procedure requires the observer to code the alternating supervisor and supervisee behaviors at 15-second intervals. That means that the supervisee's behaviors, as listed in Table 11.2, would normally be observed during a supervision session by recording the frequency of each of these six behaviors at the precise half-minute time point. In this way, a sample of the supervisee's work, normally recorded on videotape or audiotape, can be coded and a learning profile produced. To illustrate, Milne and Westerman (2001) profiled three supervisees, over an 8-month period. This profile indicated the huge preponderance of reflecting within these supervision sessions (87% of observations), a common finding, in my experience. That is, the observed supervisees spent the great majority of their time in supervision talking— providing information, describing sessions, recalling details, clarifying items, and generally telling the story of what had happened in their therapy work. By contrast, there were only modest frequencies of experiencing (10.0%) and very few instances of conceptualizing (0.5%), planning (2.0%) or experimenting (0.5%). (In Teachers' PETS, we distinguish between the affective and behavioral aspects that Kolb, 1984, subsumed under "experiencing.")

Such data get to the heart of evaluation, because they indicate that the supervision is functionally deficient: The supervisee is not achieving the basic learning objectives. According to experiential learning theory, supervisors should enable the supervisees to engage fairly equally in all of the modes of learning. As Kolb (1984) put it, people need to use all of the modes to be effective: "integration of . . . the adaptive modes is the hallmark of . . . growth" (p. 30). The kind of profile noted above should therefore alert the supervisor to a fundamental lack of impact on learning within supervision. This is not to devalue the importance of reflection, which has a hugely significant role to play within supervision. However, dominating the other modes to this extent is unlikely to produce trainee competence, safe practice, or clinical benefit. Therefore, profiles of this kind represent feedback to the supervisor and indicate the need to work in different ways to increase the use of the other modes (i.e., the evaluation function labeled *shaping* in Table 11.1). Because supervision is by definition a relationship, it also makes sense to treat this kind of information as feedback to the trainee, although on our experiential model we would probably expect the supervisor to accept the lead responsibility in rectifying the profile.

An example of how such a partial profile was rectified through the supervisor is provided in Milne and James (2002; see also Milne et al., 2002, for an illustration from a training workshop). Essentially, as noted in those studies, a consultant furnishes feedback to the supervisor, then provides advice and guidance on the use of a wider range of supervisory methods (and especially, in these examples, on the need for more guiding experiential learning—using role play and other action methods to promote experiencing and experimenting). On the basis of this consultancy, both studies indicated some improvements in the obtained learning profile.

Practical Example

Given the profile above, how might a supervisor feed back this information so as to engage in joint problem solving with a supervisee? One answer, assuming that the supervisee is not a complete novice, is to invite him or her to interpret the profile. This has the added benefit of clarifying the learner's needs, as his or her level of proficiency in the area will be indicated by his or her ability to make sense of and interpret the (Teachers' PETS) data. In this way, supervisees who engage as illustrated in the imaginary dialogue immediately below would be strongly commended—not only have they accurately understood the analysis, they have also demonstrated the ability to use these data to plan the next step.

With a novice, one might first ensure that the model is understood (and ideally that it is deemed acceptable). An excerpt from such a conversation might look like this:

Supervisor: Jenny, here is my summary of how you seem to be responding to supervision. How well do you currently understand this approach?

Supervisee: I've read a couple of papers and have a general grasp, but I am struggling to fully understand the approach in my own case.

Supervisor: Have a look at this diagram [shows her Figure 11.1]. According to this [pointing to the innermost circle], your development as a supervisee can be understood as involving movement between five fundamentally different ways of learning. For example, which mode are we in right now?

Supervisee: That's a tough question . . . I guess that you are making me reflect?

Supervisor: Well, almost there: Reflection is fundamentally different from conceptualizing in that reflecting is private, whereas conceptualizing involves public knowledge. Given that definition, would you like to try again?

Supervisee: OK, I get it—since this is a well-established, published model of learning, I must be involved in conceptualizing right now.

Supervisor: Exactly. And if we look at your profile, how much conceptualizing was going on in the observed sessions?

Supervisee: I can see now—this means that I did very little conceptualizing and spent almost the whole time reflecting.

Supervisor: That's absolutely right. You've clearly got the hang of it now. And what would this indicate we should do next?

Through such an interaction, the skillful supervisor provides feedback in an empowering way, which has the effects of strengthening the learning alliance with supervisees and of helping them to develop the vital skill of self-supervision.

Supervisee Behaviors in Therapy

Although Teachers' PETS has not been used to measure the related impact that supervisee experiential learning has on the client, it has been linked to simple qualitative and quantitative measures approximating to this ultimate level of evaluation. Milne, Pilkington, Gracie, and James (2003) carried out an intensive case study analysis of the generalization of cognitive behavior therapy (CBT) supervision to therapy, drawing on 10 successive pairs of supervision and therapy sessions for one supervisee (working as a therapist with one client). Fourteen themes were identified in the 10 supervision sessions, such as agenda setting and setting behavioral tasks. All 14 of these themes were then observed to occur in the immediately following therapy sessions provided by the supervisee. On average, 5.6 themes occurred in each of these 10 subsequent therapy sessions, and they were applied skillfully.

These are important stepwise evaluation criteria, building toward the direct evaluation of clinical impacts. This is typically achieved by assessing the clients' functioning during the course of therapy, as illustrated under Point 4.

Summary

In this section, I illustrated how one particular observation instrument, Teachers' PETS, can provide an objective evaluation of the supervisor and the supervisee. It demonstrates good psychometric status (satisfying one of the requirements stated by Lambert & Ogles, 1997) and provides a very detailed account of supervision, in terms of its main theoretically derived function—facilitation of the supervisee's experiential learning. However, it should also be noted that Teachers' PETS is a labor-intensive approach, and so it is appropriate to acknowledge that other instruments may be more useful on a day-to-day basis. Lambert and Ogles (1997) and Falender and Shafranske (2004) list some of these instruments, which include simple observations and ratings of specific skill areas, such as interviewing and formulating. Additional approaches to the observation of the supervisee include specific (ad hoc) approaches designed by the supervisor for particular purposes, such as rating how well the supervisee interacts with other staff, plus general instruments drawn from the therapy literature (e.g., alliance assessments).

POINT 2: ILLUSTRATION OF EVALUATING
THE THERAPEUTIC ALLIANCE

The previous example also illustrates another dimension of supervisory (and clinical) practice, the alliance, which has received considerable attention in the clinical literature (Lambert & Ogles, 1997; see also chap. 7, this volume). The use of measures of alliance within supervision advance the practical application of this literature and provide an empirical procedure that readers can readily apply to enhance their own supervisory work.

The Agnew Relationship Measure (ARM; Agnew-Davies, Siles, Hardy, Barkham, & Shapiro, 1998) is a suitable instrument with which to measure the trainee's therapy relationships. It is a psychometrically sound self-report instrument, with the advantage of having parallel forms for therapist and client. Consisting of 28 items, the ARM assesses the alliance dimensions of bond, sense of partnership, confidence, openness, and client initiative. A possible supplement or alternative to the ARM is the Working Alliance Inventory (Bahrick, 1989), a 36-item rating form that is designed to assess how the supervisee and supervisor perceive their working alliance (Appendix B, Falender & Shafranske, 2004). The next sections present additional methods and examine different levels of supervisee functioning.

POINT 3: ILLUSTRATION OF USING MULTIPLE MEASURES

There is a bewildering array of instruments available for the evaluation of supervision. The relevant parameters include their focus (thoughts, feelings, or behaviors); purpose of the evaluation (diagnosis, monitoring, or outcome evaluation); domains of functioning that are of interest (intrapersonal, interpersonal, or social); perspectives to be considered (supervisors, supervisees, clients, significant others); data collection methods (self-report, independent observations or ratings, psychometric tests, permanent products or archival records); and finally, the time-point parameter (past, present, or future). Given these six parameters and their multiple definitions, it is clear that supervisees can be evaluated in a number of ways. The parent text (Falender & Shafranske, 2004) or the *Handbook of Psychotherapy Supervision* (Watkins, 1997) can furnish the reader with examples of these forms of evaluation.

In this section, I focus on the second of Lambert and Ogles's (1997) criteria, the use of several perspectives to evaluate supervision. To complement the rather scientific emphasis of the previous section (Teachers' PETS), this section details straightforward applications of evaluation that are in routine use by Newcastle University's Doctorate in Clinical Psychology program. I start with how supervisors can evaluate the competence of their supervisees.

Supervisor's Ratings of Supervisee's Competence

Just as competencies have been defined for the supervisor (Falender & Shafranske, 2004), they have also been defined for the supervisee. These include cultural diversity, ethical practice, interpersonal and relationship skills, critical thinking, and knowledge of oneself (Kaslow et al., 2004). Other definitions of *competence* (and indeed other examples of measurement of the supervisee's competence) can again be found in Falender and Shafranske (2004), Watkins (1997), and other valuable textbooks on clinical supervision, such as that of Bernard and Goodyear (2004).

My own experience of evaluating supervisees' competencies was as the clinical tutor responsible for organizing practical experience for supervisees associated with the Newcastle Upon Tyne–based doctorate in clinical psychology, an intensive 3-year training program in the United Kingdom. Drawing explicitly on consensus-building work with the local supervisors (and on linked literature searching), I developed the Trainee's Competence Checklist (TraCC). This assesses five main dimensions of competence (assessment, therapy, indirect work, teaching and training, professional standards) by means of 40 items. Each item is rated by the supervisor in terms of whether the given competence is "not yet demonstrated," is "progressing satisfactorily," or is "demonstrated." The evidence supporting this rating is then noted (a list of such forms of evidence is provided with suitable keys so the supervisor can readily complete TraCC). A copy of this instrument, which has stood the test of time locally, is in Appendix A and may be used with acknowledgment. Clearly, it is important that this approach be suitably tied to the relevant competencies within a given training program and that it builds on a consensus with the local stakeholders. Like any good instrument, other implications follow, such as the need to train supervisors in the use of competency evaluations and to ensure that the information is properly fed back through the system, so that supervision is enhanced.

The following typical (but fictitious) transaction illustrates how the TraCC information can contribute to the enhancement of the supervisee's learning (and guide supervision). Again, considerable emphasis is placed on empowering the supervisee.

Supervisor: As you know, Jenny, we are approaching the half-way point in your practicum. As I do with all of my supervisees, I would like to provide you with a current summary of how I think your competence is developing. Did I let you know that we would be doing this today?

Supervisee: Yes—you mentioned it last time. You also asked me to consider how much detail and constructive criticism I would like. I have given this some thought and, since I'm not feeling too confident at the present time, I would be grateful if you would just give me the basic feedback.

Supervisor: OK. Can you also tell me which part of the TraCC you would like me to concentrate on?

Supervisee: Could we please concentrate on formulation, as this troubles me most?

Supervisor: Fine—that's one of the areas where I, too, felt we needed to place some of our emphasis. I have completed a draft version of the TraCC and would like to go through the formulation section with you now (supervisor provides supervisee with a photocopy of the TraCC form, folding it at the relevant section.). As you will see, Jenny, I am really impressed by the way that you have demonstrated skills in assessment and formulation. This is recorded in TraCC Items A1 and A3. You clearly have an ability to assess and formulate. Do you have any insight as to why you should be strong in these areas?

Supervisee: I guess it's to do with my pretraining experience as a researcher. My project work revolved around formulation, and so I reckon I became familiar with this before I even started my training here.

Supervisor: That makes good sense, and it's great that your practicum here builds on that relevant experience. On the other hand, the TraCC that I have completed for your work to date indicates that you have not yet shown me the requisite competence in relation to Items A4 (reformulation) and A5 (negotiating realistic goals). This concerns the way that you modify your initial formulation, in the light of new information (e.g., input from a family member), and how you work alongside carers to specify suitable intervention objectives. Could I ask you to let me know whether you think that is a fair assessment?

Supervisee: Yes, I have been feeling particularly weak in these areas. That's why, in preparing for this session today, I thought that this was an area where we should focus.

Supervisor: I am glad that we share that perception, as it makes our task easier and suggests that you have a sound orientation to your own competence. What I would require from you to demonstrate competence in these identified areas is more active reviewing of your current formulations and some evidence that you have worked with at least one carer to negotiate intervention goals. Does that seem reasonable to you?

Supervisee: I'm wondering if we could postpone any extra work assignments. It's just that I'm not feeling too great right now. But can you help me to demonstrate the reformulation competency—for example, by providing me with more opportunities to see you practice these skills in supervision?

Supervisor: Of course! I assume that it is my responsibility to give you appropriate learning opportunities and any necessary support in demonstrating key competencies. Next, let's work out a plan of action on that. In view of how you're feeling today, let's go through the rest of my draft TraCC ratings next time.

Self-Evaluation by the Supervisee

As noted in passing already, the supervisee has a legitimate and important role to play within evaluation. Like a service-user perspective in relation to a clinical program, the supervisees' perceptions of supervision have an obvious legitimacy. They represent the initial level of evaluation within the well-established Kirkpatrick (1967) framework. Referred to as "reaction evaluation," this dimension assesses such considerations as whether the supervision is conducted competently, with interpersonal effectiveness, and in an acceptable way (Waltz, Addis, Koerner, & Jacobson, 1993).

Of course, supervisees often struggle to engage fully in evaluation, as illustrated by the dialogue above. As this fictitious example illustrates, avoidance is a popular strategy in dealing with the inherent power imbalance that tends to affect evaluation adversely, as in the supervisee's characteristically glowing feedback to the supervisor. Supervisors should be alert to this dynamic, raising it for sympathetic and careful professional discussion (e.g., recognizing the supervisee's vulnerable position, trying to reduce perceived threat, and normalizing mutual evaluation). In these and other ways, supervisors need to work explicitly with the supervisee to find ways to minimize difficulties and to promote development in this crucial core competence of professional practice.

A case in point is to use simple, relatively nonthreatening methods to facilitate feedback. For instance, the significant events paradigm offers a simple, user-friendly Helpful Aspects of Therapy Questionnaire (Llewellyn, Elliott, Shapiro, Hardy, & Firth-Cozens, 1988). I adapted this, with permission from the authors, for supervision. Rechristened the Helpful Aspects of Supervision Questionnaire (HASQ; see Appendix B), this simple instrument asks the supervisee to evaluate a particular supervision session without the pressure associated with more formal, end-of-practicum evaluation. Not only does this sort of instrument provide the supervisor with potentially useful feedback, it engages the supervisee in reflecting on his or her own learning, supporting the learning alliance with the supervisor. Self-evaluations by the supervisee traditionally include estimates of his or her ability to carry out key technical aspects of therapy (see Falender & Shafranske, 2004, for examples).

A further simple, practical tool for supervisee self-evaluation drawn from my local work is the Placement (Practicum) Record Form (PlaceR Form). Part of the PlaceR Form is the Supervision Record, and this is the part reproduced in Exhibit 11.1. As noted in Exhibit 11.1, the PlaceR Form covers various types of supervisory activity, each of which is recorded to indicate its frequency.

EXHIBIT 11.1

Items in the Supervision Record, Part of the Placement Record Form (PlaceR)

1. Discussion
2. Providing information
3. Modeling
4. Observation by
   (a) Audiotape
   (b) Videotape
   (c) One-way mirror
   (d) Live supervision
   (e) Sitting in on trainee
   (f) Sitting in on the supervisor
   (g) Cotherapy
   (h) Self-observation data (e.g., coding tape of own therapy)
   (i) Other (e.g., transcript of a therapy session)
5. Educational role play _____
6. Simulated clinical problem solving _____
7. Examination of trainee and supervisors written work
8. Work outcomes analysis
9. Group, Cosupervision, or other formats
10. Restorative methods
    (a) Receiving general support
    (b) Feeling accepted
    (c) Receiving recognition
    (d) Experiencing "core relationship conditions"
    (e) Facilitation of reflection
11. Normative methods
    (a) Administration
    (b) Planning and managing
    (c) Evaluating
    (d) Problem solving
12. Other methods (e.g., information and feedback provided by other staff, referrers)

The supervisee, who is responsible for completing this form, is also encouraged to make qualitative observations about the contribution that they have made to the use of these methods (a measure of the learning alliance and an adult learning stance). The PlaceR Form also records the work done by the supervisee within the practicum (i.e., functions as a log of experience and, hence, a tool to help us to place the trainee's status within the training program), such as the number and range of clients seen.

Procedurally, the PlaceR Form has to be tabled at the regular meetings that are held between the trainee, supervisor, and the visiting Newcastle course tutor. This nicely complements the information provided by the supervisor, including TraCC. As with the HASQ, requiring supervisees' to complete information records on supervision and placements is a vital part of their professional development, aiding the emergence of the master skill of self-supervision. If such self-evaluations show insight and are presented in constructive ways, then the supervisor or tutor may properly acknowledge the supervisees' competence in this form of evaluation (as per the example in the verbatim account provided earlier). Similarly, this information may guide future supervision.

Audit of the Supervision System

Another use for information such as that provided by the PlaceR Form is at the systems level. The PlaceR Form provides the kind of information that can assist the overall training system to operate more effectively. This is part of the context for supervision, as indicated in Figure 11.1. Clearly, to develop optimally, supervisors and supervisees require good systems of informational feedback. The example I now present is that of treating a year's worth of PlaceR Forms as an audit. This is one of the many evaluation options outlined above and in this instance draws on archival data.

The collated supervisees' PlaceR Forms from a calendar year were collated, a total of 59, and the Supervision Record element of the form was summarized (Milne & Gracie, 2001). In this way, we were able to show that on 100% of occasions the supervisors used discussion and examinations of written work. High frequencies of guided reading and observation were also recorded (95% and 93%, respectively). Less frequently recorded were analyses of the outcomes of work (such as clinical measures of therapy; 63% of occasions). Several other methods of supervision were also noted.

This is an audit of supervision in the sense that the training program has as an agreed standard that there will be mutual observation on at least one occasion for each practicum. Therefore, although this audit is generally favorable on the observation criterion, it is apparent that on at least four occasions, supervisees went through entire practicum rotations without being observed. This is useful feedback for the training program, and it should feed into the work of the visiting tutors, our supervision forms and guidelines, and the workshops we provide on supervision competencies for the local supervisors.

Auditing the Learning Alliance

Such audits should also feed into the way that we prepare supervisees for the challenging business of receiving supervision. There is a tendency to assume that the effectiveness of supervision is the sole responsibility of the supervisor. As noted by Milne and Gracie (2001), the Watkins (1997) text appeared to devote only 9 of its 613 pages (1.5%) to the role of the supervisee in supervision. This is clearly a psychologically naive perspective, and one that devalues the status of the supervisee as adult learner and active collaborator in effective supervision.

To reflect the importance of collaboration in supervision, we therefore also assessed to what extent and in what ways our supervisees were contributing to the supervisory relationship. When we audited the PlaceR Forms for this same sample of 59 supervisees, we found a wealth of affirmative qualitative data. There were a total of 239 meaning units recorded by these trainees, which were then categorized into themes: collaborating (40% of recorded contributions made by the supervisee), prompting the supervisor (22%), preparing properly (16%), feeding back to the supervisor (7%), and helping to organize supervision (4%). The remaining 11% of meaning units were treated as miscellaneous.

Again, such evaluation data can be extremely helpful to individuals or to the general system underpinning clinical supervision. These data tell us, for example, that although collaboration is marked, there is considerable room for improvement, particularly if one takes the view that this should always happen. An implication is to provide workshops to our supervisees, attending to things like correct record keeping and encouraging them to develop some of the key skills of effective collaboration (e.g., based on the ARM specification above). It is also apparent that very little sharing of responsibility occurred, something that is of concern if one again takes an adult learner perspective on supervision. Similarly, discussing tape-recorded therapy sessions is rare in this sample, and yet such practice provides a powerful, if not essential, means of facilitating learning.

POINT 4: ILLUSTRATION OF EVALUATING THE BENEFITS TO CLIENTS

If one considers the kinds of learning mini-impacts recorded in Teachers' PETS to be the first step toward evaluating the effectiveness of supervision, then the ultimate one is surely that of client benefit. Although it has been noted that a number of powerful variables intercede between supervision and effective therapy (as provided by a supervisee), there is a consensus that the acid test of supervision efficacy is client outcome (Falender & Shafranske, 2004, p. 202). Falender and Shafranske (2004) helpfully summarized a number of outcome measures that can help to contribute to this test, such as the Outcome Questionnaire (Wells, Burlingame, Lambert, Hoag, & Hope, 1996).

Analyses of the effectiveness of supervision that use at least one such evaluative measure are actually relatively uncommon, with the great majority of evaluation studies analyzing earlier stages of the educational pyramid (such as the supervisees' perceptions of supervision). For example, Ellis and Ladany (1997) were able to locate only nine published studies since 1981 that evaluated client outcome as the criterion for effective supervision. After detailing the profound and multiple methodological weaknesses of these studies, Ellis and Ladany concluded that the literature was so beset by problems as to make conclusions problematic. They also identified "the continued dearth of viable measures specific to clinical supervision" (p. 493) as a significant problem in the field. Similarly, in a subsequent systematic review, Milne and James (2000) were able to locate only 14 studies of supervision in which clinical outcomes had been evaluated. These studies made use of a wide range of evaluation tools and methods. However, there was a significant emphasis within the sample on using objective measures to quantify clinical outcomes, often by use of simple ad hoc behavioral records in the learning disability field. Taken together, the evaluations of clinical outcome indicated to the authors that supervision had demonstrated mixed success (this equated to between 50% and 69% impact on clients; see Milne & James, 2000, p.121).

There are, of course, hundreds of instruments available for outcome evaluation. To illustrate, Froyd, Lambert, and Froyd (1996) identified over 1,400 psychotherapy outcome measures in their review, and the number has surely increased since then. Froyd et al. also highlighted the finding that 60% of these instruments were only used once, and 278 of the papers provided no psychometric data. The most commonly used instruments included the Beck Depression Inventory (BDI; Beck, Ward, Mendelson, Mock, & Erbaugh, 1961), the Beck Anxiety Inventory (BAI; Beck, Epstein, Brown, & Steer, 1988), and the Hamilton Rating Scale for Depression (HRSD; Hamilton, 1960). Perhaps it is not surprising, then, that these three instruments were routinely administered as part of the evaluation protocol at the local CBT training department and were, therefore, applied routinely to the clients seen by the supervisees in the Milne and James (2002) analysis. The convention was for these measures to be administered at least at baseline and termination of therapy (normally after 10 sessions), and ideally, a focal instrument (such as the BAI in the case of a panic presentation) would be administered at regular intervals throughout therapy. Although these clinical outcomes were not actually reported in the 2002 study (because the data set was incomplete), use of such measures can have helpful influences on the direction and nature of the clinical intervention, and in turn shape the approach taken within supervision.

The subsequent, more detailed sequential analysis of a single supervisee–supervisor dyad (Milne et al., 2003) provides an example (although again these clinical outcome data were not reported in the article). In this instance, the supervisor asked her client, a 27-year-old woman presenting with panic attacks and a second client who was a 40-year-old woman presenting with depression to complete two symptomatic questionnaires each. In the case of the woman with panic, her BDI score at baseline was 9 and was reduced to 5 at the end of therapy. However, her BAI scores reduced much more markedly from a suitably high 35 at baseline to only 2 following 20 sessions of therapy. In the case of the second client, her HRSD scores reduced from 15 to 11 and her BDI, from 27 to 17, by the end of therapy. Of particular value, the woman with panic completed the BAI on 6 intermediate occasions, providing therapist and supervisor with a cumulative record of progress. In this particular instance, there was a clear but stepwise reduction in her accounts of panic.

After 3 sessions, the BAI had reduced from 35 to 26. However, by the 4th session, this was much reduced to 15, what might be thought of as a "good gain" in her particular therapy (Tang & DeRubeis, 1999). Her BAI scores continued to reduce nicely thereafter, decreasing to 2 by the end of therapy. Both clients therefore presented with symptoms falling within the clinical range and completed their CBT with their symptoms in the "normal" range (with the exception of the BDI score for the depressed client, which at 17, fell within the moderately depressed range). Although not convincing in scientific terms (as an interpretable research design is missing), these data show how clinical outcomes can be measured and how they might feed into supervision (especially the example of longitudinal BAI data) and are at least consistent with the view that supervision was effective, by this acid test criterion.

CONCLUSION

Evaluation implies objectives, and within the experiential learning model the supervisor is expected to help supervisees to become more aware of the affective accompaniments to their work; reflect on their experience, from a personal perspective; conceptualize this experience, from the perspective of public knowledge (e.g., the scientific literature); and to experiment and plan on the basis of this process.

There is much that remains to be done in pursuit of enhancing clinical supervision through careful evaluation of these and related objectives. Quite aside from issues such as the psychometric caliber of the instruments that are used (and related issues about evaluation designs and methodologies, not discussed here), there remain significant challenges ahead. In addition to the four aspects picked out by Lambert and Ogles (1997), namely focusing on trainees' behavior in therapy and on their therapeutic alliances, drawing on multiple perspectives, and concentrating on criterion measures, my own personal list would include more upstream, detailed ($N = 1$), process–outcome analyses. This would allow for a better understanding of how supervision achieves its valuable results. It would also help researchers to better conceptualize supervision, providing the basis for more informed developments and evaluations of supervision.

As part of this effort, another key strategic consideration is the potential benefits of drawing on parallel literatures, of reasoning by analogy. In particular, the psychotherapy process–outcome literature appears to afford numerous potential insights. As touched on in this chapter, when mentioning tools such as the Helpful Aspects of Therapy Questionnaire, it seems self-evident that domains such as supervision and therapy can advantageously be linked (Milne, 2006). As Falender and Shafranske (2004) noted, "the area of evaluation is central to the training of psychologists" (p. 225) and therefore can be meaningfully used to enhance supervisory practice. I hope that this chapter has illustrated how evaluation might be pursued in a helpful way and that readers find some of the appended instruments relevant to their own evaluation practice in the pivotal sphere of supervision.

REFERENCES

Agnew-Davies, R., Stiles, W., Hardy, G. E., Barkham, M., & Shapiro, D. A. (1998). Alliance structure assessed by the Agnew Relationship Measure (ARM). *British Journal of Clinical Psychology, 37*, 155–172.

Bahrick, A. (1989). *Working Alliance Inventory—Training (WAI–T).* Unpublished doctoral dissertation, Ohio State University, Columbus.

Beck, A. T., Epstein, N., Brown, G., & Steer, R. A. (1988). An inventory for measuring clinical anxiety: Psychometric properties. *Journal of Consulting and Clinical Psychology, 56*, 893–897.

Beck, A. T., Ward, C. H., Mendelson, M., Mock, J. E., & Erbaugh, J. K. (1961). An inventory for measuring depression. *Archives of General Psychiatry, 4*, 561–571.

Bernard, J. M., & Goodyear, R. K. (2004). *Fundamentals of clinical supervision* (3rd ed.). Boston: Pearson.

Blackburn, I.-M., James, I. A., Milne, D. L., Baker, C., Standart, S., Garland, A., & Reichelt, F. K. (2001). *Behavioral and Cognitive Psychotherapy, 29*, 431–436.

Bransford, J. D., Brown, A. L., & Cocking, R. R. (Eds.). (2000). *How people learn: Brain, mind, experience, and school.* Washington, DC: National Academy Press.

Concise Oxford English Dictionary. (2004). New York: Oxford University Press.

Ellis, M. V., & Ladany, N. (1997). Inferences concerning supervisees and clients in clinical supervision: An integrative review. In C. E. Watkins (Ed.), *Handbook of psychotherapy supervision* (pp. 447–507). New York: Wiley.

Falender, C. A., Cornish, J. A. E., Goodyear, R., Hatcher, R., Kaslow, N. J., Levental, G., et al. (2004). Defining competencies in psychology supervision: A consensus statement. *Journal of Clinical Psychology, 60*, 771–785.

Falender, C. A., & Shafranske, E. P. (2004). *Clinical supervision: A competency-based approach.* Washington, DC: American Psychological Association.

Flanders, N. A. (1970). *Analyzing teaching behavior.* New York: Addison-Wesley

Froyd, J. E., Lambert, M. J., & Froyd J. D. (1996). A review of practices of psychotherapy outcome measurement. *Journal of Mental Health, 5*, 11–15.

Hamilton, M. A. (1960). A rating scale for depression. *Journal of Neurological and Neurosurgical Psychiatry, 23*, 56–62.

Kaslow, N. J., Borden, K. A., Cullans, F. L., Forest, L., Illfelder-Kaye, J., Nelson, P. D., et al. (2004). Competencies conference: Future direction in education and credentialing professional psychology. *Journal of Clinical Psychology, 60*, 699–712.

Kirkpatrick, D. L. (1967). *Evaluation of training.* In R. L. Craig & L. R. Bittel (Eds.), *Training and development handbook* (pp. 87–112). New York: McGraw-Hill.

Kolb, D. A. (1984). *Experiential learning.* Upper Saddle River, NJ: Prentice-Hall.

Komaki, J. L., & Citera, M. (1990). Beyond effective supervision: Identifying key interactions between superior and subordinate. *Leadership Quarterly, 1,* 91–105.

Lambert, M. J., & Arnold, R. C. (1987). Research and the supervisory process. *Professional Psychology: Research and Practice, 18,* 217–224.

Lambert, M. J., & Ogles, B. M. (1997). The effectiveness of psychotherapy supervision. In C. E. Watkins (Ed.), *Handbook of psychotherapy supervision* (pp. 421–446). New York: Wiley.

Llewelyn, S. P., Elliott, R., Shapiro, D. A., Hardy, G., & Firth-Cozens, J. (1988). Client perceptions of significant events in prescriptive and exploratory periods of individual therapy. *British Journal of Clinical Psychology, 27,* 105–114.

McCullough, L., Winston, A., Farbes, B. A., Porter, F., Pollock, J., Laikin, M., et al. (1991). The relationship of patient–therapist interaction to outcome in brief psychotherapy. *Psychotherapy, 28,* 525–533.

Milne, D. (2006). Developing clinical supervision research through reasoned analogies with therapy. *Clinical Psychology and Psychotherapy, 13,* 215–222.

Milne, D., & Gracie, J. (2001). The role of the supervisee: Twenty ways to facilitate clinical supervision. *Clinical Psychology, 5,* 13–15.

Milne, D., Hanner, S., Woodword, K., & Westerman, C. (2004). Formulation and feedback: An illustration of two methods for improving access to effective therapies. *International Journal of Healthcare Quality Assurance, 17,* 268–274.

Milne, D., & James, I. A. (2000). A systematic review of effective cognitive behavioural supervision. *British Journal of Clinical Psychology, 39,* 111–127.

Milne, D., & James, I. A. (2002). The observed impact of training on competence in clinical supervision. *British Journal of Clinical Psychology, 41,* 55–72.

Milne, D., James, I. A., Keegan, D., & Dudley, M. (2002). Teachers' PETS: A new observational measure of experiential training interactions. *Clinical Psychology and Psychotherapy, 9,* 187–199.

Milne, D., Pilkington, J., Gracie, J., & James I. A., (2003). Transferring skills from supervision to therapy: A qualitative and quantitative $N = 1$ analysis. *Behavioural and Cognitive Psychotherapy, 31,* 119–202.

Milne, D., & Westerman, C. (2001). Evidence-based clinical supervision: Rationale and illustration. *Clinical Psychology & Psychotherapy, 8,* 444–457.

Moos, R. H. (1992). Coping responses inventory manual. In D. Milne (Ed.), *Assessment: A mental health portfolio* (pp. 30–40). Windsor, England: NFER-Nelson.

Robiner, W. N., Saltzman, S. R., Hoberman, H. M., Semrud-Clikeman, M., & Schirvar, J. A. (1997). Psychologies supervisors' bias in evaluations and letters of recommendations. *The Clinical Supervisor, 16,* 49–72.

Rossi, P. H., Lipsey, M. W., & Freeman, H. E. (2004). *Evaluation: A systematic approach* (7th ed.). London: Sage.

Scriven, M. (1972). The methodology of evaluation. In C. H. Weiss (Ed.), *Evaluating action programs: Readings in social action and education.* Boston: Allyn & Bacon.

Tang, T. Z., & DeRubeis, R. J. (1999). Sudden gains and critical sessions in cognitive–behavioral therapy for depression. *Journal of Consulting and Clinical Psychology*, 67, 894–904.

Waltz, J., Addis, M. E., Koerner, K., & Jacobson, N. S. (1993). Testing the integrity of a psychotherapy protocol: Assessment of adherence and competence. *Journal of Consulting and Clinical Psychology*, 61, 620–630.

Wampold, B. E., & Holloway, E. L. (1997). Methodology, design, and evaluation in psychotherapy supervision research. In E. Watkins (Ed.), *Handbook of psychotherapy supervision* (pp. 11–30). New York: Wiley.

Watkins, C. E. (Ed.). (1997). *Handbook of psychotherapy supervision*. New York: Wiley.

Weiss, C. H. (1972). *Evaluation research*. Englewood Cliffs, NJ: Prentice-Hall.

Wells, M. G., Burlingame, G. M., Lambert, M. J., Hoag, M. J., & Hope C. A. (1996). Conceptualization and measurement of client change during psychotherapy: Development of the outcome questionnaire and youth outcome questionnaire. *Psychotherapy: Theory, Research, Practice, Training, 33*, 275–283.

APPENDIX A: TRAINEE'S COMPETENCE CHECKLIST (TraCC)

INSTRUCTIONS

TraCC lists the essential and transferable competences within the clinical experience part of training in clinical psychology. Opportunities to demonstrate these competences should be arranged by the supervisor, who also assesses the extent to which they are demonstrated by the trainee. During the placement, the supervisor enters the appropriate 'evidence' (e.g. 'FD'—focus of discussion in supervision) and a suggested competence level (under 'L'). Competences are either 'demonstrated' (tick placed alongside) or 'not yet demonstrated'. In the case of the latter, either 'a' (concerns), 'b' (no opportunity) or 'c' (progressing satisfactorily) should be entered alongside each competence.

The functions of the TraCC are to provide a basic structure for learning on placement (i.e. defining the minimal clinical experience aspect of training); to allow all parties to review this learning in a systematic and cumulative manner during the whole training period; to provide a reference point for mutual evaluation; and to form part of the evaluation database.

Please note that the TraCC is only intended to provide a statement of the <u>minimum</u> range of competences to be developed on placement. It is expected that all trainees will target and demonstrate additional competences, which should be recorded alongside TraCC items in the Learning Contract.

Name of Trainee:
Name of Supervisor:
Dates of Training Sequence:

RECORD OF PLACEMENTS

	DATES	SITE	ROTATION	SUPERVISOR
1				
2				
3				
4				

Editors Note: This checklist provides a format to articulate clinical competencies across training rotations and may be adapted with acknowledgement of the author. The use of the TraCC or other checklists provide the means to articulate clinical competencies to be developed within clinical training. Such tools are useful in identifying the knowledge, skills, values and attitudes which contribute to specific clinical competencies. Copyright 2006 by Derek Milne. Reprinted with permission of the author.

A. ASSESSMENT

	COMPETENCE	TI	EVIDENCE	L*
A1	Ability to carry out a thorough assessment by the accumulation of appropriate information regarding the client, significant others and/or staff across relevant settings.			
	Rotation 1 Rotation 2			
A2	Uses standardised psychometric testing (including tests & questionnaires)			
	Rotation 1 Rotation 2			
A3	Formulation: able to present an account of the aetiology, maintaining factors and intervention implications, based on A1 and A2 above.			
	Rotation 1 Rotation 2			
A4	Reformulates: able to modify the problem formulation in response to new information (e.g., response to initial intervention).			
	Rotation 1 Rotation 2			
A5	Negotiates realistic goals and objectives with the client and/or carers.			
	Rotation 1 Rotation 2			

*Level : enter either a tick, to indicate that the specific competence has been demonstrated, or 'a' (indicating a concern), 'b' (no opportunity to demonstrate competence) or 'c' (progressing satisfactorily)

B. PSYCHOTHERAPY

	COMPETENCE	TI	EVIDENCE	L*
B1	Demonstrates the ability to relate empathically to clients, communicates an understanding of client's experiences, and can establish a rapport.			
	Rotation 1 Rotation 2			
B2	Demonstrates the ability to work within a behavioural framework by: a) the use of anxiety management techniques b) the use of functional analysis: i) recording antecedents, behaviours and consequences			

	ii) coming to a behavioural formulation and related intervention strategy c) Understanding the impact of the physical and social environment on the client			
B3	Rotation 1 Rotation 2 Demonstrates the ability to work within a cognitive framework by: a) establishing a collaborative therapy relationship b) explaining the links between thoughts and emotions c) enabling clients to identify negative automatic thoughts (NATS) d) enabling clients to generate alternative thoughts			
B4	Rotation 1 Rotation 2 Demonstrates the ability to work within a systemic framework by: a) thinking in terms of interactive systems regarding individual, family and organisational issues b) using circular questioning c) interviewing at a systems level with families and/or organisations			
B5	Rotation 1 Rotation 2 Demonstrates the ability to work within humanistic & psychodynamic frameworks by: a) discussing the humanistic aspects of therapeutic relationships and their contribution to change (e.g. the contribution to change of acceptance, accurate empathy & genuineness; recognising the client's inherent potential for growth and development) b) discussing when defence and transference phenomena may be involved in a therapy relationship c) maintaining a generally neutral stance or attitude in relation to the client d) interviewing at a systems level with families and/or organisations Rotation 1 Rotation 2			

B6	Demonstrates the ability to consider more than one strategy for intervention			
	Rotation 1 Rotation 2			
B7	Demonstrates the ability to work with couples			
	Rotation 1 Rotation 2			
B8	Demonstrates the ability to work with groups			
	Rotation 1 Rotation 2			
B9	Demonstrates the ability to work with families			
	Rotation 1 Rotation 2			
B10	Works directly with at least one patient in long-term care (e.g. psychiatric rehabilitation setting)			
	Rotation 1 Rotation 2			
B11	Demonstrates competence in managing breaks and endings in therapy			
	Rotation 1 Rotation 2			
B12	Ensures the provision of a secure, safe and reliable therapeutic 'space' (e.g. by addressing issues relating to the therapeutic 'frame'—as in the timing of sessions, or the location or duration of therapy)			
	Rotation 1 Rotation 2			
B13	Can monitor and <u>evaluate</u> the effectiveness of an intervention (e.g. pre-post measures)			
	Rotation 1 Rotation 2			
B14	Adjusts interventions according to the physical and social characteristics of the clients environment (e.g. material resources or social support)			
	Rotation 1 Rotation 2			

C. INDIRECT SERVICE

	COMPETENCE	TI	EVIDENCE	L*
C1	Demonstrates the ability to guide other professionals in their own interventions with clients (including supervision and co-working) Rotation 1 Rotation 2			
C2	Supports staff, carers etc (including counselling and education) Rotation 1 Rotation 2			
C3	Demonstrates the ability to develop effective working relationships with other professionals and carers (including multi-disciplinary teamwork), as well as with relevant others (inc. secretaries & managers) Rotation 1 Rotation 2			
C4	Poses research or service evaluation questions Rotation 1 Rotation 2			
C5	Carries out research or service evaluation (e.g., survey of needs in a client group) Rotation 1 Rotation 2			
C6	Disseminates results from research or evaluation (e.g. report or presentation to a meeting) Rotation 1 Rotation 2			

D. TEACHING AND TRAINING

	COMPETENCE	TI	EVIDENCE	L*
D1	Conducts a needs assessment (e.g. determines the delegates' existing knowledge) Rotation 1 Rotation 2			
D2	Negotiates and specifies realistic objective (with delegates and/or person organising the training) Rotation 1 Rotation 2			

D3	Able to devise and present a relevant experiential learning exercise (including role play, etc) Rotation 1 Rotation 2			
D4	Demonstrates familiarisation with, and use of, a number of different teaching aids (e.g., OHP, flipchart, slide projector)			
D5	Contributes to a didactic teaching programme (e.g. lecturing) Rotation 1 Rotation 2			
D6	Applies an appropriate method of feedback (e.g., learner 'satisfaction' ratings) Rotation 1 Rotation 2			

E. PROFESSIONAL STANDARDS

	COMPETENCE	TI	EVIDENCE	L*
E1	Ability to examine the impact of <u>own behaviour</u> in a problematic situation (e.g. to take responsibility for own contribution to a clinical failure) Rotation 1 Rotation 2			
E2	Ability to access relevant <u>literature</u> when required Rotation 1 Rotation 2			
E3	Ability to apply relevant <u>theory</u> and <u>empirical knowledge</u> to clinical and indirect work Rotation 1 Rotation 2			
E4	Shows <u>initiative or enterprise</u> (e.g. considers ways of addressing challenges without need for prompting) Rotation 1 Rotation 2			
E5	<u>Communicates</u> and records information effectively (written and verbal; participation in audit procedures; letters to referrers; project reports etc) Rotation 1 Rotation 2			

E6	Behaves professionally (including adherence to current standards; reliability; 'hardiness'; confidentiality; enthusiasm; independence; discretion)			
	Rotation 1 Rotation 2			
E7	Demonstrates Awareness of own limits of competence			
	Rotation 1 Rotation 2			
E8	Makes appropriate use of any feedback received			
	Rotation 1 Rotation 2			
E9	Manages own time and resources effectively (e.g. prioritisation)			
	Rotation 1 Rotation 2			

GUIDELINES FOR COMPLETION OF THE TRAINEE COMPETENCY CHECKLIST

The checklist should be completed in the following way:

a) The supervisor and the trainee will note what form of evidence has been produced to verify the competence (record this in the 'evidence' column, using this set of abbreviations):

DO	Direct Observation (by supervisor)
R	Reports (written evidence)
IS	Indirect Inference via supervision
D3	Discussion in 3-way demonstrates competence (e.g. conceptual issue)
FD	Focus of discussion during placement
PW	Project Work/'Permanent Product' evidence (e.g. teaching handout)
VA	Video or Audio evidence

b) The supervisor will also record whether <u>competence</u> has been demonstrated.

It is possible to complete training and qualify without demonstrating some competences, as they may be subject to available opportunity. It is, however, expected that the majority of competences will be demonstrated. This is the standard expected by the end of the course.

COMPETENCE LEVEL	FEATURES
First Level: <u>Competence not yet demonstrated</u>	a) cause for concern b) due to lack of suitable opportunity c) progressing satisfactorily: not yet level 2
Second Level: <u>Competent</u>	Equivalent to graduate level of proficiency.

c) Finally, the clinical tutor discusses a sample of the observed and rated competences in the final 'three way' meetings (e.g. to verify and to moderate), and then <u>initials</u> them (the TI or 'tutors initials' column) following the final assessment and feedback meeting. <u>Ultimately, it is the job of the trainee and supervisor to provide evidence of the trainee's competence, for the supervisor to evaluate and record this competence, and for the tutor to moderate the supervisor's evaluation.</u>

TraCC also provides a row to record competences demonstrated within each rotation. This is partly to recognise that 'competence' is a state not a trait: it may well vary under different placement circumstances. It is possible that a rating of competence in an earlier rotation may not be rated at this level by a subsequent supervisor. If this is the case, this will need to be discussed with and moderated by the clinical tutor.

The supervisor's and tutor's evaluations of the trainee's competence are based on the available evidence. In some instances a trainee may only have to undertake a particular task on one occasion to demonstrate one or more competences. In other cases it may be judged that additional data are required before an evaluation can be made. Therefore, the tutor (and supervisor) have to assess all the available evidence and arrive at an evaluation of the trainee's competence as demonstrated <u>at the end of placement stage.</u>

Research & Theory Guiding Practice

"Underpinning knowledge"

Please note that the competences assume (or explicitly require) a knowledge base. '<u>Competence' is defined as the ability to perform the activities of an occupation to the standards expected in employment</u>. This ability is derived from research and theory in psychology, particularly clinical psychology. Indeed, perhaps the most fundamental competence in clinical psychology is the ability to develop new skills and knowledge so as to find solutions to new problems. Section E ('professional standards') sets this out most clearly, though there are relevant items in other sections. In judging competence, therefore, the tutor and supervisor should routinely ask the trainee to outline the reasoning underpinning his or her performance of a competence. <u>Only when this reasoning demonstrates an acceptable grasp and application of research and theory should the competence be credited to the trainee.</u>

Value Base Guiding Practice

In tandem with the knowledge base, it is essential that the trainee also demonstrates an awareness of, and adherence to, the appropriate standards of ethical clinical practice. This includes:

a) Commitment to Professional Values
   The trainee should demonstrate self-awareness and commitment in implementing professional values in practice. This involves demonstrating:
   1) An ability to understand and to implement anti-discriminatory, anti-oppressive, and anti-racist principles;
   2) Respect for clients' dignity, privacy, autonomy and rights as service users;
   3) An ability to manage complex ethical responsibilities and to value conflicts;
   4) An ability to empower others; and
   5) Adherence to methodological values (such as a commitment to rigorous procedures of assessment and continuing monitoring of effectiveness).

b) Continuous Professional Learning
   Demonstrates a commitment to, and capacity for, reflection on practice, leading to progressive deepening of professional understanding. This involves demonstrating a willingness and capacity to:
   1) learn from others, including clients;
   2) recognise that professional judgements are always open to question; and
   3) engage in self-evaluation, recognising and analysing one's strengths and limitations.

c) Affective Awareness
   Demonstrates understanding and effective management of emotional responses in relation to others. This involves:
   1) Demonstrating sensitivity to the unique complexity of different situations; and
   2) Developing effective collaborative relationships with others.

APPENDIX B: HELPFUL ASPECTS OF SUPERVISION QUESTIONNAIRE (HASQ)

Your name: _____

Placement: _____

Date of session: _____ Today's date: _____

1. Please rate how helpful this session was overall:

		Neither helpful		
Very unhelpful	Fairly unhelpful	nor unhelpful	Fairly helpful	Very helpful
1	2	3	4	5

2. Of the events that occurred in this session, which one do you feel was the most helpful for you personally? It might be something you said or did, or something the supervisor said or did. Can you say why it was helpful?

3. How helpful was this particular event? Rate this on the scale:

Neither helpful nor unhelpful	Fairly helpful	Very helpful
3	4	5

4. Did anything else of particular importance happen during this session? Include anything else that may have been helpful or anything that might have hindered your learning.

Editors' Note. This brief questionnaire illustrates a simple means to obtain feedback on processes and experiences within clinical supervision. From "Client Perceptions of Significant Events in Prescriptive and Exploratory Periods of Individual Therapy," by S. P. Llewelyn, R. Elliott, D. A. Shapiro, G. Hardy, and J. Firth-Cozens, 1988, *British Journal of Clinical Psychology, 27*, pp. 105–114. Adapted with permission.

INDEX

ABOUT THE EDITORS

Carol A. Falender, PhD, is adjunct professor at Pepperdine University in Los Angeles, California, and clinical professor in the Department of Psychology, University of California, Los Angeles. Dr. Falender has served as president of the American Psychological Association (APA) Division 37 (Society for Child and Family Policy and Practice), communications officer for the Supervision and Training Section of Division 17 (Society of Counseling Psychology), chair of the California Psychological Association (CPA) Division of Education and Training, and chair of continuing education for the CPA. She directed APA-accredited internships at community mental health centers for more than 20 years. She received the Outstanding Supervisor of the Year award from the CPA Division of Education and Training and the Silver Psi award from the CPA for outstanding service. She provides training and workshops internationally on the subject of clinical supervision and contributes scholarship in this clinical specialty area. Dr. Falender's publications include *Clinical Supervision: A Competency-Based Approach.*

Edward P. Shafranske, PhD, ABPP, is professor of psychology and director of the doctoral program in clinical psychology at Pepperdine University in Los Angeles, California. He also lectures in the Department of Psychiatry, David Geffen School of Medicine, University of California, Los Angeles. A fellow of the American Psychological Association (APA), Dr. Shafranske has served as president of APA Division 36 (Psychology of Religion) and chair of the California Psychological Association (CPA) Division of Education and Training. A former Luckman Distinguished Teaching Fellow, he received Pepperdine's Howard A. White Award for Teaching Excellence in 2006 and the CPA Award for Distinguished Contributions to Psychology as a Profession in 2007. He has supervised clinicians at all levels of professional development. His publications include *Clinical Supervision: A Competency-Based Approach, Religion and the Clinical Practice of Psychology,* and *Spiritually Oriented Psychotherapy.* In addition to academic, research, and consultation activities, Dr. Shafranske maintains a private practice in clinical psychology in Irvine, California.